AUG 2012

The NEW ENCYCLOPEDIA *of* SOUTHERN CULTURE

VOLUME 5 : LANGUAGE

Volumes to appear in

The New Encyclopedia of Southern Culture

are:

The NEW

ENCYCLOPEDIA *of* SOUTHERN CULTURE

CHARLES REAGAN WILSON General Editor

JAMES G. THOMAS JR. Managing Editor

ANN J. ABADIE Associate Editor

VOLUME 5

Language

MICHAEL MONTGOMERY & ELLEN JOHNSON

Volume Editors

Sponsored by

THE CENTER FOR THE STUDY OF SOUTHERN CULTURE

at the University of Mississippi

THE UNIVERSITY OF NORTH CAROLINA PRESS

Chapel Hill

© 2007 The University of North Carolina Press

All rights reserved

This book was published with the assistance of the Anniversary
Endowment Fund of the University of North Carolina Press.

Designed by Richard Hendel

Set in Minion types by Tseng Information Systems, Inc.

Manufactured in the United States of America

The paper in this book meets the guidelines for permanence and
durability of the Committee on Production Guidelines for Book
Longevity of the Council on Library Resources.

Library of Congress Cataloging-in-Publication Data

Language / Michael Montgomery & Ellen Johnson, volume editors.

p. cm. — (The new encyclopedia of Southern culture ; v. 5)

"Sponsored by The Center for the Study of Southern Culture
at the University of Mississippi."

Includes bibliographical references and index.

ISBN 978-0-8078-3114-4 (alk. paper) —

ISBN 978-0-8078-5806-6 (pbk. : alk. paper)

1. English language—Southern States—Encyclopedias. 2. English
language—Dialects—Southern States—Encyclopedias. 3.English
language—Variation—Southern States—Encyclopedias.
4. Southern States—Language—Encyclopedias. I. Montgomery,
Michael. II. Johnson, Ellen. III. University of Mississippi. Center
for the Study of Southern Culture. IV. Series.

F209 .N47 2006 vol. 5

[PE2922]

975.003 s—dc22

2007700131

The *Encyclopedia of Southern Culture*, sponsored by the Center for
the Study of Southern Culture at the University of Mississippi, was
published by the University of North Carolina Press in 1989.

cloth   10 09 08   5 4 3 2

paper   10 09 08 07 06   5 4 3 2 1

Tell about the South. What's it like there.

What do they do there. Why do they live there.

Why do they live at all.

WILLIAM FAULKNER

Absalom, Absalom!

CONTENTS

GENERAL INTRODUCTION

In 1989 years of planning and hard work came to fruition when the University of North Carolina Press joined the Center for the Study of Southern Culture at the University of Mississippi to publish the *Encyclopedia of Southern Culture*. While all those involved in writing, reviewing, editing, and producing the volume believed it would be received as a vital contribution to our understanding of the American South, no one could have anticipated fully the widespread acclaim it would receive from reviewers and other commentators. But the *Encyclopedia* was indeed celebrated, not only by scholars but also by popular audiences with a deep, abiding interest in the region. At a time when some people talked of the "vanishing South," the book helped remind a national audience that the region was alive and well, and it has continued to shape national perceptions of the South through the work of its many users—journalists, scholars, teachers, students, and general readers.

As the introduction to the *Encyclopedia* noted, its conceptualization and organization reflected a cultural approach to the South. It highlighted such issues as the core zones and margins of southern culture, the boundaries where "the South" overlapped with other cultures, the role of history in contemporary culture, and the centrality of regional consciousness, symbolism, and mythology. By 1989 scholars had moved beyond the idea of cultures as real, tangible entities, viewing them instead as abstractions. The *Encyclopedia*'s editors and contributors thus included a full range of social indicators, trait groupings, literary concepts, and historical evidence typically used in regional studies, carefully working to address the distinctive and characteristic traits that made the American South a particular place. The introduction to the *Encyclopedia* concluded that the fundamental uniqueness of southern culture was reflected in the volume's composite portrait of the South. We asked contributors to consider aspects that were unique to the region but also those that suggested its internal diversity. The volume was not a reference book of southern history, which explained something of the design of entries. There were fewer essays on colonial and antebellum history than on the postbellum and modern periods, befitting our conception of the volume as one trying not only to chart the cultural landscape of the South but also to illuminate the contemporary era.

When C. Vann Woodward reviewed the *Encyclopedia* in the *New York Review of Books*, he concluded his review by noting "the continued liveliness of interest in the South and its seeming inexhaustibility as a field of study." Research on the South, he wrote, furnishes "proof of the value of the *Encyclopedia* as a scholarly undertaking as well as suggesting future needs for revision or supplement to keep up with ongoing scholarship." The decade and a half since the publication of the *Encyclopedia of Southern Culture* have certainly suggested that Woodward was correct. The American South has undergone significant changes that make for a different context for the study of the region. The South has undergone social, economic, political, intellectual, and literary transformations, creating the need for a new edition of the *Encyclopedia* that will remain relevant to a changing region. Globalization has become a major issue, seen in the South through the appearance of Japanese automobile factories, Hispanic workers who have immigrated from Latin America or Cuba, and a new prominence for Asian and Middle Eastern religions that were hardly present in the 1980s South. The African American return migration to the South, which started in the 1970s, dramatically increased in the 1990s, as countless books simultaneously appeared asserting powerfully the claims of African Americans as formative influences on southern culture. Politically, southerners from both parties have played crucial leadership roles in national politics, and the Republican Party has dominated a near-solid South in national elections. Meanwhile, new forms of music, like hip-hop, have emerged with distinct southern expressions, and the term "dirty South" has taken on new musical meanings not thought of in 1989. New genres of writing by creative southerners, such as gay and lesbian literature and "white trash" writing, extend the southern literary tradition.

Meanwhile, as Woodward foresaw, scholars have continued their engagement with the history and culture of the South since the publication of the *Encyclopedia*, raising new scholarly issues and opening new areas of study. Historians have moved beyond their earlier preoccupation with social history to write new cultural history as well. They have used the categories of race, social class, and gender to illuminate the diversity of the South, rather than a unified "mind of the South." Previously underexplored areas within the field of southern historical studies, such as the colonial era, are now seen as formative periods of the region's character, with the South's positioning within a larger Atlantic world a productive new area of study. Cultural memory has become a major topic in the exploration of how the social construction of "the South" benefited some social groups and exploited others. Scholars in many disciplines have made the southern identity a major topic, and they have used a variety of methodologies to suggest what that identity has meant to different social groups. Literary critics have adapted cultural theories to the South and have raised the issue of postsouthern literature to a major category of concern as well as exploring the links between the literature of the American South and that of the Caribbean. Anthropologists have used different theoretical formulations from literary critics, providing models for their fieldwork in southern communities. In the past 30 years anthropologists have set increasing numbers of their ethnographic studies in the South, with many of them now exploring topics specifically linked to southern cultural issues. Scholars now place the Native American story, from prehistory to the contemporary era, as a central part of southern history. Comparative and interdisciplinary approaches to the South have encouraged scholars to look at such issues as the borders and boundaries of the South, specific places and spaces with distinct identities within the American South, and the global and transnational Souths, linking the American South with many formerly colonial societies around the world.

The first edition of the *Encyclopedia of Southern Culture* anticipated many of these approaches and indeed stimulated the growth of Southern Studies as a distinct interdisciplinary field. The Center for the Study of Southern Culture has worked for more than a quarter century to encourage research and teaching about the American South. Its academic programs have produced graduates who have gone on to write interdisciplinary studies of the South, while others have staffed the cultural institutions of the region and in turn encouraged those institutions to document and present the South's culture to broad public audiences. The center's conferences and publications have continued its long tradition of promoting understanding of the history, literature, and music of the South, with new initiatives focused on southern foodways, the future of the South, and the global Souths, expressing the center's mission to bring the best current scholarship to broad public audiences. Its documentary studies projects build oral and visual archives, and the New Directions in Southern Studies book series, published by the University of North Carolina Press, offers an important venue for innovative scholarship.

Since the *Encyclopedia of Southern Culture* appeared, the field of Southern Studies has dramatically developed, with an extensive network now of academic and research institutions whose projects focus specifically on the interdisciplinary study of the South. The Center for the Study of the American South at the University of North Carolina at Chapel Hill, led by Director Harry Watson and Associate Director and *Encyclopedia* coeditor William Ferris, publishes the lively journal *Southern Cultures* and is now at the organizational center of many other Southern Studies projects. The Institute for Southern Studies at the University of South Carolina, the Southern Intellectual History Circle, the Society for the Study of Southern Literature, the Southern Studies Forum of the

European American Studies Association, Emory University's SouthernSpaces .org, and the South Atlantic Humanities Center (at the Virginia Foundation for the Humanities, the University of Virginia, and Virginia Polytechnic Institute and State University) express the recent expansion of interest in regional study.

Observers of the American South have had much to absorb, given the rapid pace of recent change. The institutional framework for studying the South is broader and deeper than ever, yet the relationship between the older verities of regional study and new realities remains unclear. Given the extent of changes in the American South and in Southern Studies since the publication of the *Encyclopedia of Southern Culture*, the need for a new edition of that work is clear. Therefore, the Center for the Study of Southern Culture has once again joined the University of North Carolina Press to produce *The New Encyclopedia of Southern Culture*. As readers of the original edition will quickly see, *The New Encyclopedia* follows many of the scholarly principles and editorial conventions established in the original, but with one key difference; rather than being published in a single hardback volume, *The New Encyclopedia* is presented in a series of shorter individual volumes that build on the 24 original subject categories used in the *Encyclopedia* and adapt them to new scholarly developments. Some earlier *Encyclopedia* categories have been reconceptualized in light of new academic interests. For example, the subject section originally titled "Women's Life" is reconceived as a new volume, *Gender*, and the original "Black Life" section is more broadly interpreted as a volume on race. These changes reflect new analytical concerns that place the study of women and blacks in broader cultural systems, reflecting the emergence of, among other topics, the study of male culture and of whiteness. Both volumes draw as well from the rich recent scholarship on women's life and black life. In addition, topics with some thematic coherence are combined in a volume, such as *Law and Politics* and *Agriculture and Industry*. One new topic, *Foodways*, is the basis of a separate volume, reflecting its new prominence in the interdisciplinary study of southern culture.

Numerous individual topical volumes together make up *The New Encyclopedia of Southern Culture* and extend the reach of the reference work to wider audiences. This approach should enhance the use of the *Encyclopedia* in academic courses and is intended to be convenient for readers with more focused interests within the larger context of southern culture. Readers will have handy access to one-volume, authoritative, and comprehensive scholarly treatments of the major areas of southern culture.

We have been fortunate that, in nearly all cases, subject consultants who offered crucial direction in shaping the topical sections for the original edition have agreed to join us in this new endeavor as volume editors. When new volume editors have been added, we have again looked for respected figures who can provide not only their own expertise but also strong networks of scholars to help develop relevant lists of topics and to serve as contributors in their areas. The reputations of all our volume editors as leading scholars in their areas encouraged the contributions of other scholars and added to *The New Encyclopedia*'s authority as a reference work.

The New Encyclopedia of Southern Culture builds on the strengths of articles in the original edition in several ways. For many existing articles, original authors agreed to update their contributions with new interpretations and theoretical perspectives, current statistics, new bibliographies, or simple factual developments that needed to be included. If the original contributor was unable to update an article, the editorial staff added new material or sent it to another scholar for assessment. In some cases, the general editor and volume editors selected a new contributor if an article seemed particularly dated and new work indicated the need for a fresh perspective. And importantly, where new developments have warranted treatment of topics not addressed in the original edition, volume editors have commissioned entirely new essays and articles that are published here for the first time.

The American South embodies a powerful historical and mythical presence, both a complex environmental and geographic landscape and a place of the imagination. Changes in the region's contemporary socioeconomic realities and new developments in scholarship have been incorporated in the conceptualization and approach of *The New Encyclopedia of Southern Culture*. Anthropologist Clifford Geertz has spoken of culture as context, and this encyclopedia looks at the American South as a complex place that has served as the context for cultural expression. This volume provides information and perspective on the diversity of cultures in a geographic and imaginative place with a long history and distinctive character.

The *Encyclopedia of Southern Culture* was produced through major grants from the Program for Research Tools and Reference Works of the National Endowment for the Humanities, the Ford Foundation, the Atlantic-Richfield Foundation, and the Mary Doyle Trust. We are grateful as well to the individual donors to the Center for the Study of Southern Culture who have directly or indirectly supported work on *The New Encyclopedia of Southern Culture*. We thank the volume editors for their ideas in reimagining their subjects and the contributors of articles for their work in extending the usefulness of the book in new ways. We acknowledge the support and contributions of the faculty and staff at the Center for the Study of Southern Culture. Finally, we want especially to honor the work of William Ferris and Mary Hart on the *Encyclopedia of Southern Culture*. Bill, the founding director of the Center for the Study of Southern Culture, was coeditor, and his good work recruiting authors, editing text, selecting images, and publicizing the volume among a wide network of people was, of course, invaluable. Despite the many changes in the new encyclopedia, Bill's influence remains. Mary "Sue" Hart was also an invaluable member of the original encyclopedia team, bringing the careful and precise eye of the librarian, and an iconoclastic spirit, to our work.

New York City and Los Angeles may claim to have speakers of more different languages today, but historically no section of the country has been more linguistically diverse than the American South. No other region can—or ever could—rival its many recognizable varieties of English, and English is only one part of the region's linguistic fabric, as this volume seeks to show. Few volumes of *The New Encyclopedia of Southern Culture* will be newer in more ways than this one. It has grown from the 26 entries of the "Language" section of the first *Encyclopedia of Southern Culture* to 67 entries here. In reviewing the earlier edition, the editors soon realized how much additional material could be—indeed, must be—tapped if the region's linguistic richness was to be reflected adequately. Thus, coverage of language topics and themes now takes a much more inclusive and wide-ranging view of the South and its many languages and language varieties. In addition to all the new entries, earlier ones have been updated, with only two or three exceptions.

The overview takes a broad, chronological look at the many languages and varieties that have been spoken in the southern states, beginning with the indigenous languages (e.g., Natchez and Yuchi) or language families (e.g., Muskogean, Algonquian, and Iroquoian) that were here when Europeans arrived. Some of these languages are still spoken today, but many are not. The overview then surveys the languages brought by Europeans and discusses the input of African cultures into southern ways of speaking.

In addition to entries on indigenous language families and individual languages, this volume includes an essay on the phenomenon of trade languages, which were used to communicate widely in multilingual areas and settings. From one entry on native languages in the first edition, coverage has grown to 11. Entries about other non-English languages (e.g., French and Spanish) have been expanded to reflect up-to-date research, and new entries show the cultural impact of recent immigration (e.g., Immigrant Languages, Recent, and Teaching English to Speakers of Other Languages). Language contact and borrowing are themes encountered in many entries, evidence that the multilingualism of the South has been both a historical and a modern-day reality. An important innovation has been to recognize emigration out of as well as immigration into the South and the linguistic consequences of such movement. Expatriate varieties are discussed in the Liberian Settler English, Confederate English in Brazil, and Bahamian English entries.

Besides containing a variety of languages, the southern landscape is a patchwork of English dialects. This volume naturally features entries on varieties that millions of people speak, such as African American English and Appalachian English. It also covers distinctive speech patterns used in particular cities (e.g., Charleston English and New Orleans English), in specific geographical areas (e.g., Chesapeake Bay English, Gullah, Ozark English, and Conch), and by certain ethnic groups (e.g., Lumbee English and Afro-Seminole Creole). While entries often identify usages inherited from older forms of the language, many emphasize the changing nature of the pronunciation, grammar, and vocabulary of the dialect at hand, and there are separate entries on these topics. Nowhere, however, will the reader find the simplistic and familiar lament that southern varieties of English are being completely homogenized into a national whole. Change is inherent to all languages and varieties, and not necessarily toward the mainstream even in the increasingly mobile South.

Much of the scholarly research on southern types of English has made use of information from linguistic atlas research (see the entries on the two large-scale projects of this kind, the *Linguistic Atlas of the Gulf States* and the *Linguistic Atlas of the Middle and South Atlantic States*). For a long time research on the region's English was produced by linguists who were southerners themselves (see, e.g., entries on Raven I. McDavid Jr., Lorenzo Dow Turner, and Linguists and Linguistics), including that on specific features (see, e.g., entries on Southern Drawl, *Y'all*, and *Fixin' to*). The last two decades have seen the blossoming of sociolinguistic research in the South, and many entries reflect this. In addition to language varieties and features, sociolinguists often study how language is used in cultural contexts. Topics such as politeness, discourse (see, e.g., entries on African American Discourse Features, Narrative, and Storytelling), and special language uses like preaching and naming (e.g., Place-Names and African American Naming Patterns) all describe ways language is woven into southern culture. Outsiders as well as southerners have recognized diverse characteristics and uses of language in the South, so this volume also considers how southern dialects are portrayed in popular culture (see, e.g., Southern English in Television and Film, Perceptions of Southern English, and Literary Dialect).

Language is a subject that has long captivated natives and visitors to the South alike. The editors of this volume, as well as its gracious contributors, hope that some of our own sense of fascination with language, linguistics, and southern culture will be conveyed to our readers.

The NEW ENCYCLOPEDIA *of* SOUTHERN CULTURE

VOLUME 5 : LANGUAGE

Few traits identify southerners so readily as the way they talk. It is often the first thing nonsoutherners notice about them, sometimes ridiculing southern speech as being "uneducated" or "incorrect" but at other times admiring it as "down-to-earth," "friendly," or "polite." Southerners are frequently renowned for their linguistic skills and verbal dexterity, whether as raconteurs, preachers, politickers, or just good talkers. When Georgian Jimmy Carter and Arkansan Bill Clinton ran for the presidency, the country took notice of their speech, and the media gave it much attention, curious about and often baffled by it. Carter's campaign spawned a rash of paperbacks of the *How to Speak Southern* ilk in 1976. Bubba jokebooks and one-liners played off the candidacy of "the man from Hope" in 1992, and when Clinton responded to a reporter's question on the campaign trail with the common regionalism "That dog won't hunt," journalists were quick to phone linguists at southern universities for a translation. For many southerners, the way they speak English marks their loyalties, their upbringing, their roots, and their identity, even if it often provokes stereotypes and prejudice when they travel, and not infrequently in southern schoolrooms as well.

Although the South is the most distinctive speech region in the United States, it is also the most diverse, little more uniform than the nation as a whole. Outsiders may think that all southerners talk pretty much alike, but southerners certainly know better. Some of the most unusual types of American English are found on the periphery of the South, in areas such as the southern Appalachian and Ozark mountains and such coastal areas as the Outer Banks of North Carolina, the Chesapeake Bay Islands of Virginia, and the Sea Islands of South Carolina and Georgia. But these varieties only begin to outline the linguistic picture of the region. Even so, many accounts, both popular and scholarly, have regrettably obscured the diversity of speech within the region by contrasting a generalized "Southern English" with "General American English" or "Standard English," the latter two being abstract, even hypothetical entities never described and certainly not homogeneous. Even the well-worn stereotypes so often featured in cinematic and other media portrayals of southern speech do not typify speakers throughout the South. For example, the lack of *r* after a vowel, once a hallmark of much of the region, is fast disappearing and is increasingly confined to older and African American speakers. The expression *y'all*,

1

(John L. Hart FLP, and Creators Syndicate, Inc.)

though as trademark a southernism as one can find and routinely acquired by transplants from outside the South, is still replaced by *you'uns* in some parts of southern Appalachia.

The South has never been a linguistic region unto itself. Nearly all features of English usually ascribed to the region can be found outside the former Confederacy among older-fashioned or rural speakers in one or another part of the country. Neither the Mason-Dixon Line nor any other geographical or political demarcation has ever set off the region linguistically. This became even less the case after World War I as countless African Americans took their southern-derived speech to northern cities in several large waves of migration. Southern English has also been exported abroad from time to time for more than two centuries, by African Americans to Nova Scotia, Sierra Leone, and the Bahamas in the 1780s and 1790s and to Liberia in the 1820s–1850s, and by disaffected whites after the Civil War to Brazil (where their English-speaking descendants are still known as Confederados). (Interestingly, Bahamian English was later brought back to the United States to form a prime constituent of Conch, a variety spoken in the Florida Keys.) The diaspora of southerners thus left its mark on the use of English in several areas overseas.

Early immigrants to the South from Europe were as heterogeneous as migrants to any other region (more so when those from Africa are considered), and into at least the antebellum period the South was no more isolated as a whole than other regions of the United States. Some cosmopolitan types of Southern English, such as those of New Orleans and Charleston, are among the nation's most recognizable, showing that ethnic mixes and social dynamics often produced distinctive American dialects. These factors were at play even in "isolated" areas. Most Americans, southerners and nonsoutherners alike, tend to view the South as a speech region (perhaps because of its shared history), even though linguistic research can hardly identify common features that definitively mark a "southern accent" or a "southern dialect."

Although no one common linguistic denominator distinguishes the South, linguists still identify it as a speech region, on the basis of three main characteristics: (1) a unique combination of linguistic features, (2) the use of these features more often and by a wider range of the population than elsewhere in the country, and (3) the consciousness of the people in the South that they form a region with distinctive speechways. These characteristics are clearly interrelated, in that a person's use of "southern features" can usually be correlated with his or her attachment to the region.

The persistent folk notions alleging distinctive speech in the region often refer vaguely to a "drawl" or "twang" and attribute it to the influence of the hot climate, the slower pace of life, or similar factors. However, the heart of why the region's speech is distinctive lies in the mundane realms of history, demography, and social factors, on one hand, and in the realm of psychology — in the consciousness of the region's people — on the other.

Indigenous Languages. Long before the many varieties of English in the South developed or other European languages arrived, the linguistic landscape of the region was an intricate patchwork of indigenous languages from five important families: Iroquoian, Algonquian, Siouan, Muskogean, and Caddoan. There were also other unaffiliated languages and scattered languages from other families in Texas, making several dozen indigenous tongues in all. Some had been in the region for millennia, but others had arrived in comparatively recent times (e.g., the Biloxi came to Mississippi from what is now the Midwest). Already by the 16th century, contact with the Spanish in Florida and South Carolina had put the existence of many small groups under threat of extinction from forced labor, disease, competition for land, and capture and sale into slavery (a common practice in British colonies into the 18th century). The identity, even the existence, of some tribes and the languages they spoke are known only from a highly fragmentary record that often contains only a few place-names. Though missionaries and other early workers were handicapped in their efforts to analyze languages very different in nearly every way from European ones, having only a Latin-based grammatical framework to base their descriptions on and lacking such tools as a phonetic alphabet, they left behind an impressive record on these languages for later scholars and tribal officials. The literature they produced dates from the early 17th century, when the Spanish and, later, British, French, Americans, and native peoples themselves began collecting word lists, devising systems of spelling, and describing the indigenous languages of the South.

By the beginning of the 21st century all remaining indigenous languages in

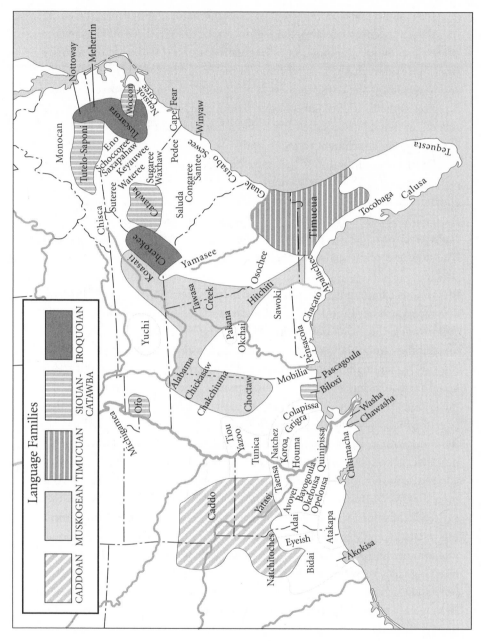

Map 1. Native Languages of the American South

Language Families

- IROQUOIAN
- SIOUAN-CATAWBA
- TIMUCUAN
- MUSKOGEAN
- CADDOAN

Nottoway
Meherrin
Monocan
Tutelo-Saponi
Eno
Schoccoree
Saxapahaw
Keyauwee
Suteree
Wateree
Waccon
Nottoree
Tuscarora
Cape Fear
Pedee
Sugaree
Waxhaw
Catawba
Winyaw
Saluda
Congaree
Santee
Sewee
Cusabo
Guale
Chisca
Cherokee
Koasati
Yamasee
Osochee
Timucua
Tocobaga
Calusa
Tequesta
Tawasa
Creek
Hitchiti
Sawoki
Chacato
Apalachee
Yuchi
Pakana
Okchai
Pensacola
Ofo
Alabama
Chickasaw
Chakchiuma
Choctaw
Mobilia
Pascagoula
Biloxi
Natchitoches
Colapissa
Grigra
Washa
Chawasha
Tiou
Yazoo
Tunica
Taensa
Natchez
Koroa
Houma
Quinipissa
Chitimacha
Bayogoula
Okelousa
Opelousa
Caddo
Yatasi
Adai
Avoyel
Natchitoches
Eyeish
Atakapa
Bidai
Akokisa

the South were endangered, as few of them had any native speakers under the age of 20. Extinction of indigenous languages seemed inevitable, abetted by the dominance of English speakers economically, numerically, and politically and by such official policies as the forcible removal in the 19th century of native speakers to Indian Territory (present-day Oklahoma) and prohibition against the use of native languages in tribal schools until recent years. However, revival and revitalization movements have begun sprouting around the region, even where the ancestral language is known only from decades-old recordings (e.g., among the Catawba in South Carolina). Today more courses in tribal languages are offered in schools and community centers than ever before, so their future is by no means so uncertain as it was a few short years ago.

Algonquian and Iroquoian speakers lived in the east. There were several varieties of Algonquian, with Powhatan, spoken in Virginia, being the best-known southern member of the family; it survived until almost 1800. Of the Iroquoian languages, Tuscarora was spoken in eastern North Carolina until 1722, when a remnant of its war-decimated speakers moved to New York, where a handful of older speakers remain on two reservations. Cherokee is still used today in both Oklahoma and among some of the Cherokee who remained behind and now live in western North Carolina. The Cherokee linguist Sequoyah devised a writing system for the language by 1821, bringing rapid literacy to his people; newspapers are still printed using this Cherokee syllabary. The number of Cherokee speakers declined dramatically during the 20th century; but some groups are promoting education in and about the language, and it has for the first time become a required course in a local high school in North Carolina. Speakers of Siouan languages (to which Catawba is distantly related) also lived in Virginia and the Carolinas as well as in Tennessee and Mississippi.

The Muskogean language family, the largest in the region, covered the central portion of the South in present-day Mississippi, Alabama, Georgia, northern Florida, and eastern Tennessee in the 19th century. It has nine members: Choctaw, Chickasaw, Alabama, Koasati, Mikasuki, Hitchiti, Creek, Seminole, and Appalachee. Choctaw and Chickasaw are closely related to each other and, like Cherokee, have been written languages since the 19th century; both have current revitalization efforts under way. Hitchiti was a dialect of Mikasuki. Creek and Seminole encompass three mutually intelligible dialects: Oklahoma Creek (also called Muskogee), Oklahoma Seminole, and Florida Seminole. Appalachee, a language originally spoken in the Florida panhandle, became extinct in the early 19th century, but not before the name of the tribe was applied on early Spanish maps to a vague range of mountains in the southern interior, which are today known as the Appalachians. The linguistic diversity of the lower Mississippi Valley led to the creation of a lingua franca known as Mobilian Jargon based on Muskogean vocabulary. It and other Indian trade languages (some of which became pidgins) arose in parts of the South that were particularly heterogeneous or where many groups had contact (as along rivers or seacoasts), in order to facilitate communication and trade between native groups. With between 30 and 60 distinct languages, the American South was a region more linguistically diverse than any other part of North America except California and the Pacific Northwest coast.

Of the Caddoan family, Caddo was the only member in the South, spoken in east Texas, Arkansas, and Louisiana. Other indigenous languages have no known relatives, either in the South or elsewhere. Timucua was spoken in northern Florida and southern Georgia; Yuchi is thought to have been spoken in central Tennessee (it survives, but barely, in Oklahoma); Natchez, Tunica, Chitimacha, and Atakapa were spoken in Louisiana and Mississippi.

Beyond east Texas indigenous languages were sparse. Comanche, a member of the Uto-Aztecan language family, was formerly spoken in west Texas and is used now by a small band in Oklahoma. In south Texas there were one or two Apache dialects spoken, primarily Lipan, an Athapaskan language that is now apparently extinct. The seminomadic Kiowa may have gotten as far South as the Texas panhandle on occasion. Beyond these, there were several poorly known languages along the Gulf Coast in east Texas: Karankawa, Tonkawa, Comecrudo, Cotoname, and Atakapa.

The principal linguistic contribution of indigenous languages to English in the South, as elsewhere in the Americas, is in place-names, especially for watercourses (e.g., *Tennessee* and *Yazoo*). What they (as well as other languages) gave to regional American English can be judged most accurately and authoritatively from the *Dictionary of American Regional English*; these borrowings are mainly names for plants. In the dictionary's first three volumes (encompassing *A* through *O*), one finds seven terms from Choctaw (e.g., *appaloosa*, *bayou*), three from Cherokee (e.g., *conohany*), one from Seminole (*coontie*), and two from Creek (e.g., *catalpa*). What English has borrowed from native sources in the South is surprisingly modest and obscure, the exception being from Algonquian languages (especially Powhatan or a pidginized form of it) in Virginia, from which John Smith and other early Virginia colonists took *opossum*, *raccoon*, *persimmon*, and other common terms for things novel to Europeans. In western North Carolina, eastern Tennessee, and northern Georgia, the Cherokee intermarried with whites and introduced a substantial part of their traditional culture (e.g., their pharmacopoeia) to them, but their linguistic influence was minuscule except for place-names.

Other Non-English Languages. The American South has witnessed nearly five centuries of contact between Old World and New World languages originating on three continents. Speakers of major European languages arrived in permanent settlements in the early 16th century with Spanish in Florida, in the 17th century with English in Virginia and French in Louisiana, and in the 18th century with German in Virginia. In the colonial period these languages were sometimes found more widely than they are today (e.g., Spanish, French, and German in South Carolina). Many other, less prominent languages, such as Ladino (to South Carolina) and Scottish Gaelic (to North Carolina), having fewer speakers and less permanence, came in the 18th century. Immigrant languages have continued to arrive, meaning that the South remains quite a heterogeneous place linguistically and has become even more so in the past two or three decades, with speakers of Haitian Creole, many types of Spanish, and other tongues (especially from East Asia) forming sizable immigrant communities in southern towns large and small. In addition, thousands of deaf southerners use American Sign Language, which has its own structure different from that of English. Because of the history of deaf education in the United States, southern varieties of American Sign Language are not markedly different from nonsouthern varieties.

During the centuries of the slave trade, enslaved West Africans brought dozens of languages, mostly from the vast Niger-Congo family (e.g., Ewe, Mandinka, and Ngola) to the South. African languages contributed to the vocabulary of the region as a whole and to the vocabulary and grammar of African American English throughout the country. Except for small fragments (such as a Mende funeral chant recorded in coastal Georgia in the early 1930s), these languages disappeared rapidly. Given the lack of a shared African tongue (or usually even similar languages) and the need for Africans to communicate with one another and with whites, contact between speakers of African languages and European ones produced creole forms of both French (in Louisiana) and English (in coastal South Carolina and Georgia) similar to those that developed in the Caribbean.

The only English-based creole spoken in the mainland United States is Gullah (sometimes also known as Geechee), whose speakers live in coastal Georgia and South Carolina. Perhaps half of the estimated 200,000 speakers of Gullah use it daily, but such an estimate is quite tentative. Gullah is not distinct from English in the way that French and Spanish are. Some types of Gullah are close to the local English, but others are much less so. Speakers can typically shift back and forth from one extreme of Gullah to the other, depending on their purposes and whom they are talking to. Nearly all Gullah vocabulary is shared with English (only about 5 percent comes from African or Caribbean sources), but Caribbean-like grammatical patterns, rhythms, and sometimes the meanings of words may make Gullah incomprehensible to English speakers elsewhere, including African Americans from the nearby rural South. Today the Sea Islands are experiencing a cultural renaissance, and interest in Gullah food, music, storytelling, literature, and traditions has extended to language. The most dramatic indication of this is a translation undertaken by the Sea Island Translation Team of Wycliffe Bible Translators, at work since 1979. The Gospel of Luke, *De Good Nyews Bout Jedus Christ Wa Luke Write*, was published in 1995, and the entire New Testament was issued in November 2005. Gullah, Cherokee, Creek, and Choctaw are the only languages native to the South to have their own translation of Scripture.

Spanish, the first European language to establish itself in the region, left an imprint on the place-names of Florida and Texas and, to a much less extent, on South Carolina, Louisiana, and other colonies/states. Among the oldest Spanish-speaking communities in the region are those in Florida deriving from Cuba more than a century ago (greatly enlarged in the 1960s) and the Isleños of southeastern Louisiana, who came from the Canary Islands in the 1770s. Today the number of Spanish speakers is growing exponentially in the Carolinas, Georgia, Tennessee, Virginia, and elsewhere (it had been increasing steadily in Florida and Texas for decades). According to the 2000 census, 4.24 million (6 percent) of the 67.5 million people in the 13-state region spoke Spanish, a figure that will certainly continue to increase. Texas led with 31 percent, followed by Florida with 15 percent, Georgia (5.3 percent), North Carolina (4.7 percent), and Virginia (4.4 percent). With its many varieties of Spanish from the Caribbean, Central America, and South America — among other languages — south Florida has become the most linguistically diverse and polyglot part of the South.

French first came to Louisiana more than three centuries ago and was once spoken in much of the lower Mississippi Valley in several varieties. Just as Gullah developed along the South Atlantic Coast, Louisiana French Creole arose as the native tongue among the linguistically heterogeneous slave population. It is used today by an estimated 4,000 to 5,000 speakers in scattered communities. A type of French close to the Parisian standard was used as the language of administration and wider communication until the Louisiana Purchase of 1803. Its prestige, gained in plantation society when children were sent to France for education, waned in the 19th century as the population of Louisiana shifted from majority-French- to majority-English-speaking (however, English was not compulsory in public schools until 1916). Cajun French, which arrived from Acadia (Nova Scotia and New Brunswick) in the 1760–80s, thrived in much of southern Louisiana until the early 20th century, but it is now in steep decline and is being acquired by relatively few children, despite preservationist efforts. Much more than other varieties of Louisiana French, Cajun French has influenced the English of the state.

The heartland of German language use and influence in the United States has always been Pennsylvania, and much of the German found in the South was or is a product of later migration from that colony/commonwealth. Two centuries ago, German dialects were commonly heard in the Shenandoah Valley of Virginia, where their speakers arrived as early as 1726. By the time of the American Revolution, German speakers comprised 5 percent of Virginia's population. In the colonial period, German-speaking Moravians immigrated to central North Carolina in the 1750s. Lutherans, in four stages, moved into the interior of South Carolina beginning in the 1730s, contributing such terms as *saddle horse, sawbuck, spooks*, and *I want off* to the state's English. In the mid-19th century, several thousand Germans immigrated to the vicinity of New Braunfels in central Texas. Today a few elderly speakers remain in Virginia, West Virginia, and Texas in remnants of early communities, but they are not passing the language on. In the 20th century, Old Order Amish and Old Order Mennonite speakers of German from Pennsylvania or the Midwest have formed communities in Florida, Virginia, Georgia, Texas, and South Carolina. The Pennsylvania German that is heard in the South today is the result of these more recent settlements.

Underappreciated is the cultural and linguistic diversity of arrivals from the British Isles. To be sure, those who came from Scotland and Ireland (less so for Wales) usually spoke English rather than a Celtic language, but sometimes they were bilingual or came from communities that had recently shifted from Irish or Scottish Gaelic to English. Immigrants from Lowland Scotland and Ulster also frequently spoke Scots, that close sibling to English, or Scots-influenced English. None of this historically eclectic lot, which came mainly in the 18th century, considered themselves to be "English," nor did their spoken English approximate that of southern England. These groups rarely formed their own communities or used a Celtic language, even within the home, for more than a generation. The major exception involved Presbyterian Highland Scots who came to the Upper Cape Fear Valley of North Carolina beginning in the 1730s. They had Scottish Gaelic as their first language and used it in the home for well over a century. Some early church services were in Gaelic, but schooling apparently never was. Highlanders continued to arrive throughout the 19th century, and the last native speaker died only in the 1950s. Even in southeastern North Carolina, however, Gaelic has apparently left no permanent mark.

For two centuries following the American Revolution, with the exception of Africans brought involuntarily, fewer immigrants came to the southern United States, especially to the region's interior parts, as compared with the rest of the country. Beginning in the 1970s immigration increased significantly, and it is accelerating. In decades yet to come its impact on the South can be expected to increase, producing ethnic diversification in urban areas, small towns, and rural areas. It remains to be seen whether stable multilingual communities will remain in areas of the South with growing immigrant populations. Children of adult immigrants are learning English as quickly as the second generation always has in other parts of our country of immigrants. Alongside English, however, heritage languages may remain, reinforced in part by continuing arrivals. Newcomers' countries of origin include Mexico, Brazil, China (including Hong Kong and Taiwan), Iran, Iraq (in Tennessee), Kenya, Laos, Mongolia, Nigeria, Pakistan, the Philippines, South Korea, Thailand, the former USSR, and Vietnam, as well as a number of Spanish-speaking countries in Central and South America. Monolingual southerners are certain to be exposed in the coming years to languages they have never heard before, and new varieties of English will undoubtedly be created.

English. The English language that arrived in Virginia 400 years ago had yet to develop a standard written form, much less a spoken one. Spelling was quite irregular, even among educated classes. For a century or more the English of coastal Virginia and the Carolinas was in large part an Atlantic variety having much in common with the language of the New England colonies and of Britain. It was in constant and rapid flux from the continuing arrival of speakers, in the 17th century mainly from southwestern and southeastern England and in the 18th century from Scotland, northern England, and Ulster. It grew by constant borrowing from other tongues, both indigenous and European. Because few records survive with direct evidence until well into the 18th century, comparatively little is known about the English of early settlers, but all indications are that colonists from the British Isles brought quite different types of speech to North America. No doubt the competition among languages and dialects throughout the settlement period led to the smoothing and amalgamating of differences, producing middle grounds between dialects in many places.

Scholars speak of three main streams in the formation of Southern English.

The first, the speech that came from southern England, is most pronounced in the Lower South. The second, that of north Britain (Scotland and northern England) and Ulster (the settlers from this northern province of Ireland have usually been known as the Scotch-Irish), is more akin to the speech found in the Upper South. A third stream, dozens of languages spoken by large numbers of Africans from along a 2,000-mile coast from Senegambia to Angola over a period of two-and-a-half centuries and sometimes (especially before the 1730s) creole types of English from the Caribbean, made the linguistic constituents of Southern English immensely more complex. Certainly no type of English came to American shores without almost immediate change. Dialects and languages competed and rubbed against one another everywhere, even in remote places. Statements widely encountered today about isolated areas of the South — whether the Outer Banks, the Chesapeake Bay Islands, or the southern Appalachian and Ozark mountains — preserving Elizabethan or Shakespearean English are great exaggerations (but not without social value in implying that varieties that may have little social prestige today have a legitimate and notable history). No matter how powerful or appealing such characterizations may be, how persistently or unquestionably they are believed by outsiders, how fervently they are espoused (or promoted) by the local population, or how ardently they are championed by the early linguistic literature on the region, they are myths.

As shown by research of the Linguistic Atlas Project (see below), the South is divided into two broad regions in speech, based on settlement history: the Lower South and the Upper South. The Lower South (sometimes known as the Coastal South or the Deep South) covers the Atlantic Coastal Plain from eastern Virginia to Texas. The speech of the Coastal South (such as Tidewater English) was carried southwestward and westward from the colonial settlements in Virginia and the Carolinas (especially Lowcountry South Carolina) into southern Georgia, Alabama, and Mississippi and then northward into Arkansas, western Tennessee, and Kentucky; into Louisiana and east Texas; and into Florida. The Upper South (sometimes known as the Upland South or South Midland) encompasses the Piedmont and the southern Appalachians from interior Virginia through South Carolina, the hill areas above the Piedmont in Georgia and Alabama, and northwestern Arkansas. Its speech derives in considerable part from the colonial settlements in the Delaware Valley of Pennsylvania. Beginning in the 1730s this speech was taken southwestward into western Virginia, North Carolina, Kentucky, and Tennessee. In the 19th century it spread across northern Georgia, Alabama, and Mississippi and also across Tennessee, Kentucky, and Arkansas and into east Texas.

Crossing migration patterns have blended these two general varieties of speech in the interior South, so that the more clear-cut distinctions found in the Atlantic states diminish as one moves west (Map 2). Contact between English-speaking migrants and non-English speakers also affected the varieties of English in the South. The French influence produced Cajun English in Louisiana, Mexican Spanish formed Texas English, and indigenous languages produced Afro-Seminole Creole in Texas (via Florida). Then there is the rich mixture of languages resulting in the distinctive sounds and vocabulary of New Orleans English.

When the speech of the South became distinct from that of the rest of the country is unclear, but this likely occurred in the first half of the 19th century, when the South attained a strong sense of sectional consciousness. At the end of the 18th century, Noah Webster of Connecticut and the Reverend John Witherspoon of Philadelphia noted (and objected to) characteristic southern usages as contrary to the national ideal. The South was developing (or was perceived to have) its own speech by then, a trend that would continue in some respects to the present. In the early 19th century one can find extended published comments by travelers about speech in the South, and southern commentators (as in Georgia, Virginia, and Tennessee) began compiling glossaries and observations of local speech.

Just as the South has been conservative in its cultural institutions and agrarian habits, so has the region's English in general been more conservative than other American regional varieties, preserving many usages common to 19th-century British speech that today are rarely found in either Great Britain or other parts of the United States. Most of these so-called quaint older forms in southern speech are lexical (e.g., *carry* 'take, escort'; *poke* 'paper bag') or grammatical usages (e.g., the past-tense verb forms *knowed, clum*), but several of the region's distinctive pronunciations are holdovers from the 18th century. For example, the pronunciation of *get* as *git* and of the suffix *-ing* as *-in* in words like *singing* and *dancing* were fashionable British usage 200 years ago, even though today they are labeled as nonstandard and are discouraged in American classrooms. The literary critic Cleanth Brooks claimed such pronunciations were more prevalent in the American South, as opposed to New England and elsewhere, because the South's stronger oral tradition has resisted admonitions of schoolteachers to pronounce words as they are spelled. On this basis southerners can with some justice claim, if they wish, that their speech is somewhat closer to the "Queen's English" than is that of most other Americans, although it is certainly not Elizabethan.

Many grammatical forms brought by immigrants from Britain or Ireland

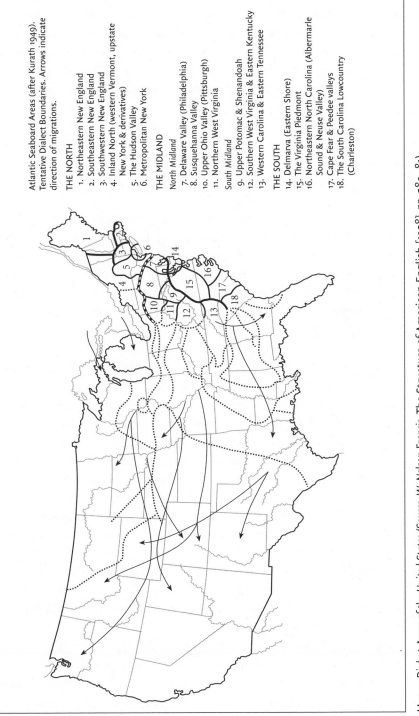

Atlantic Seaboard Areas (after Kurath 1949).
Tentative Dialect Boundaries. Arrows indicate
direction of migrations.

THE NORTH
1. Northeastern New England
2. Southeastern New England
3. Southwestern New England
4. Inland North (western Vermont, upstate
   New York & derivatives)
5. The Hudson Valley
6. Metropolitan New York

THE MIDLAND
North Midland
7. Delaware Valley (Philadelphia)
8. Susquehanna Valley
10. Upper Ohio Valley (Pittsburgh)
11. Northern West Virginia

South Midland
9. Upper Potomac & Shenandoah
12. Southern West Virginia & Eastern Kentucky
13. Western Carolina & Eastern Tennessee

THE SOUTH
14. Delmarva (Eastern Shore)
15. The Virginia Piedmont
16. Northeastern North Carolina (Albermarle
    Sound & Neuse Valley)
17. Cape Fear & Peedee valleys
18. The South Carolina Lowcountry
    (Charleston)

Map 2. Dialect Areas of the United States (Source: W. Nelson Francis, The Structure of American English [1958], pp. 580–81)

have developed new patterns or meanings in the South. For example, the verb *be* (especially among African Americans) came to refer to a habitual or frequent activity (*He be talking* 'He talks all the time'). *Might could* is known in Ulster and Scotland (its place of origin), but many other similar southern combinations of helping verbs, such as *might would* and *might should*, are not. Other patterns are new to the South altogether. Speakers of English everywhere use *whatever* and *whoever*, but in the South (especially in the hills) these developed the inverted forms *everwhat* and *everwho* (*Everwho it was didn't call back*). *One* when stressed and put after a pair of nouns to indicate a possible alternative (*I want to speak to Jack or Karen one* [i.e., either Jack or Karen]) is also unknown in Britain or Ireland.

African American English. Because the races have historically lived such intertwined yet separated lives in much of the South and because their varieties of English have at once striking similarities and striking differences, how and why the speech of blacks and whites differs in the South has long intrigued scholar and layperson alike. These questions remain as sensitive and intractable as the general issue of the social relations between the races throughout the country. This is because one's speech is often and intimately tied to views in society at large about one's social potential, one's intelligence, and one's background, among other things, and because American schools are expected to teach a colorblind "standard" or "correct" English. The "Ebonics" controversy in Oakland, Calif., that leaped into public attention in December 1996 was only one demonstration of the strong feelings people hold about the kind of language allowed in schools. The pedagogical issues of how teachers can handle diverse dialects in the teaching of literacy skills and do this most effectively hinge, in part, on an appreciation of minority speech varieties as having a history and validity of their own. Linguists can inform these issues by answering questions such as "What are the origins of African American English speech patterns?" and "What are the relative influences of African, Caribbean, and British Isles linguistic heritages?" Parallel questions pertain to white varieties, of course. With the possible exception of Appalachia, however, for white speech patterns, pedagogical issues have rarely reached the critical concern that they have for African American children and the long legacy of unequal schooling they have received.

On historical questions concerning similarities and differences, countless researchers and commentators in the South have weighed in with evidence, speculation, and proposals. White English and African American English are not monolithic; but African American English does share many features throughout the country, and for the sake of comparison it is frequently treated as monolithic. Views about their relationship run the gamut and show little sign of reaching consensus. At one extreme is the view that the speech of blacks (except for Gullah) retains from African languages only names and a small handful of nouns (e.g., *goober* 'peanut,' *yam*, *gumbo* 'okra,' *juke*) and that the otherwise distinctive features of black speech derive from 17th- and 18th-century American or regional varieties from Britain or Ireland, these having been acquired from whites and perpetuated by segregation. Analyzing the speech of expatriate African Americans in Nova Scotia and the Dominican Republic, a school of linguists from Canada has for some years vigorously championed this "Anglicist" view that African American English has no creole roots at all but derives entirely from the speech of whites.

A view at an opposite extreme is that present-day black speech is only superficially English and is derived from a plantation creole language similar to Gullah. The vocabulary and to some extent the grammar of this creole was, it is claimed, heavily influenced by African languages and Caribbean creoles and was ultimately derived from a pidgin language spoken in West Africa. About 40 years ago linguists began noting profound structural similarities (e.g., the absence of the auxiliary verb in sentences like *She kiddin'* 'She is kidding') between many English-based creole languages of the West Indies, from the Bahamas to Belize to Trinidad and Guyana. It became clear that in Gullah/Geechee many similar features could be found, and African American English shared a few as well. Historical research revealed that approximately 40 percent of African slaves entering American colonies came through Charleston and that many of the early arrivals were brought from the Caribbean (Jamaica and especially Barbados). Only later were slaves brought directly from Africa. Thus, both linguistic and historical factors made it plausible that African American English could have evolved from and retained vestiges of a creole.

The first significant and still most important study of Gullah is Lorenzo Dow Turner's *Africanisms in the Gullah Dialect* (1949). It is the foundation upon which all later work rests, though its focus is primarily on items that can probably or possibly (i.e., without certainty) be traced to West African languages. In all, Turner identified approximately 4,000 Africanisms, around 90 percent of which were personal names, rather than usages in the everyday language of the Gullah community. Following Turner's footsteps, popular attention has focused on Gullah's African roots, but the more immediate historical connections of Gullah to Caribbean creoles have drawn more scholarly interest. It is in fact the Caribbean flavor that visitors more often notice when they hear the lilt of Gullah for the first time, imagining they are in Jamaica.

There is an immense middle ground between the polar positions on the historical relationship between black and white speech in the South, and though extreme views have narrowed in recent years, they have done so only slightly. Few scholars now argue that a Gullah-like creole was spoken throughout the plantation South in the antebellum era, and more are increasingly coming to see African American English as having developed from a range of varieties.

The case for a distinct Black English or African American English is easier to make in the urban North than in the South, where far fewer linguistic forms are used exclusively by either blacks or whites. African American English in Cleveland and Chicago is to a large extent, especially in pronunciation, Southern English transported and quite different from local white speech varieties. Social differences are often more significant than racial ones, and a key problem with much of the research comparing white and black speech is that groups having equivalent education and social status have not typically been contrasted. In the South relatively few specific linguistic forms are now used exclusively by either blacks or whites. The differences are probably greatest in intonation and rhythm, the parts of language structure most difficult to describe and to generalize about.

There is much evidence that for the past century the speech of African Americans has been one of the most innovative varieties (or collection of varieties) in the country, both in the South and in the urban North. African American English has developed many new grammatical features in the past two to three generations. However, northern teachers and linguists have routinely labeled as Black English many other features, such as the helping verb *done* (*I done told you to stop that*), that are present in southern white speech. A common experience of white linguists native to the South has been to read or hear research conducted in northern cities that labels features as Black English that are characteristic of their own speech.

Innovation and change have been constants in all categories of southern speech. The social and political alienation that affected the former Confederacy for decades after the Civil War apparently intensified the region's dialect identity, so much so that some scholars argue that Southern English as we now know it (e.g., the pronunciation of *pen* as *pin*, a feature found up and down the social scale in most of the South) developed mainly after the Civil War. Thus, some of the most radical changes in southern speech began, or at least rapidly spread, in the late 19th and 20th centuries as the South became more and more urbanized and industrialized.

The influence of these and other social forces has meant two things: (1) social dialects have been replacing the diversity of regional dialects in the South, and

(2) regional dialect boundaries have been shifting in the South. Lower South urban centers such as Charleston, Savannah, and Richmond exercised prestige from the 18th century well into the 20th century as centers of wealth, power, and the social elite. In focal areas dominated by such cities, the older types of patrician Lower South speech developed that are found in the former plantation belt that spread from the coast all the way to east Texas and north along the Mississippi River into Kentucky. This prestige has been eroding steadily, and this erosion is attributable not to the influence of a national standard so much as to the increasing dominance of Upper South speakers and of former lower- and middle-class speakers who have climbed the social ladder. Whereas older speakers in Columbia, S.C., often pronounce *Mary*, *merry*, and *marry* with three different Lower South vowel sounds, their grandchildren more often than not pronounce all three with the vowel of *merry*, the Upper South pattern. The nonpronunciation of *r* after a vowel, once a sure sign of Lower South speech (as spoken by Jimmy *Cah-tah*), shows a similar generational progression. Nowadays the newer metropolises at the edge of the Upper South, such as Birmingham, Charlotte, Nashville, and Atlanta, are the centers for linguistic change and development of regional standards of speech. These cities, beyond the reach of the Coastal Plain but not quite in the southern Appalachian territory, mark a transition zone between the Upper South and the Lower South. The spread of their mixed dialect to smaller cities both toward the coast and toward the mountains is eroding many regional differences in speech between former plantation and upland areas.

Southern speech underwent major changes in the latter half of the 20th century, as did all regional varieties of English in an increasingly mobile, urbanized American society. This does not mean, as linguistic research reveals, that Southern English is necessarily simply converging with other varieties of American English or losing its distinctiveness. Changes in vocabulary are the most dramatic and occur primarily in the direction of homogeneity with the rest of the country (southerners, especially younger ones, increasingly use *green beans* rather than *string beans*, *bag* rather than *sack*, *soda* rather than *Coke* or *soft drink*, and even *stuffing* rather than *dressing*).

But grammar and especially pronunciation, while evolving, are by no means following suit. One recent study has shown, for instance, that young people in a small Alabama city extensively use the southern drawl (the lengthening and splitting of vowels into two syllables: *bed* as *bay-uhd*, *hit* as *hee-uht*), an important indication of their intent to preserve their speech. The "southern shift" (sounding *beagle* as *bagel*), which differentiates some Southern English pronunciations from other U.S. varieties, appears to be spreading rapidly, and pronouncing long *i* as *ah* is holding its own, as the speech of the two main contestants (George W. Bush and Al Gore) in the 2000 presidential election attested.

The sentimental may bewail linguistic change, especially in vocabulary, as the demise of a language that had more color, expressiveness, charm, and tradition (as when *dinner* referred to the midday meal every day of the week). They assume that the standardized, nondescript speech of the national media, of newscasters in particular, is responsible for homogenizing the speech of Americans in our television-addicted age. There is little empirical evidence for this belief, and it presupposes conditions unlikely to be true for most individuals: that newscasters possess sufficient prestige to function as models and that Americans talk back to their television sets. Linguists believe people usually pattern their speech after real-life models. Television has an influence on vocabulary, but it is hardly standardizing the pronunciation and grammar of Americans. There is also scant evidence that the recent settlement of northern migrants and retirees in the region is making southerners speak more like these new arrivals. One of the last things that most southerners want is to talk "like a Yankee." In fact, it is the transplanted northerners who pick up southern features such as *y'all* and *fixin' to*.

Features and Use. Among the representative grammatical features that are southern, some of which do not have exact equivalents in other varieties of American English, are the following: (1) *y'all* and *you all* (the latter, with the accent on *you*, being the somewhat more formal variant) as second-person plural pronouns; (2) by analogy, adding *all* after other pronouns to indicate inclusion, as in *what all, who all* (*Who all did you see?*); (3) "double modal" or "multiple modal" constructions such as *might could, may can,* and *might should*; (4) "perfective" *done* used for emphasis, as in *I done told you that*; (5) *liked to* 'almost,' as in *I liked to died*; (6) frequent use (especially in Appalachia) of the *a-* prefix with verbs ending in *-ing,* as *a-walkin'* and *a-talkin'*; (7) "personal dative" pronouns, as in *I bought me a dog*; and (8) *fixin' to* 'be about to, getting prepared to.' Southerners may also use verbs with the same form in all tenses (*come, run*) or verbs whose principal parts are made regular in the past tense and past participle (*blowed, heared*).

Among representative features of Southern English pronunciation are the following: (1) the tendency to pronounce the diphthong /ai/ (the so-called long *i*) as something like *ah,* so that words like *tide* and *time* sound like *tahd* and *tahm* (and for some southerners, *like* sounds like *lahk*); (2) r-lessness, for blacks and older upper-class and some middle-class whites, in words like *beer, bird,* and *better*; (3) the southern drawl, especially common in the Lower South;

(4) the southern shift, the "breaking" of some vowels, especially common in the Upper South and Texas, so that *steel* is pronounced like *stale*, and *stale* like *style*; (5) similar pronunciation of front vowels before nasal consonants, so that *pen* sounds like *pin*, and *hem* like *him*; (6) nasalization of vowels, as in the first syllable of *pumpkin*; (7) shifting of accent to the first syllable of words (*EN-tire*, *UM-brella*); and (8) final *l* reduced to a vowel or lost in words like *ball* and *boil*. Lower South speech has some affinities (as in the pronunciation of vowels) to that of London and southern counties of England, while Upper South speech is akin (especially in grammar) to the speech of the north of England, Scotland, and Ulster. The contribution by Scotch-Irish immigrants from Ulster, the dominant group in much of the Carolina and Virginia backcountry in pre-Revolutionary days, had until recently been significantly underappreciated, perhaps because of the popularity of the purported and more romantic Elizabethan origin of southern speech (especially for the southern mountains and the Outer Banks). To Southern English the Scotch-Irish contributed *cracker* (originally "a boaster," then "a person from the backwoods," and now "a rural white person from Georgia or Florida"); *galluses* 'suspenders'; *gumption* 'common sense, good judgment, shrewdness'; *wait on* 'wait for'; and many other terms and grammatical patterns, perhaps even *y'all*.

The two regions once differed from each other most in vocabulary. Typical Lower South vocabulary items include *lightwood* or *lighterd* 'kindling' and *piazza* 'porch.' Typical Upper South vocabulary includes *blinds* 'window covering,' *little piece* 'short distance,' *skillet* 'frying pan,' *red worm* 'earthworm,' and *quarter till* 'quarter to.' While the Lower South has *red bug* and *earthworm*, the Upper South has *chigger* and *red worm* (see Map 3).

Besides its grammar, pronunciation, and vocabulary, Southern English is distinctive because of other ways southerners use their language. Southerners are well known for their ability to stump on the campaign trail, to tell stories, and to preach. Old-fashioned proverbs remain in use, and the region is known for its colorful storytelling, whether by tellers of traditional folktales, by nationally known comedians, or by family elders. Stories are swapped in many informal settings, and anyone with a narrative of personal experience or a family tradition to relate can become a storyteller. In keeping with the image of the South as a place where life proceeds at a slower pace, the art of conversation remains alive and well. Southern hospitality is part of this way of life, and politeness strategies are still strongly maintained and valued, as in the use of *ma'am* and *sir* and elaborate greetings, leave-takings, and other rituals of social conversation. Politeness is sometimes turned on its head, as with the ritualistic toasts and dozens performed by young African American males, creative forms of rhythmic stories and insults that became the basis for the hip-hop music style. Other public performances and oratorical themes enliven the southern linguistic landscape as well, most notably preaching. The rhetorical styles of the black folk preacher have been thoroughly documented and researched; the more eclectic white preaching styles, less so. There is even a southern style of Jewish English that can be found in both urban areas and small towns throughout the South.

Finally, there is the special use of language for naming. Place-names for cities and counties come from Old World namesakes (*Richmond*), military and political life (*Jackson*), indigenous languages (*Tallahassee*), and other sources. Personal names derive from antiquity (classical and biblical names), family tradition, and many other sources as well. Unconventional names abound in the South, especially in African American given names. Yet creativity is also a tradition that continues today from the African custom of assigning "basket names," or nicknames, to babies.

Perceptions. Many southerners feel their speech is as much a part of their heritage as grits, football, and barbecue, inseparable from local and regional pride and cultural traditions. Yet southerners are acutely aware of how their speech is often caricatured elsewhere in the country. This mockery can make them insecure, even schizophrenic, about their speech, and they are unsure whether they want to be set off from the rest of the country. Over the past two generations many middle-class parents have sought to eradicate the more obtrusive regional features of their children's speech, labeling these as "country." Most southerners, however, defy the notion that they have any reason to change how they talk. When a community college in Tennessee offered a course not long ago for southerners wanting to change their accents, particularly those aspiring to traffic with nonsoutherners, the instructor of the course was publicly vilified and harassed. Regional consciousness accounts in part for the South's speech patterns, which, like much social behavior, express one's identity (whether local, regional, ethnic, or national) and indicate the group one prefers to be associated with. The strong attachments many southerners tend to have to the region are perhaps the surest buffer against the disappearance of Southern English; as long as there is regional consciousness in the South, a discernible variety of speech will likely express and embody it.

Because native southern dialect usually commands regional, but rarely national, prestige, southerners often acquire additional varieties of speech and develop a repertoire of speaking styles depending on the audience or situation. Many have long had the ability to shift between more formal, nationally influenced English and something resembling folk speech, or they command more than one variety of Southern English because of the class and ethnic structure of the area in which they grew up. Alabamians who have moved to New York City may alter their speech for New Yorkers, but among other Alabamians their speech will shift back quickly and naturally.

The self-consciousness that southerners have about their speech is perhaps most acute when a southern politician is in the national limelight or they hear portrayals of southern speech in films and television shows such as *The Beverly Hillbillies* or *The Dukes of Hazzard* (what might charitably be called "Hollywood Southern"). The use of dialect in such portrayals exploits both positive and negative stereotypes. While it is frequently intended only to indicate a character's regional origin, it can also suggest that character is unintelligent or uneducated. However embarrassing media portrayals of mountain bumpkins and stock car addicts may be, frequently southerners are depicted using their country smarts to thoroughly outwit their city counterparts.

The national media's consuming attention to southern speech whenever a southern politician gets his or her due alternately pleases and pains southerners. Carter's presidential run sparked countless newspaper stories by Washington, D.C., feature writers who feared they would have to learn a second dialect. In the 1984 campaign the populace was presented with such a caricature of the speech of South Carolina's Ernest Hollings that few knew his position on any issue or took him seriously (a national columnist claimed that Hollings's "lockjaw Southern drawl is almost unintelligible"). But southern politicos are also often recognized for having superior linguistic and rhetorical skills. Sam Ervin of North Carolina captured the country's imagination with his downhome banter and anecdotes when he chaired the special Watergate investigating committee in 1973. And Jesse Jackson of South Carolina roots has enlivened the Democratic presidential primaries with his powerful rhetoric in more than one campaign.

While southerners frequently find themselves striving to overcome stereotypes, they are not slow to capitalize on them, as on the Nashville stage or in a growing number of *Oprys* nationwide. Throughout the region, tourist-shop booklets featuring exaggerations of local speech are vastly overpriced, but they sell regularly, expressing pride in the local speech and profiting from outlanders at the same time.

Study of Southern Speech. There is more commentary on the speech of the American South than on any other region. Much of this, especially recently, has been produced by scholars, but much has come as well from nonacademics in a wide range of publications, from newspaper columns to state historical journals, suggesting the curiosity and pride southerners have about their own speech. Though often sentimental, their work is motivated by a fascination with local usages or an antiquarian interest in the picturesque expressions used by older, less-educated, less-traveled speakers and perceived to be dying out. However, the frequent attention to such expressions has in some respects exaggerated the exoticism of the region's speech, particularly the speech of African Americans and mountain whites.

The discrepancy between linguistic facts, as established by research, and folk perceptions and beliefs is not simple to explain. Take the putative southern drawl, for instance. Linguists have only begun to describe it and are now relying on spectrographic analyses to do so; to them *drawl* refers to the lengthening and raising of accented vowels, normally accompanied by a change in voice pitch. It involves the addition of a second or even a third vowel (so that *bed* becomes *bay-uhd* or even *bay-ee-uhd*) but does not necessarily involve a slower overall speech tempo. To the general public, however, the term is much broader and more inclusive, referring to the speech cadence, voice quality, and general language patterns most often associated with southerners.

The South is the only American region to have a book-length bibliography devoted to its speech, *The Annotated Bibliography of Southern American English* (1989). The early literature on southern speech, until roughly 1930, consisted of items such as word lists, collections of vivid and unusual localisms, and notes and speculations on etymology. Rarely rigorous or based on a survey of any kind, these writings dealt mostly with vocabulary but occasionally commented on pronunciation and grammar. With few exceptions, they discussed speech impressionistically, without relating the use of language to social variables such as age, social status, level of education, occupation, or gender. Neglecting these variables led, and continues to lead, to presentation of southern speech as more uniform and more different from the rest of the country than has ever been the case. Social variation and change are the rule even for small localities.

The systematic study of language patterns in the region began in earnest with fieldwork for the *Linguistic Atlas of the Middle and South Atlantic States* in the mid-1930s. Field-workers noted the age, level of education, occupation, gender, and social habits and contacts of each of the 1,162 speakers interviewed for the project. Summary volumes with maps covering this territory, which includes Virginia, North Carolina, South Carolina, eastern Georgia, and the northeasternmost corner of Florida, include Hans Kurath's *Word Geography of the Eastern United States* (1949), E. Bagby Atwood's *A Survey of Verb Forms in the Eastern United States* (1953), and Hans Kurath and Raven I. McDavid Jr.'s *Pronunciation of English in the Atlantic States* (1961). The *Linguistic Atlas of the Gulf States* (LAGS), directed by Lee Pederson from 1968 to 1992, carried the same survey into the interior South and contained interviews with 1,121 people in Alabama, Arkansas, Florida, Georgia, Louisiana, Mississippi, Tennessee, and east Texas, a territory of nearly a half-million square miles. Data from LAGS was published in microtext in 1981 and in seven interpretive volumes (1986–92). Atlas methodology, investigating hundreds of specific items using a standardized questionnaire for features of grammar, vocabulary, and pronunciation, has been highly influential in the region and has spawned a number of smaller-scale studies.

Central to Linguistic Atlas and other regionwide projects has been determining the number and the identity of subregions of Southern English. Early subjective studies divided American speech into three areas: New England, the South, and General America (i.e., Western or Midwestern). But in 1949 Hans Kurath first made the systematic case, on the basis of vocabulary, that the eastern states have three general dialect areas—Northern, Midland, and Southern—and that these were based on 18th-century settlement patterns and subsequent migration. In dividing the Midland area into two subareas, the North Midland (from Pennsylvania into northern West Virginia) and the South Midland (southern West Virginia and western Virginia, extending southward into South Carolina), Kurath made the proposal, which remains controversial, that the speech of the southern mountains and hills had more affinities with that of Pennsylvania, the colony from which interior parts of Virginia and the Carolinas were settled in the 18th century, than it did with that of the Lower South. Other research, based on the *Dictionary of American Regional English*, puts the main geographical dividing line between the Lower North and Upper South and thus challenges Kurath's identification of the Midland region.

LAGS sought to identify and characterize the primary speech varieties of the region, both regional and social. In a 1986 formulation based on grammar and pronunciation as well as vocabulary, Pederson and his associates identified at least 11 major subregional dialects in the eight states (comprising two basic regional configurations, Coastal and Interior) and as many as 14 urban dialects. Some usages correlate with geography (for example, Map 3 shows the distribution of *chigger* in the Upper South vs. *red bug* in the Lower South for the mite that crawls under the skin and causes an itch). But other terms show a pattern that is more social (for example, *wishbone* was found to cluster in urban areas; *pulley bone*, in rural ones) (see Map 4). Kentucky remains the only southern state yet to be mapped for its dialect areas. Fieldwork was conducted there in

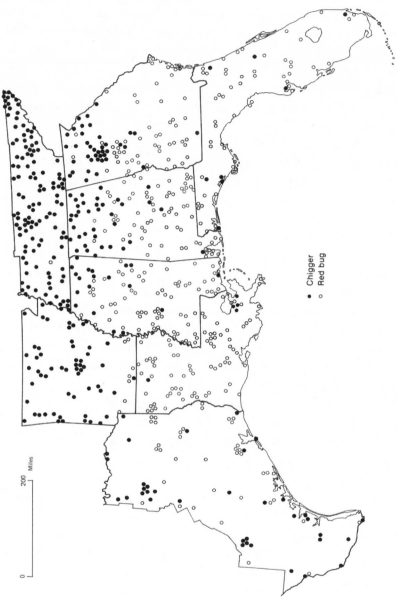

Map 3. Distribution of the Use of Chigger and Red Bug (Source: Lee Pederson, Susan McDaniel, Guy Bailey, and Marvin Bassett, Linguistic Atlas of the Gulf States, vol. 1, Handbook [1986], p. 75; cartography by Borden D. Dent)

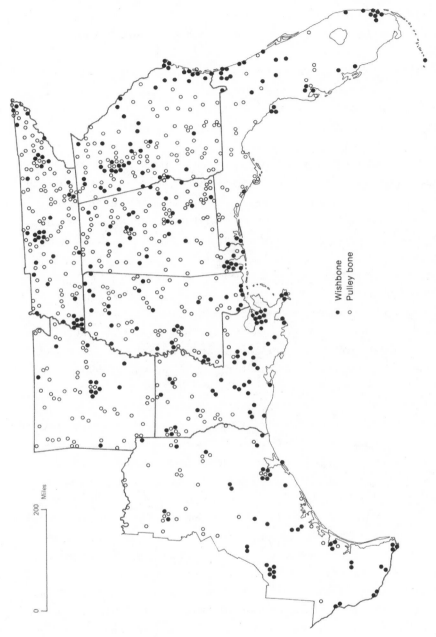

Map 4. Distribution of the Use of Wishbone and Pulley Bone (Source: Lee Pederson, Susan McDaniel, Guy Bailey, and Marvin Bassett, eds., Linguistic Atlas of the Gulf States, vol. 1, Handbook [1986], p. 74; cartography by Borden D. Dent)

Wishbone
Pulley bone

Miles
0   200

the 1950s as part of the *Linguistic Atlas of the North-Central States* (which also included Michigan, Ohio, Indiana, Illinois, and Wisconsin), but the data has never been analyzed.

The southern passion for determining roots applies to language no less than to bloodlines, so efforts to establish cross-Atlantic ties and the earlier history of features of Southern American English continue to be undertaken, by both linguists and nonlinguists. Hans Kurath, the founder and longtime director of the Linguistic Atlas of the United States and Canada project, designed its questionnaire to collect linguistic items that could be compared to regional British dialects, and he and other scholars have made tentative comparisons of individual terms. The odds against establishing unambiguous relationships between varieties on the two sides of the Atlantic are considerable, but the quest continues. The issue of time span is not as problematic as the means of establishing proof. For more than 50 years Cleanth Brooks advocated a linguistic version of the Cavalier myth, arguing that southern speech, including general features such as the drawl and specific archaic pronunciations such as *gyarden* 'garden' and *bile* 'boil,' came primarily from southwestern England. In his efforts to hear the rhythm and record the echoes of the southern idiom in the old country, Brooks tried to compare the intonation of English speech with that of southern speech, a quest far more difficult than pinning down individual words.

For more than a century researchers in the South, often nonlinguists, have published studies detailing analogues of southern features in British English. Most often these have been lists comparing the speech of mountaineers, blacks, islanders, or southerners in general with forms found in the works of Chaucer, in Shakespeare and other Renaissance writers, and even in Old English. A combination of regional and local pride and defensiveness about Southern English has motivated such efforts. Michael Montgomery's work in tracing grammatical features of Southern (especially Appalachian) English to the Scotch-Irish immigrants from Ulster has increased our knowledge of its roots. Though he has found many forms dating back to the British Isles, he debunks the myth that any southern speakers retain pure speech from immigrants.

Careful historical work like that of Montgomery and other scholars comparing British and Irish varieties of English to American dialects and parallel research exploring the origins of African American English have brought us much closer to an understanding of the historical development of Southern American English in many of its varieties. There is not yet a consensus on some general issues, but present-day linguistic research in the South is very active and promises to bring a fuller understanding not only to questions of historical interest but also to ones involving the continuing variation and change within the region.

MICHAEL MONTGOMERY
University of South Carolina

ELLEN JOHNSON
Berry College

Rudy Abramson and Jean Haskell, eds., *Encyclopedia of Appalachia* (2006); E. Bagby Atwood, *A Survey of Verb Forms in the Eastern United States* (1953); Cynthia Bernstein, Thomas Nunnally, and Robin Sabino, eds., *Language Variety in the South Revisited* (1997); Cleanth Brooks, *The Language of the American South* (1985); Craig M. Carver, *American Regional Dialects: A Word Geography* (1987); Frederic G. Cassidy et al., eds., *Dictionary of American Regional English* (1985–); J. L. Dillard, *Black English: Its History and Usage in the United States* (1972); Ives Goddard, ed., *Handbook of North American Indians*, vol. 17, *Languages* (1996); Heather K. Hardy and Janine Scancarelli, eds., *Native Languages of the Southeastern United States* (2005); Ellen Johnson, *Lexical Change and Variation in the Southeastern United States, 1930–1990* (1996); William A. Kretzschmar Jr., ed., *Dialects in Culture: Essays in General Dialectology by Raven I. McDavid Jr.* (1979); Hans Kurath, *Word Geography of the Eastern United States* (1949); Hans Kurath and Raven I. McDavid Jr., *Pronunciation of English in the Atlantic States* (1961); William Labov, Sharon Ash, and Charles Boberg, *The Atlas of North American English: Phonetics, Phonology, and Sound Change* (2005); Raven I. McDavid Jr., in *The Structure of American English*, ed. W. Nelson Francis (1958); James B. McMillan and Michael B. Montgomery, eds., *Annotated Bibliography of Southern American English* (1989); Modern Language Association Language Map, <www.mla.org/map_main>; Michael Montgomery, *From Ulster to America: The Scotch-Irish Heritage of American English* (2006); Michael B. Montgomery and Guy Bailey, eds., *Language Variety in the South: Perspectives in Black and White* (1986); Michael B. Montgomery and Joseph S. Hall, eds., *Dictionary of Smoky Mountain English* (2004); Stephen J. Nagle and Sara L. Sanders, eds., *English in the Southern United States* (2003); Lee Pederson et al., eds., *Linguistic Atlas of the Gulf States*, 7 vols. (1986–92); Edgar W. Schneider, in *Legacies of Colonial English: Studies in Transported Dialects*, ed. Raymond Hickey (2004); Erik K. Thomas, *An Acoustic Analysis of Vowel Variation in New World English*, Publication of the American Dialect Society, no. 85 (2001).

African American English

African American English is now the preferred term for the wide spectrum of varieties of English used by African Americans, ranging from Gullah, a creole language spoken along the coasts of South Carolina and Georgia that is similar to Anglophone Creoles spoken in the Caribbean (as in Jamaica), to varieties identical to those used by whites. Most linguistic research, however, focuses on African American Vernacular English (AAVE), the variety spoken by many working- and lower-class African Americans, especially in the inner cities of large urban areas. In fact, over the last half century more research has been done on AAVE than on any other variety of American English. This level of interest is a consequence of several things, including the substantial structural differences between AAVE and white varieties of vernacular English, the poor performance of many African American students on standardized measures of academic achievement and in the public schools, and the close relationship between AAVE and African American cultural identity.

While the level of interest in AAVE has remained high for half a century, the issues that have sustained this interest have changed over time. Initially, the three issues that fueled scholarly interest in AAVE were the dialect's adequacy as a mode of communication, its uniqueness, and its history. During the 1960s and early 1970s some educators argued that AAVE was simply a deficient form of English, with features (e.g., the absence of the linking verb *be* in sentences such as *They sick* and of the past-tense suffix *-ed* in sentences such as *Yesterday he walk to school*) that, they claimed, made it illogical and hence a barrier to educational success. Linguists have now thoroughly discredited this view. AAVE is not only adequate as a vehicle for communication but also powerful in many of its expressive uses (e.g., blues and hip-hop music). In general, linguists also now agree that AAVE, if not completely unique, is the "most different" of American dialects. AAVE, of course, shares many features with southern white varieties: for example, the identical pronunciation of *pen* and *pin* (as *pin*) and similar word pairs; flat /ai/ in words like *ride* and *nine* (so that these are pronounced with a sound something like *ah*); and grammatical forms such as perfective *done* (as in *Are y'all done finished?*), *y'all*, and *fixin' to* (as in *I was fixin' to leave when you called*). However, features like habitual *be* to express frequent or regular activity (as in *I be working at the Dairy Queen every afternoon*), the absence of *be* (as in *She sleeping*), the absence of the third-singular *-s* suffix (as in *She live in Dallas*), and the use of *had* plus a past-tense verb to express the simple past tense (as in *Yesterday she had went to Hearne*) are all either unique to AAVE or appear otherwise only in those varieties of American English heavily influenced by it.

The history of AAVE, though, remains controversial, and in fact, the controversy has increased as new issues relating to its development have emerged. For much of the last half century, historical issues have focused on the origins of AAVE, with two rather distinct views dominating the discussion. So-called Anglicists argue that the distinctive features of AAVE can be traced to the regional dialects of Britain and Ireland that were brought to the Atlantic seaboard during the 17th and 18th centuries. They note that features like perfective *done* and the absence of the third-singular suffix have analogues in rural British dialects even today and that the whites with whom slaves would have had contact were speakers of these regional vernaculars. Creolists, on the other hand, point out that AAVE features such as the absence of *be* have no analogues in either current or earlier British regional dialects but that they closely parallel similar features in Anglophone Caribbean Creoles. Creolists argue that AAVE is a latter-day descendant of an earlier creole language, much like Gullah and other Anglophone Creoles, that was used in the American South, especially on plantations. The creole arose first as a pidgin, a grammatically simplified contact language that resulted from the mixing of English and African elements either in Africa or in the United States among recently imported slaves who spoke diverse native African languages. As this pidgin was passed along to the children of slaves as a first language, it became grammatically more complex and developed into a creole. Current-day AAVE is said to represent a "decreolized" version of this earlier creole, one that has become more like other varieties of American English but that retains vestiges of its creole heritage.

Neither of these views is without merit, and both Anglicists and Creolists have marshaled impressive evidence in support of their claims. For instance, Creolists point out that in AAVE the absence of *be* is conditioned by the type of predicate that follows the copula. When the following predicate is *gonna* or a verb ending in *-ing* (as in *She gonna be late* or *The bus leavin' in fifteen minutes*), the verb is more likely to be absent than when the predicate is an adjective or a locative adverb (as in *She mad* or *They in Houston*). It is least likely to be absent when the following predicate is a noun or noun phrase (as in *Mr. Johnson the principal*). This distinction is important because a similar hierarchy occurs in Anglophone Creoles of Jamaica and elsewhere in the Caribbean. AAVE and those creoles, then, are alike not only in the absence of the verb but also in having the occurrence of the feature conditioned by the following predicate in the same way.

Anglicists have used similar types of evidence to support their arguments. For example, they note that in the English of Scotland and Ulster (and in American varieties strongly influenced by those dialects), *-s* occurs on third-person plural verbs (as in *Those boys works for me*) as well as on third-person singular ones (*He works for me*). The occurrence of *-s* on third-person plural verbs, however, is strongly conditioned by what kind of subject precedes the verb and by the proximity of the subject to the verb: *-s* is far more likely to occur when the subject is not the personal pronoun *they* (e.g., *They work for me*) or when the subject and verb are adjacent. Using data from a variety of sources, Anglicists show that earlier varieties of AAVE used *-s* on verbs in much the same way. Again, earlier AAVE (especially in the 19th century) parallels the dialects of Scotland, Ulster, and some areas of the United States (e.g., Appalachia) not just in the presence of a feature, plural verbal *-s*, but also in the factors that condition its occurrence.

In spite of the sophisticated arguments that Creolists and Anglicists have put forward for their positions, the debate over the origins of AAVE is far from resolved. Neither position alone can account for all of the distinctive features of AAVE, and many linguists now believe that the truth lies somewhere between the two. In certain respects (e.g., absence of *be*), AAVE clearly shows the imprint of its language contact history, a history that is similar but not identical to that of Anglophone Caribbean Creoles. At the same time, many other common features of AAVE (e.g., perfective *done*) clearly have or had use in British regional dialects. Even this compromise position, however, cannot account for all of the distinctive features of AAVE; the attempt to explain these other features continues to lead to controversy and debate.

Since the mid-1980s, a second historical issue has generated as much controversy as the question of origins. William Labov and his research team, based on work in Philadelphia, and Guy Bailey and his team, based on research in Texas, proposed independently that whatever its origins, AAVE was not simply becoming more like other varieties of American English but, rather, was developing along an independent trajectory. This position became known as the divergence hypothesis, although "independent development" more accurately describes what is happening. The evidence for independent development is of two types. First, Labov and, later, Bailey and Erik Thomas demonstrated that African Americans generally did not participate in the changes in vowel pronunciations that have increasingly distinguished the regional vernaculars of white Americans from one other during the course of the 20th century. The phonological relationships between African Americans and whites in the American South provide an excellent example of this development. During the late 19th century both blacks and whites participated in the vowel changes that made *pin* and *pen* sound alike (both sound like the former) and that produced the monophthongal or flat /ai/ in words like *hide* (so that it sounds like *hahd*). It was primarily whites, however, who participated in the series of 20th-century vowel changes known as the southern shift. Among other things, these changes in white speech make the nucleus of the diphthong in *way* (i.e., the first part of the vowel) sound something like the vowel in *bad* (so that *way* sounds close to *why* and correspondingly *we* sounds close to *way*) and the nucleus of the diphthong in *note* sound something like the vowel in *net*. The independent development of the black and white vowel systems during the 20th century accounts in part for the fact that ethnic identity can often be determined from speech alone, without any visual cues, and it makes those vowel systems in some respects more different now than they were a century ago.

Second, the research teams of Labov and Bailey have demonstrated that certain crucial grammatical features of AAVE did not emerge until the middle of the 20th century and that some older features of AAVE are more frequent now than they were in the past. For example, Bailey and his associates show that both habitual *be*, long seen as one of the hallmarks of AAVE, and *had* plus the past tense used as a simple past did not fully emerge in AAVE until around World War II, while the absence of third-singular *-s*, a feature that seems to have been present since the beginning of the vernacular, occurs more extensively now than at any time in the last 150 years. The independent development of AAVE grammar occurs in more subtle ways as well. For instance, although perfective *done* almost certainly has its origins in early contact with British vernaculars, Labov shows that in AAVE it has developed new meanings (e.g., moral indignation) in addition to the meanings (e.g., completion, intensification) that it carries in other varieties of English.

The evidence for the continuing independent development of AAVE comes largely from new sources of data that have emerged since the mid-1980s. That evidence, along with a better understanding of the complex demographic history of African Americans, has helped reshape the conversation about both the origins and the later history of AAVE. Until the 1980s much of the evidence on AAVE came from sociolinguistic interviews conducted in large northern cities such as New York, Detroit, and Washington, D.C. Conclusions about the origins of AAVE were the result of inferences made from contemporary data, much of which came from adolescents. Over the last 25 years four additional types of data have emerged: (1) data from extensive studies of rural southern communities that include interviews with African Americans born as early as the 1880s; (2) historical evidence from a variety of sources, including mechanical recordings made between the late 1930s and the early 1970s with former slaves born as early as 1844; (3) Freedmen's Bureau letters and other documents written by former slaves; and (4) "diaspora varieties" from places like Liberia, Nova Scotia, and the Dominican Republic.

As it became clear that a number of AAVE features are relatively recent developments rather than relics of the colonial period, linguists began to explore African American history more closely, shaping their research designs to better reflect its complexities. For instance, Walt Wolfram and his research teams in North Carolina have examined several insular communities that reflect different historical patterns of black-white interaction, including different types of slave communities, while Bailey and Cukor-Avila have over a 17-year period examined the relic of an old tenant-farming community organized around a general store that remained in operation until 2004. The evidence that has emerged from the historical research and from the study of different types of southern communities suggests a rich, multitextured history for AAVE that neither the Creolist nor the Anglicist position captures. As might be expected from the different patterns of slaveholding in the South, present-day AAVE seems to have had no single, monolithic ancestor but, rather, a complicated group of ancestors that ranged from Gullah, spoken in areas where slaves comprised an overwhelming majority of the population, to varieties of speech that incorporated much of the local white dialect, typically spoken in areas with proportionately much smaller slave populations. In spite of this extensive variation, however, a number of features seemed to have been present in all varieties of early AAVE, including the absence of *be* and third-person singular *-s*. These features reflect the language contact situation that existed everywhere slaves were imported and have been among the most durable features of AAVE, perhaps because of their widespread use.

The increasing geographic mobility that African Americans experienced after slavery and particularly during the 20th century gradually led to the erosion of many more localized dialect features, while the Great Migration that began with World War I and accelerated after World War II led to the formation of new African American communities in large northern cities that provided a context for the development of new grammatical features, such as habitual *be*, and the expansion of older ones. As these new urban communities were formed, most purely local AAVE variants disappeared, the more common AAVE forms persisted or even expanded, the newly emerging forms (such as habitual *be*) spread, and a supraregional variety emerged, one that correlates not with place but with ethnicity. While many of the details of the history of AAVE remain to be worked out, it is clear that features of the present-day variety reflect its language contact history, its historically close relationship with southern white vernaculars, and its continuing grammatical development.

The origins and current trajectory of AAVE have largely been topics of academic debate, but they became matters of public discussion and controversy in December 1996 when the Oakland, Calif., school board passed a resolution proclaiming Ebonics to be the official language of the 28,000 African American students within its district. Motivated by a desire to reverse the long-standing failures of the public school system to educate African American students successfully, the school board focused on the linguistic issues that seemed to be the fulcrum of that failure. Although the focus on language was not surprising, both the approach that the school board took and the public response were. The term *Ebonics* (a blend of *ebony* and *phonics*) was coined by Robert Williams in the early 1970s to refer to the complete set of linguistic behaviors (including not only grammar and pronunciation but also the social uses of language) that distinguish African Americans from whites in the United States. More recently the term has come to suggest the Afrocentrist belief that the distinctive features of AAVE derive entirely from the languages of the Niger-Congo family that were spoken by many slaves brought to the New World.

While almost all linguists applauded the Oakland school board's focus on linguistic issues, virtually none would agree with the assertion that AAVE derives entirely from Niger-Congo languages. Although some of the rhetorical traditions of AAVE may have African antecedents, the phonology and grammar of AAVE are clearly more English than African. Using evidence from mechanical recordings with former slaves, Thomas and Bailey do in fact identify several vowel features of early AAVE that seem to be African retentions, the most prominent of which are monophthongal /e/ in words like *fate*, and /o/ in words like *boat* (the monophthongs sound as if the English vowel were cut in half). These features, however, had largely disappeared by the beginning of the 20th century, and there is little evidence of them in current AAVE.

What linguists found far more troubling than the school board's version of the linguistic history of AAVE, though, was the public reaction to the controversy. Mainstream media commentators often showed a remarkable dearth of linguistic knowledge in their equation of AAVE features with a lack of intelligence and with communicative inadequacy, myths that linguists assumed they had refuted decades ago. Even more troubling, AAVE provided a surrogate for the expression of ridicule and racist views by some people. Ultimately, what the Ebonics controversy demonstrated was the large gap between linguists' views of nonstandard dialects and the perceptions and beliefs of the general public. If linguists see those dialects (including AAVE) as linguistically adequate but socially stigmatized, much of the general public sees them simply as the products of ignorance and laziness — as just poor English.

The public reaction to the Oakland school board's focus on Ebonics was also problematic in its failure to recognize that not all African Americans use AAVE.

Some, especially middle-class African Americans, do not use the set of features (especially the grammatical features) normally associated with AAVE at all, while others use them to varying degrees and with varying frequencies. Nevertheless, many of these African Americans participate in the African American speech community in the ways they use language and in African American rhetorical traditions (e.g., "talking that talk"). Participation in traditional speechways, some of which may have roots in African language traditions, provides the linguistic substance that defines a larger African American English, of which AAVE is only one manifestation.

Ironically, even as many in the general public decry Ebonics as a sign of ignorance and laziness, the uses of AAVE continue to expand into the mainstream, most notably in hip-hop music and other forms of cultural expression. If much of the country regards AAVE with disdain, for many African Americans it is a mechanism for establishing their identities as African Americans, for integrating themselves into their community, for building and maintaining relationships, and for expressing pride in their racial heritage. These positive values have ensured the existence of AAVE even in the face of astonishing social and educational pressures, such as those evidenced by the Ebonics controversy, to eradicate it. For African Americans, as for white southerners, their language is their most important vehicle for establishing who they are. That bodes well for the future of AAVE.

GUY H. BAILEY
University of Missouri–Kansas City

Guy Bailey and Natalie Maynor, *Language and Society* (vol. 16, 1987); Guy Bailey, Natalie Maynor, and Patricia Cukor-Avila, eds., *The Emergence of Black English: Texts and Commentary* (1991); John Baugh, *Out of the Mouths of Slaves: African American Language and Educational Malpractice* (1999); William Labov, *Language in the Inner City* (1972); Sonja J. Lanehart, ed., *Sociocultural and Historical Contexts of African American English* (2001); Michael B. Montgomery and Guy Bailey, eds., *Language Variety in the South: Perspectives in Black and White* (1986); Michael Montgomery, Janet Fuller, and Sharon DeMarse, *Language Variation and Change* (vol. 5, 1993); Salikoko Mufwene, John Rickford, Guy Bailey, and John Baugh, eds., *African-American English: Structure, History, and Use* (1998); Shana Poplack and Sali Tagliamonte, *African American English in the Diaspora* (2001); John R. Rickford, *African American English: Features, Evolution, and Educational Implications* (1999); Erik Thomas and Guy Bailey, *Journal of Pidgin and Creole Languages* (vol. 13, 1998); Walt Wolfram and Erik R. Thomas, *The Development of African American English* (2002).

Afro-Seminole Creole

Afro-Seminole Creole (also called Shiminol or Maskogo) is an offshoot of 17th- and 18th-century Gullah, traceable to the Africans who escaped from the British plantations in the southeastern Crown colonies of Georgia and South Carolina. These slaves, along with Creeks and other indigenous tribes, were allowed refuge in Spanish Florida, where they were called *cimarrones* 'fugitives,' possibly from a native word meaning a kind of wild grass. *Seminole* comes from the Creek pronunciation (*siminoli, similoni*) of this Spanish word. When Florida joined the United States, slavery was still legal, and the African Seminoles petitioned to move west to Indian Territory (now Oklahoma), which they did in 1837. Others went to the Bahamas or Cuba. Still subject to slave raids in the United States, in 1849 they again petitioned to move, this time into northern Mexico, where they were granted 25 square miles of land at Nacimiento, in the state of Coahuila. In 1870 they were invited by the Texas Rangers to become scouts to help clear south Texas of Lipan Apaches and other tribes for European settlement. This they did, basing themselves in Fort Clark in Brackettville and Fort Nicholas at Eagle Pass. In 1914 with the dissolution of the garrisons some returned to Nacimiento and some remained in Brackettville. Today the three main areas inhabited by Afro-Seminoles are Brackettville, Nacimiento (where they are known as Maskogos), and Wewoka, Okla. (where they are known as Freedmen). Their genetic and cultural makeup is traceable to various African and Native American peoples. They refer to themselves as "Negro Indians."

The food and the culture of Afro-Seminoles also include African and American Indian elements. At a revival meeting, African gospel rhythms eventually move into the "Seminole stomp," which is clearly Native American, as is the preparation of frybread, *suffki*, and a flour from the royal palm (called a *coonteh*). Use of a large pestle and mortar to grind rice and corn probably has dual origins.

Historically Gullah has developed into two independent branches: Sea Island Creole (SIC) and Afro-Seminole Creole (ASC). Their separation took place before the large-scale influence from Upper Guinean languages into the Georgia/Carolina region in the mid-18th century modified Gullah to become the variety described by Lorenzo Dow Turner and others in the 20th century. By contrast, ASC has been influenced by Spanish and indigenous languages. SIC resembled ASC more in the late 19th century than it does today. ASC negates solely with *no* (*hunnuh no bin yeddy um* 'You didn't hear her') and pluralizes with postnominal *dem* (*duh wisseh de knife dem dey?* 'Where are the knives?'), both of which are now rare in contemporary SIC. It retains forms such as *warra* 'what' and *darra* 'that' recorded only as archaic in other creoles, such as Jamaican. Its future marker is *en*, from *gwen* 'going' (*e n'en talk turrum* 'She won't talk to her'), not found in SIC, where the similar-sounding *ain'* is today the common verbal negator. Some indigenous American words in ASC include *suffki, stamal,* and *polejo*, all foodstuffs prepared from corn. Spanish words include *calpintero* 'woodpecker,' *banya* 'wash,' *metati* 'mortar,' and many others. Quite a few African-derived words are shared with SIC (*pinda* 'peanut,' *coota* 'turtle,' *tabby* 'mud'), but that language has many more African-derived words not found in ASC. SIC also has African phonological features, such as the doubly articulated stops /kp/ and /gb/, not found in ASC. ASC does not share with SIC such words as *buntas* 'buttocks,' and *skiffi* 'pudenda' (though variants of both of these occur in some Caribbean creoles).

ASC is a very private language, and when asked, its speakers typically deny any knowledge of it. At a gravestone dedication attended by the Seminole and non-Seminole Brackettville community, a lady greeted her friend in English from a distance as she approached her, then repeated the whole greeting in ASC quietly in her ear as she bent to hug her. ASC is not being passed on to younger generations. While ASC speakers know what they are speaking — Creole or English — at any given time, the English of the oldest generation is clearly influenced grammatically and phonologically by ASC. Speakers are also aware that ASC was "deeper" in earlier times; a younger speaker who said *trow-way* for *spill* was corrected by an older speaker, who told her that the proper pronunciation was *chuwway*. Likewise, the "proper" pronunciation of the name of the language is said to be *Shiminóleh*, not *Siminóle*, as it is commonly pronounced. Young people today can mimic the distinctive English pronunciation of their elders but cannot produce the language.

None of the pidgin or creole languages spoken in the South is in good shape today. Mobilian Jargon (or Mobilian Yamá), once used in the lower Mississippi Valley, is extinct. Louisiana Creole French has only a few thousand speakers and is not being learned by children. Sea Island Gullah of South Carolina and Georgia shows ongoing drift toward English. Fewer than 400 people, none of whom is younger than about 60, can speak Afro-Seminole Creole fluently today.

IAN HANCOCK
University of Texas

Thomas A. Britten, *A Brief History of the Seminole-Negro Indian Scouts* (1999); Cloyde I. Brown, *Black Warrior Chiefs: A History of the Seminole Negro Indian Scouts* (1999); Joshua R. Giddings, *The Exiles of Florida* (1858); Ian Hancock, in *Language Variety in the South: Perspectives in Black and White*, ed. Michael B. Montgomery and Guy Bailey (1986), *Hablar, Nombrar, Pertenecer* (1998).

Algonquian Languages

Algonquian languages indigenous to the South were limited to those known today as Virginia Algonquian (Powhatan) and Carolina Algonquian, two groups of sparsely documented dialects spoken in coastal Virginia and coastal North Carolina, respectively. Powhatan remained spoken until the 1790s. Little is known about the fate of other languages in the area.

A third Algonquian language, Shawnee, was represented by wandering bands along the Savannah River for a brief time, from the 1680s until shortly after 1700, when they left to join other Shawnee bands in Pennsylvania and elsewhere in the North. The Algonquian family as a whole was centered around the Great Lakes, with the Shawnee homeland in the Ohio River Valley. Nonetheless, the Shawnee were regarded by many white Americans as a southern tribe with no legitimate claim to a northern homeland. Their brief sojourn along the Savannah River has given rise to the supposition that the river name was taken from their name for themselves: *Shawanwa*, commonly contracted to *Shawano*. The latter is the purported source of *Savannah*, but the river name actually comes directly from *savanna* 'grassland,' borrowed into English from Spanish in the mid-1500s. Shawnee is still spoken by older tribal descendants now living in and around the towns of Shawnee and Tecumseh in central Oklahoma, where some younger tribal members continue to learn the language with the intention of preserving traditional ceremonies.

Powhatan contact with Spanish explorers began as early as 1525, but it was contact with the English settlers of Jamestown after 1607 that provided all that is known of the language. Existing documentation is limited to that obtained in the early 1600s. English borrowings from Virginia Algonquian, dating from the time of the Jamestown settlement, include *moccasin, persimmon, opossum, raccoon,* and *pone* 'bread' (as in *corn pone*). Numerous other Algonquian terms were borrowed into English through contact with Algonquian tribes in New England.

Algonquian languages, like many indigenous North American languages, are characterized by complex grammatical structures in which the verb, accompanied by prefixes and suffixes, often constitutes a complete sentence. Intransitive verbs distinguish between animate and inanimate subjects, while transitive verbs make similar distinctions for animate and inanimate objects. Thus, the Powhatan intransitive form for "He is short" can be analyzed as *tahkw-esi-w*. It is built on the root *-tahk-* 'short,' an animate verbal suffix *-esi*, and a third-person marker *-w*. The inanimate form would be *tahkw-ee-w* 'It is short,' built on the same root, with an inanimate verbal suffix and the same third-person marker.

A transitive verb like *smell* also has two forms: *ne-meraam-aa-w* 'I smell him' and *nemeraantaan* (from underlying *ne-meraam-taa-n* with shift of *m* to *n* before *t*) 'I smell it.' The prefix in both cases represents the first person, and both forms share the same root. The distinction is made by the transitive suffixes *-aa* for animate and *-taa* for inanimate, and third-person markers *-w* for animate and *-n* for inanimate. In transitive verbs, the choice of prefix is determined by a hierarchy of person. Second person takes priority as prefix, then first person, and finally third person. This is true regardless of which person is subject or object. The direction of action is then shown by a special suffix, while other suffixes indicate whether either category of person is plural. Thus, the Powhatan word meaning "I feed you [singular]" can be analyzed as *ke-t-assam-es*, in which *ke-* denotes *you* (singular), *-assam-* denotes the root *feed*, and *-es* denotes first person acting on second person. By contrast, the expected form for "I feed him" is *ne-t-assam-aa-w*, in which *ne-* denotes first person, *-aa* signifies action flowing from prefix to suffix, and *-w* marks third person. The intrusive *-t-* is inserted to separate a sequence of two vowels.

Shawnee has similar grammatical patterns, as do the other Algonquian languages. In Shawnee the form meaning "I feed him" can be analyzed as *ni-t-sham-a-w*. The individual elements making up the word correspond exactly to those in the Powhatan word, although the pronunciation has diverged over the centuries as the original community separated into independent branches.

The distinction between animate and inanimate appears in nouns as well as verbs. The Powhatan word for *fish* is *nameess*, with a plural *nameess-ak*. The corresponding Shawnee words are *nameth-a* for singular and *nameth-aki* for plural. Inanimate nouns take a different plural suffix and, in the case of items inseparably associated with someone, must carry a possessive prefix as well. Thus, Powhatan has *me-sit* for *someone's foot* and *me-sit-as* for *someone's feet*. The root *-sit-* denotes *foot*, while *me-* is an impersonal possessive prefix and *-as* marks inanimate plural.

In comparison, Shawnee has *ni-thich-i* for *my foot* and *ni-thit-ali* for *my feet*. The prefix *ni-* marks first person. The suffix *-i* marks inanimate singular, and the suffix *-ali* denotes inanimate plural. The root for *foot* is *-thit-*, although the final *t* becomes *ch* before *i*.

The Virginia and Carolina Algonquian tribes were substantially reduced in numbers through conflict with Europeans and exposure to European diseases. Most surviving descendants eventually lost their separate identity through intermarriage with Europeans or merger with neighboring tribes, as tribes with declining populations welcomed other Indians, runaway slaves, and Europeans who preferred the Indian way of life. Descendants of these remnant bands identifying themselves as the Powhatan Renape Nation have relocated north of their original homeland and, since 1982, have owned a reservation near Rankokus, N.J. The name *Renape* (a three-syllable word meaning "people") is cognate with the form *Lenape*, found in related languages such as Delaware.

BRUCE L. PEARSON
University of South Carolina

Bruce L. Pearson, *International Journal of American Linguistics* (vol. 53, 1987), *Southern Journal of Linguistics* (vol. 24, 2000); Frank T. Siebert Jr., in *Studies in Southeastern Indian Languages*, ed. James M. Crawford (1975).

American Sign Language

The history of American Sign Language in the South is directly linked to the history of deaf education in the United States. The first school, the American School for the Deaf (originally called the American Asylum for the Deaf and Dumb), was founded in 1817 in Hartford, Conn., by Thomas Hopkins Gallaudet. He was assisted by Dr. Mason Cogswell and Laurent Clerc, a graduate of and teacher at the Institute for Deaf Mutes in Paris, a school that was teaching deaf children through sign language as opposed to using a strictly oral method. Because the American School for the Deaf was the first institute of its kind to gain permanence in the United States, others looked to it when setting up schools for deaf students in their states. Furthermore, Gallaudet University (originally the Columbia Institution for the Instruction of the Deaf and Dumb and the Blind) was founded in Washington, D.C., in 1864, and many of its graduates helped found and develop schools for the deaf in various states. Thus the sign language used by southern white deaf children and adults has direct historical ties to northern varieties. For example, students from Georgia were sent to Hartford before their own school was founded in 1846; before the Mississippi school was established in 1854, children were sent to a school in Kentucky with strong American School for the Deaf ties and to New York. The first superintendent of the Florida school (founded in 1885) was from Gallaudet, while the North Carolina school in Raleigh (1845) and the Virginia school in Staunton (1839) both enjoyed the support of the American School for the Deaf. By 1834 a single signed dialect was used throughout the schools for deaf students in the United States.

There are many regional lexical differences from state to state, but the basic structure of American Sign Language—its phonology, morphology, and syntax—is shared throughout northern and southern states. The terms *phonology*, *morphology*, and *syntax* refer to the same entities to which they refer in spo-

Gallaudet College, Chapel Hall, 1933 (Library of Congress [HABS DC, WASH, 428A-], Prints and Photographic Division, Washington, D.C.)

ken languages: the basic building blocks of a language, the units used to form signs and sentences. In the case of phonology, the basic units are handshape, location, palm orientation, movement, and nonmanual signals (facial expressions). The term *phonology* is now widely accepted by spoken-language and sign-language linguists alike.

The situation is somewhat different for black signers. While the American School for the Deaf was established in 1817 for white children, no attempt was made to provide for black deaf children until the 1850s. Following the Civil War, some states established schools or departments for black children within already established schools in the South. North Carolina established the first school for black deaf children in 1869. One school for black deaf children in Hampton, Va., was founded by a white deaf man, William Ritter, in 1928. In the early 1950s, 13 states still had segregated schools for black deaf children, and as late as 1963, eight states still did. Many teachers in these schools could hear and did not know how to sign. While southern black American Sign Language users share the same linguistic system used by white signers, there are many lexical differences. For 28 of 34 lexical signs analyzed in one study, black signers had signs that white signers did not use; earlier research accounted for this in part by hypothesizing that black signers tend to use older forms of signs. The black

Louisiana signers in one study also tended to use the citation form (the form of the sign as it appears in sign language dictionaries, as it occurs in formal situations, and how it is generally taught in sign language classes) of signs like "deaf," signing it from ear to chin as opposed to chin to ear, and "know," signing it at the forehead level or even in the middle of the forehead, as opposed to lowering it on the face. Other structural differences that distinguish black signing as a variety, such as larger signing space and more movement of the body, are currently being researched.

CEIL LUCAS
Gallaudet University

CAROLYN MCCASKILL
Gallaudet University

Jack Gannon, *Deaf Heritage* (1981); Ernest Hairston and Linwood Smith, *Black and Deaf in America: Are We that Different?* (1983); Hannah Joyner, *From Pity to Pride: Growing Up Deaf in the Old South* (2004); Harlan Lane, Robert Hoffmeister, and Ben Bahan, *Journey into the DEAF-WORLD* (1996); Ceil Lucas, Robert Bayley, and Clayton Valli, *Sociolinguistic Variation in American Sign Language* (2001); Carolyn McCaskill, "The Education of Black Deaf Americans in the 20th Century: Policy Implications for Administrators in Residential Deaf Schools" (Ph.D. dissertation, Gallaudet University, 2005); James Woodward and Carol Erting, *Language Sciences* (vol. 37, 1975).

Appalachian English

Appalachian English is a broad term for the social and geographical varieties found in a large mountain and valley region encompassing all or parts of eight southern states: West Virginia, eastern Kentucky and Tennessee, western Virginia and North Carolina, northern Georgia and Alabama, and northwestern South Carolina. Historically and structurally it is closely related to Ozark English, and it shares many features with the English of the Lower South.

The English of Appalachia has long been subject to popular misconceptions and stereotypes, in large part because of the low socioeconomic status of many of its speakers and numerous stock representations and caricatures in fiction, comic strips, films, and television programs. It has also been the object of curiosity and even romanticization, perhaps mostly because of its old-fashioned flavor and its colorful and seemingly quaint usages. Since the late 1800s writers have searched for and noted its retention of older elements, often suggesting that it was a remnant of the past that preserved Elizabethan, Shakespearean, or even Chaucerian word forms. The isolation of the mountains, it was claimed, had stalled it in time from centuries earlier, when settlers from the British Isles arrived in Appalachia. While such labels were often well intended (as when used to counter negative images of mountain people) and are widely believed both inside and outside the mountains today, scholars had by the mid-20th century discounted them as highly exaggerated and based on only a relative handful of terms shared with well-known earlier English literature (such as *afeard* 'afraid,' *postes* 'posts,' and *pack* 'carry'). A more accurate assessment is that, among American regional dialects, Appalachian English preserves an unequaled record of usages common in colonial American English that have disappeared elsewhere (*jine* 'join,' *holler* 'hollow,' and *a-* prefix on verbs, such as *a-goin'*). Recent scholarship has also shown that the Old World roots of Appalachian English lie less in Shakespeare's England than in 18th-century Ulster, the northern province of Ireland. Settlers from there are most often called the Scotch-Irish, and they brought words such as *piece* 'short distance,' *ill* 'bad-tempered,' and *you'uns* 'you' (plural). Contributions to Appalachian English from other languages, such as German, French, Spanish, and Cherokee, are negligible.

Though retaining an unusually rich vein of older usages, Appalachian English is otherwise typical of American English in exhibiting features in various stages of change (such as verb principal parts) and in producing many new words and meanings. As in other varieties, its features give social and regional identity and cultural cohesion to its speakers and so tend to be used most between natives. Few of the characteristics identified below are unique to Appalachia, and even fewer are used throughout the large region. It is the concentration of quantitative differences rather than the existence of qualitative ones that constitutes the region's distinctive speechways.

The expressive richness of Appalachian English and the verbal dexterity of its speakers are widely reputed, as evidenced in fresh and earthy metaphors (*kick* 'reject in courtship,' *can see to can't see* 'dawn to dusk'); vivid similes (*meaner than a striped snake, as thick as fiddlers in hell, as ugly as a mud fence daubed with chinquapins*); and abundant proverbs (*A whistlin' woman and a crowin' hen always come to no good end*). Mountain speakers have long taken existing words and fashioned new ones from them. Sometimes this was accomplished by shortening, producing *splo* 'homemade whiskey' (from *explode*, what the substance does in the head) or *the hippoes* 'an imaginary or pretended ailment' (from *hypochondria*). Other novel coinages are conversions of one part of speech to another (*brogue* as a verb 'go on foot, wander'; *man-power* as a verb 'move by brute effort'). The use of such devices, among other things, has made Appalachian storytellers famous.

Vocabulary items and meanings that are concentrated in Appalachia include *branch* 'creek'; *bald* 'treeless area on a mountaintop'; *backset* 'relapse' (of an illness); *boomer* 'diminutive red squirrel'; *awful* 'excellent, extraordinary' (as *an awful fisherman*); *sop* 'gravy' (*We ate light bread and sop*); *poke* 'paper sack'; and *lay out*, 'play truant.' Within Appalachia vocabulary varies mainly by subregion or by the age or ruralness of the speaker. More modern, national terms have been rapidly displacing many older, rural counterparts, especially among younger inhabitants. A recent study of students at a small western North Carolina college found a dramatic loss of regional vocabulary; for instance, *living room, gutters, mantel*, and *attic* had completely replaced *big house, eaves trough, fireboard*, and *loft*.

Common grammatical patterns in the region include numerous features whose ancestry is either from England or Ulster. Among the first group are *a-* as a prefix on verb present participles (*a-goin', a-comin'*); possessive pronouns with the suffix *-n* rather than *-s* (*hern, hisn, yourn*, as *a book of yourn*); and personal dative pronouns (*I bought me a dog*). In the second, Scotch-Irish group one finds *done* as a helping verb (*He's done landed in jail again*); the personal pronoun *you'uns* 'you' (plural); addition of *all* after pronouns to indicate inclusion (*what all, who all*); verb suffix *-s* (and linking verb *is*) with plural noun subjects (but not with plural pronoun subjects: *people knows* vs. *they know*; *people is* vs. *they are*); and *they* 'there' to introduce clauses (*They's a problem with Susie*). Other grammatical patterns, such as the reversal of word elements (*everwhat* 'whatever,' *everwho* 'whoever') and prepositions in series (*Come out from up under the table*) apparently originated in America, if not in Appalachia itself. Perhaps the most conspicuous area of Appalachian grammar is the handling of verb principal parts. Three general tendencies are the making of irregular verbs regular (*knowed, heared, seed*), the use of irregular past-tense forms as past participles (*have went, have took*), and the use of the root form of a verb as also the past tense and past participle (*begin, eat, give, run*).

Features of pronunciation that are more common in Appalachia include final *-a* pronounced as *-y* (*opry* 'opera,' *extry* 'extra'); addition of the *r* sound to some words (*tomater* 'tomato,' *warsh* 'wash'); shifting of the accent to the first syllable (*IN-surance, PO-lice*); modifying long *i* to *ah* (so that *my right side* sounds something like *mah raht sahd*); use of the same vowel sound in word pairs like *pen/pin* and *hem/him* and in pairs like *steel/still* and *sale/sell*; and use of the vowel of *cat* in *care, bear*, and similar words. Modified long *i* in *my* and *side* and the merger of *pen* and *pin* are used by speakers of all social or educational levels in Appalachia, even in formal situations.

Despite the fact that the English of Appalachia is often believed to have the most respectable of roots, it remains highly stigmatized, especially outside the region, and is considered to be an inferior type of English that is an impediment to social mobility and educational progress. Even so, and while bending to the forces standardizing American culture, it will persist and develop because of the strong cultural solidarity and the regional identity it provides its speakers, even in the face of misunderstanding and pressure to conform. This is shown in the pronunciation of the third syllable of *Appalachia* as *latch* rather than *lay*, a tendency that has grown steadily since the 1960s in reaction to national perceptions of the region, especially by government representatives and members of the media, that are negative and considered unfair.

MICHAEL MONTGOMERY
University of South Carolina

Rudy Abramson and Jean Haskell, eds., *Encyclopedia of Appalachia* (2006); Linda Blanton, in *Toward a Social History of American English*, ed. J. L. Dillard (1985); Michael Montgomery, *Now and Then: The Appalachian Magazine* (Summer 2000), in *High Mountains Rising*, ed. Richard Straw and Tyler Blethen (2004); Michael B. Montgomery and Joseph S. Hall, eds., *Dictionary of Smoky Mountain English* (2004); Anita Puckett, *Seldom Ask, Never Tell: Labor and Discourse in Appalachia* (2000); Walt Wolfram and Donna Christian, *Appalachian Speech* (1976).

Bahamian English

The nonstandard English of the Bahama Islands (also called Bahamian Creole English or Bahamian dialect) is a conservative form of African American English with historical links to Gullah, the creolized English of coastal South Carolina and Georgia. Thus Bahamian is a North American creole with close ties to the English of the American South. It has a range of varieties, from near standard (spoken by most middle-class members of the black majority) to that of the local white minority (also called Conchy Joes) to a fairly deep creole, the variety least like standard English.

Variation in Bahamian English is related not only to social class and ethnicity but also to geography. Varieties nearer the standard are associated with the capital, Nassau, and the northern islands in general, while the deepest creole is characteristic of the southern islands, such as Mayaguana and Inagua. The latter were unpopulated until the 1780s after the American Revolutionary War, when they received a sudden influx of mainland loyalists and their slaves, largely from the South (particularly South Carolina) but also from such northern colonies as New York. It was once thought that the existence of this creole in the Bahamas was evidence that mainland African American English

Bahamian man sitting aboard ship, summer 1935 (Lomax Collection, Library of Congress [LOT 7414-H, no. N259], Washington, D.C.)

had been a creole in the 18th century. However, it has since been demonstrated that the language that most people brought to the southern Bahamian islands was actually Gullah, not a general creole spread throughout the U.S. South.

The Lucayan Indians were carried off as slaves by the Spanish in the early 1500s, so the islands were uninhabited when British colonists and their slaves came from Bermuda to establish the first settlement in 1648. In 1670 the Bahamas became a single colony with the Carolinas, and close ties with the mainland continued even after more direct British rule came in the 1720s. Linguistic and cultural contact between whites and blacks was likely much closer here than on the vast sugar plantations elsewhere in the Caribbean, because unsuitable soil prevented plantations from developing. Instead, whites and blacks worked together on small farms or at sea. By 1783 blacks made up 58 percent of the population. They formed about the same proportion as in South Carolina, but the higher concentrations along the coast in the latter case led to a fully creolized language (Gullah). Bahamian English remained closer to British English than did many Caribbean varieties, such as Jamaican.

With the influx of loyalists, the black population of the Bahamian island of New Providence doubled by 1786, and blacks made up 66 percent of the colony's population. However, blacks comprised almost the entire population of the southern islands after the soil proved unsuitable for raising cotton and slave owners left, even before emancipation in 1834. This suggests that the Gullah taken to the southern Bahamian islands probably underwent less decreolization there over the next two centuries than it did on the mainland.

Thus modern Bahamian English evolved from varieties of English spoken by white British and mainland American settlers, as well as from 18th-century varieties of Bahamian and African American English and the mainland creole, Gullah. This history is illustrated by features of its vocabulary (e.g., Bahamian and archaic British English *bass* 'to sing bass' or Bahamian and U.S. South *bubba* 'brother'); grammar (e.g., *The boss be sleeping*); and sound system (e.g., *first* /fʌis/), as well as many traits from African languages (e.g., Bahamian *ninny* and Mende *ɲini*, both 'breast'; Bahamian *yinna* and Limba *yina* or Mbundu *yenu*, all 'you' [plural]). A number of these features are not found in the Creole English of the Caribbean proper and West Africa, but others are (e.g., Bahamian, Jamaican, and Sierra Leonean Creole English *aks* 'ask,' all from archaic and regional British English).

JOHN HOLM
Universidade de Coimbra (Portugal)

Stephanie Hackert, *Urban Bahamian Creole: System and Variation* (2004); John Holm, *American Speech* (vol. 58, 1983); John Holm with Alison Shilling, *Dictionary of Bahamian English* (1982); Alison Shilling, *Some Non-standard Features of Bahamian Dialect Syntax* (1978).

Caddo

Prior to European contact the Caddo people were distributed over a huge area that covered what are now eastern Texas, northern Louisiana, western Arkansas, and eastern Oklahoma. Caught between Spanish, French, and British intruders, by 1855 the remnants of these people were forced to move to a small reservation on the Brazos River in Texas. In 1859, under pressure from white settlers, they moved once more to their present location in the neighborhood of Anadarko, Okla.

The Caddo language belongs to a family of languages termed *Caddoan*, whose other languages include Wichita, Pawnee, and Arikara, all spoken on the Great Plains. In spite of these linguistic affiliations, Caddo culture was not of the Plains variety but resembled that of other groups in the Southeast such as the Choctaw, Chickasaw, and related peoples. The Caddo were agriculturalists, they were not heavily dependent on the buffalo, and their religious practices and clothing were similar to those of other southeastern groups.

Aside from a few brief word lists collected in the 19th century, the Caddo language was largely neglected by scholars until the 1950s, when Daniel Da Cruz wrote an unpublished essay on the sounds of the language. The linguist Wallace Chafe began investigating Caddo in the late 1950s and has published various articles on its properties. More recently Lynette Melnar published an extensive description of Caddo verb morphology.

Caddo belongs to a language type termed polysynthetic, characterized by words that contain significantly more information than is typical of words in a language like English. It is also highly fusional, in the sense that sound changes have often obscured the internal structure of words. A word that means "We (three or more of us) heard the message" must once have been pronounced *híttsibakayiwá:bah*, with elements that conveyed past tense, first person, plural, and the ideas of a message and of hearing it. Through the loss of the third and fifth vowels, as well as a change of a *b* to *w*, this word is now pronounced *híttsiwkáywá:bah*.

Supplementing its native repertoire, Caddo has borrowed words from various neighboring languages, both indigenous and European. From the Tonkawa to the west came the Caddo word *Ká:nos*, a shortened form of *Mexicanos*, at first a way of referring to all Europeans but later only to Frenchmen, while Mexicans have come to be called *Ispayun*, from *Español*. The British and later Americans are called *Inkinishih*, from the word *English*. The Caddo word for one's mother is *ina'*, which was evidently borrowed from the Osage language. There are a number of borrowings from the three European languages with which the Caddo were in close contact. One example is *káwá:yuh* 'horse' from Spanish *caballo*. Another is *sún:dah* 'soldier' from French *soldat*. The word *íkah* comes from English *acre*.

The Caddo language is now seriously endangered, with only a handful of speakers remaining. Just as the Caddo were important players in the history of the South, their language contributes important insights to our knowledge of language in general, particularly in exemplifying an especially interesting language type that differs substantially from European linguistic patterns.

WALLACE CHAFE
University of California, Santa Barbara

Wallace Chafe, *The Caddoan, Iroquoian, and Siouan Languages* (1976), *International Journal of American Linguistics*, Native American Text Series 2, ed. Douglas R. Parks (no. 1, 1977), in *The Native Languages of the Southeastern United States*, ed. Heather K. Hardy and Janine Scancarelli (2005); Lynette Melnar, *Caddo Verb Morphology* (2004).

Cajun English

Cajun English, or Acadian English, is a vernacular variety of Southern American English spoken by many of the inhabitants of southern Louisiana who consider themselves Acadians. The word *Cajun* is a development of an ordinary, casual pronunciation of *Acadian* in which the unstressed first vowel is lost. Some speakers prefer the designation *Acadian English* because they feel that the word *Cajun* evokes negative stereotypes, yet others apply *Cajun* with pride to their speech, food, music, and other features of their culture.

Cajun English is both ethnically and regionally defined. Its speakers see themselves as descendants of the Catholic, French-speaking Acadians of New France who were expelled from the British colony of Nova Scotia (now the Canadian provinces of Nova Scotia, New Brunswick, and Prince Edward Island) beginning in 1755 and who, after great hardships, made their way to colonial Louisiana a decade later. Speaking provincial dialects of French, the earliest Louisiana Acadians spread southward and westward from New Orleans, along the bayous and rivers and into the prairies of southwest Louisiana. Other displaced Acadians joined them, as well as immigrants of various ethnicities willing to claim a new life from the wilderness. Surnames like *Edwards*, *Hebert*, *Galiano*, *Hidalgo*, *Riley*, *Szush*, and *Wagner* show the diverse elements that contributed to today's Cajun ethnicity. Until World War II ended their isolation, inhabitants of Acadian Louisiana spoke French primarily, even though English had been mandated for all schooling (in 1916) and the use of French in public settings was discouraged. Many African Americans living in southwestern Louisiana speak varieties of French and English similar to those spoken by Cajuns. However, most of them apply *Cajun* only to whites and use *Creole* for their own speech and culture. Today, except for the elderly, almost all Cajuns and African American Creoles are monolingual speakers of English.

Cajun English is heard mainly in the 22 parishes that extend roughly from New Orleans to Alexandria to Lake Charles, sometimes called the Cajun Triangle. Descendants of French speakers in other parts of Louisiana turned to English in the 19th century and do not speak Cajun English. Cajun English sounds different from the dialects of New Orleans and Baton Rouge and of the parishes north of Lake Pontchartrain and east of the Mississippi, though it shares many vocabulary items with them, such as *bayou* 'small river,' *gris-gris* 'wish of bad luck,' *jambalaya* 'tomato and rice dish with meat or seafood,' *make do do* 'for a child to go to sleep,' *parrain* 'godfather,' and *pirogue* 'type of small boat.'

Among the most noticeable Cajun English pronunciations are stress on the final syllable of a phrase; shortening and tensing of the final vowel sound in words like *today* and *pray*; pronouncing words such as *hair*, *there*, and *care* as *har*, *thar*, and *car*; and substituting *t* or *d* for *th* in pronunciations like *tink* for *think* and *dat* for *that*. A favorite device for emphasis is putting *me* at the beginning or end of a sentence (*Me, I was late* or *I was late, me*).

In the last two decades of the 20th century, Cajuns made their unique heritage and culture the basis of tourism and found an appreciative audience for Cajun food and music throughout the world. What were once stigmatized varieties of both French and English in southern Louisiana now enjoy respect and sometimes admiration as a part of Cajun identity. Many of today's Cajuns are bidialectal, using typical Cajun pronunciations and intonations when they want to claim their Cajun identity but using regionally standard pronunciation otherwise.

CONNIE EBLE
University of North Carolina

Carl A. Brasseaux, *French, Cajun, Creole, Houma: A Primer on Francophone Louisiana* (2005); Sylvie Dubois and Barbara Horvath, *English World-Wide* (vol. 18, 1998); Connie Eble, in *English in the Southern United States*, ed. Stephen J. Nagle and Sara L. Sanders (2003); Ann Martin Scott, ed., *Cajun Vernacular English: Informal English in French Louisiana* (1992).

Catawba

The earliest mention of the Catawba people in written accounts was made by Spanish explorers of the mid-16th century. A member of the Juan Pardo expedition recorded a number of names of villages and peoples of the area as they traveled up the Edisto and Santee river complexes in the Piedmont of what is now South and North Carolina. *Katapa* or *Kataba* and *Yssa* or *Esaw* are among the names easily recognized as designating Catawba peoples. It is likely that the Catawba were a loosely associated confederation of villages speaking related dialects of a language or languages distantly related to Siouan. This connection was hypothesized in the early 20th century, based on a few correspondences in sounds and basic vocabulary and was strongly advocated by Frank T. Siebert. However, the relationship of Catawba to the Siouan language family remains in dispute, in part because Catawba had absorbed words from diverse other languages before it became well documented. There were also speakers of Algonquian, Iroquoian, Yuchi, and Muskogean languages living in the general area, with whom the Catawba had contact. John Lawson, who spent time with them in 1701, wrote the most complete early description of the Catawba. He also left us the only known sample of Woccon, a Siouan language related to Catawba, in the form of a list of 150 words.

The early Catawba occupied an area where two cultural traditions—of the tribes of the Piedmont and of the southern chiefdoms of the Lowlands—met. Situated at the intersection of trade routes, they occupied a prominent position as middlemen in the trade with the British, mostly for deerskins and furs, for which both Virginia and South Carolina competed. In the 18th century their numbers were decimated by the French and Indian War and by smallpox and influenza epidemics, and although they sided with the colonials during the American Revolutionary War, they were no longer a strong military force by that time. By 1840 the Catawba had leased out all their land and signed a treaty with South Carolina, agreeing to cede their land and relocate to North Carolina. Some of them went to live with the Cherokee, once their fiercest enemies, in North Carolina, but most eventually returned to South Carolina. They fought in the Civil War, and afterward some sharecropped, leaving the reservation for short periods of time. However, they maintained their legal status as Indians, and South Carolinians continued to refer to them as a nation. The late 1930s and early 1940s, with the onset of World War II, marked the beginning of a period of assimilation for the Catawba. Many went to work in the textile mills in nearby Rock Hill or were employed by the Works Progress Administration.

Catawba has not been spoken widely by tribal members since the late 19th century, and by the mid-20th century only a handful of speakers remained. The language was studied extensively in the 1930s and 1940s, when linguists such as Frank Speck transcribed and published numerous Catawba texts. Apparently the last fluent speakers were Chief Sam Blue (d. 1952), his wife Louise (d. 1959), and his sister, Sally Brown Gordon (d. 1963). Red Thunder Cloud, who claimed to be the last native speaker and who helped collect Catawba material for the Smithsonian Institution in the 1940s, died in 1996, but he probably learned most of his Catawba as an adult. Although Catawba families had moved west at various times during the 19th century, there are no fluent speakers of the language left anywhere.

Catawba is built around verb roots, with prefixes, suffixes, and particles to express other sentence elements. One fascinating aspect of the language is that verbs indicate the speaker's source of knowledge (i.e., whether a speaker saw or heard an event, was told about it by an eyewitness, or learned of it by hearsay).

Today, the Catawba are survivors. The single most unbroken tradition of the tribe throughout all the years is pottery making, using the traditional ways. The culture has also continued to live on through dancing, singing, and storytelling. The Catawba Indian Nation now is located in north-central South Carolina, centered around a reservation about eight miles east of Rock Hill. The tribe was officially recognized by the federal government in 1993 and by the state of

South Carolina in 2003. Over 2,200 Catawba, the majority of whom live on or within 20 miles of the reservation, are listed on the official tribal roll. In recent years the Catawba Cultural Preservation Project has worked to revive the language, using archival materials recorded and collected from the mid-1900s, and to develop a new orthography, terminology, and curriculum materials for local schools. It has also fostered programs in crafts, dancing, and other traditions and sought to build self-confidence among the Catawba as well as appreciation of Catawba culture among outsiders.

CLAUDIA Y. HEINEMANN-PRIEST
Winthrop University

A. S. Chamberlain, *The Catawba Language* (1988); Ives Goddard, "The Identity of Red Thunder Cloud," *Society for the Study of the Indigenous Languages of the Americas Newsletter* (April 2000); Claudia Heinemann-Priest, comp., Catawba Lexicon, <www.ccppcrafts.com>; Charles Hudson, *The Catawba Nation* (1970); Blair A. Rudes and David J. Costa, *Essays in Algonquian, Catawban, and Siouan Linguistics in Memory of Frank T. Siebert* (2003); Frank Speck, *Catawba Texts* (1934).

Charleston English

The English spoken by natives of Charleston, founded in 1670 as one of the earliest permanent English settlements in North America and the first capital of South Carolina, has long stood apart from the English of other southern cities. Although linguists in recent decades have claimed a gradual loss of this distinctive speech, Charleston English has for centuries elicited mimicry by outsiders, intrigued visitors, and reinforced the solidarity of residents born in the city.

Long the only major southern port on the East Coast, historic Charleston was important as a colonial trading center, the point of entry for nearly half of the Africans brought as slaves to mainland North America, and the launching site of the American Civil War. Charleston's demographic and economic history, along with the centuries-old culture of its landed families and their servants, contributed to a distinctive speech that is often (if erroneously) referred to locally and in upstate South Carolina as *Geechee*, a label that recognizes the influence of Gullah, the creole spoken mainly on offshore islands, on the speech of local whites and blacks. (*Geechee* possibly developed to describe the Gullah-like speech of blacks along the Ogeechee River in coastal Georgia; alternatively, the term may have come from Gullah speakers comparing their own speech, which they often called *Geechee*, to that of the Kissy region [Liberia], whose name they pronounced in the same way and where some slaves originated.)

The linguistic features that merge in Charleston English, while not all unique to Charleston, differ from those of inland South Carolina and other parts of the South where a broadly southern dialect of American English developed. There were different influences in Charleston from the start. Entrepreneurs and gentry mainly from southern England settled there, often coming by way of Barbados to build their fortunes. French Huguenots and Sephardic Jews later joined them, followed by immigrants from Germany, Scotland, Ireland, and elsewhere, making Charleston distinctly heterogeneous compared with small inland farming communities not far away. But Charleston's wealth and its social and political institutions depended particularly on the large population of West Africans who were brought as slaves and who, with their descendants, powered the quasi-feudal plantations surrounding the city before the abolition of slavery.

The Gullah Creole spoken in segregated black enclaves of the city (as depicted in the opera *Porgy and Bess*) and especially on nearby islands lent a distinct flavor to overall Charleston speech with its pronunciation, grammar, and vocabulary. Some Gullah-speaking blacks came in contact with whites at market, in agriculture, or in fishing, and black servants and the white families they served had daily personal contact. To this day, white Charlestonians have been known to season their English with Gullah in relaxed settings, perhaps reinforcing their sense of place and identity. Today blacks and whites govern the city together and continue to share speech patterns.

Charleston English once commonly featured words such as *broadus* 'a little extra, a bonus, lagniappe' and *piazza* 'porch,' as well as words from Gullah Creole that can also be found in some form in certain West African languages. These include *buckra* 'white man' (also in Ibibio and Efik of southern Nigeria); *cooter* 'turtle' (Bambara and Malinke of West Africa); *Da* 'a black nursemaid' (Ewe of Togo and Benin); *pinder* 'peanut' (Kongo of Angola); *ninna* 'female breast to a nursing infant' (Mende of Sierra Leone); and *joggling board* 'a board suspended as a bench on which one bounces on the *piazza*' (originally perhaps *chika board*: Mandingo of West Africa). Sesame is still called *benne seed* in Charleston cookbooks. *Benne* is also found in Wolof (Senegal and Gambia) and Bambara.

Charleston grammar, which has spread from the city to other parts, includes phrases such as *I ran up with him* and *I ran across him* 'I encountered him.' One hears *them boys* 'those boys,' probably reinforced by the Gullah use of *dem boy* ('the boys') as a form of plural. One might also hear *used to didn't* as well as *fell out the bed* and *Wait on me* 'Wait for me.' Gullah's presence in Charleston produces grammatical forms such as the use of uninflected verbs in the past tense, as in *Yesterday I eat*; *for/fuh* rather than *to* or *for to*, as in *He come over for tell me*; or *I haffuh go now* 'I have to go now.'

First described by a linguist in 1887, the pronunciation of Charleston English features distinctive vowels, many of which are aligned closely with the West African–influenced vowels of Gullah Creole. Words such as *Ma* and *Pa*, *calm* and *palm* have the same vowel as *cat*. Before consonants *p*, *f*, *t*, *s*, and *k*, the initial part of the vowel sound in words like *tight* and *house* is *tuh-eeet* instead of *tah-eet* and *huh-ooose* instead of *hah-oose*, a pronunciation also found in coastal Virginia and in much of Canada. Before consonants *b*, *v*, *d*, *z*, *m*, *n*, *l*, and *g*, the initial part of the vowel in words like *five* and *kind* is *faw-ive* instead of *fah-ive* and *kaw-ind* instead of *kah-ind*. The vowels of words like *boat* and *gate* are distinctive: *bo—it* and *ge—it*. Speakers often do not pronounce an *r* when it follows a vowel sound: *fahm* 'farm,' *flo* 'floor,' and *le-tuh* 'later.' Also, Charleston speakers do not differentiate the vowel before an *r* in such words as *beer* and *bear*: both are pronounced *bay-uh*. The vowel in *milk* and *fish* sounds more like *mulk* and *fush*. Charleston speakers, like Gullah speakers, may also pronounce the *k* or *g* sound at the start of a word as if it is followed by *y*: *gyal* 'girl,' *gya-den* 'garden,' and *cya* 'car.' The Huguenot influence on Charleston speech is seen primarily in family names (*Legare*, pronounced *le-GREE*; *Huger*, pronounced *yu-JEE*) and street names, and it accounts for their distinctive pronunciation today.

Among black and white natives of the port city, Charleston English continues to evoke a sense of deep roots in a unique place, even though it may be a dialect that is losing some of its distinctiveness. It still draws attention when its speakers travel inland or abroad.

KATHERINE WYLY MILLE
Midlands Technical College

Raven I. McDavid Jr., *Publication of the American Dialect Society* (no. 23, 1955); Raymond K. O'Cain, in *Papers in Language Variation*, ed. David L. Shores and Carole P. Hines (1977); Sylvester Primer, *Transactions of the Modern Language Association* (vol. 3, 1887), *American Journal of Philology* (vol. 9, 1887); Lorenzo Dow Turner, *Africanisms in the Gullah Dialect* (1949; 2002).

Chesapeake Bay English

The diversity of southern speech is exemplified particularly well by island communities of the Chesapeake Bay that make their living by fishing, crabbing, clamming, and oystering. These include Tilghman, Deal, and Smith islands in Maryland and Saxis, Chincoteague, and Tangier islands in Virginia. Outsiders, especially journalists, have sometimes misrepresented and exaggerated the speech of the islands as "pure dialect," "fossilized language," or "Elizabethan English"—labels that are incorrect but hard to dispel. It is conservative, but to look at it as simply a preservation of Chaucerian or Shakespearean English is nonsense.

Tangier is the best known of the Chesapeake islands. It is 3.5 miles long by 1.5 miles wide and lies in the middle of the bay, part of Accomac County on Virginia's Eastern Shore. Its closest neighbor, 10 miles to the north in Maryland, is Smith Island, whose speech Tangier residents think is different and whose people they playfully call "Yarnies." Years ago Tangier Islanders had little contact with the mainland, but today many own automobiles, are highly mobile, and find the island flooded with "strangers" from April through September. The 650 permanent residents, persuaded by a national historical marker, imaginative brochures, and creative newspaper stories, believe their history dates to 1686, when a John Crockett settled the island, but a more likely founding date, according to county court records, is 1778.

Tangier Island features a community of working-class whites of English descent called "watermen." Their speech is most striking in its pronunciation. This, plus double negatives, stated opposites, clipped phrases, nicknames, and nautical terms, can amuse and baffle an outsider.

The dialect of Tangier lacks features still commonly heard in Piedmont and Tidewater Virginia: the broad *a* of *aunt*; the loss of *r* in *car, corn,* and *dinner*; or the pronunciation of *afraid* and *naked* as *a-fred* and *nek-ed*. Rustic pronunciations heard along the coastal fringes of the Chesapeake are not heard on the island either, where, for example, *can't, push, dog, fish,* and *poor* are pronounced with the vowels of *paint, pooh, doe, fee,* and *Poe,* respectively. *Mary* and *merry* are pronounced *Murray,* and *tire* and *I* have the vowel of *lard. Chair* and *scare* have the vowel of *curd,* and *year, hear, here,* and *ear* are all pronounced *yer.* All words rhyming with *trash* invariably have the vowel of *bay.* The pronunciation *zinc* is still used for *sink.*

Quite noticeable in Tangier speech is the lengthening and prolonging of vowels and diphthongs, reminiscent of a Cockney-like drawl. Tangier speakers say *beach* as *buh-eech, set* as *seh-uht,* and *dress* as *dreh-uss.* In *bat, bad, sack, dance, glass,* and *half,* the vowel is prolonged and glided as in *bae-uht, bae-uhd,* and so forth. Before *sh* the vowel sound of *pop* becomes the vowel of *die,* producing *guy-eesh* (for *gosh*) and *why-eesh* (for *wash*). The pronunciation of *dredge* as *drudge* and *mesh* (of a net) as *marsh* is shared with watermen around the bay. In Tangier speech *light, twice,* and *tide* generally do not have the long *i* of *buy*, but *uh-ee* or *oi*, like Cockney. *Out* and *house* sound something like *ow-ut* and *how-us*.

Vocabulary heard on Tangier includes *spargass* 'asparagus,' *bowsplit* 'bowsprit,' *other room* 'living room,' *gum boots* 'hip boots,' *gum band* 'rubber band,' *spider* 'frying pan,' *chinch* 'bedbug,' *agaling* 'dating,' and *New Year's Gift* 'Happy New Year' (a plea from children who expect small change from adults in return). Any window covering, including blinds and shades, is called *curtains*, and any small boat, flat-bottomed or not, is a *bateau* or *skiff*. *Mudlarking* and *progging* mean "wading around the shoreline, coves, or creeks with a dip net trying to catch crabs, especially softshells."

Conversational phrases and sentences reveal the most arresting feature of Tangier English, which islanders have called "over the left talk" or "talking backwards." Those who encounter it for the first time may not understand it, because speakers may intend the exact opposite meaning from what is said literally. This is not sarcasm or irony. At its simplest, "over the left" expresses negation. If one person asks another if he is going to the evening church services, the response may be a drawn out "no!," followed by "over the left." This means "yes!" "Over the left" did not originate on Tangier. *Worcester's Dictionary of the English Language* (1860) related it to "over the left shoulder" with the sense of "contrariwise." Consider the following sentences:

1. She's ugly!
2. He's adrift!
3. John's in good heart!
4. Kenny ain't nowhere away!
5. I didn't catch no crab today! Over the left!

The exclamation marks indicate that the sentences have full Tangier intonation, where the varying pitch, intensity, and tone of the voice conveys the opposite meaning of what one hears literally. Sentence 1 means that the girl is gorgeous; sentence 2, that the person has a well-built and seaworthy boat; sentence 3, that John has a crippling despondency; sentence 4, that Kenny was overseas; and sentence 5, that the crabber had a gigantic catch. Talking backwards is how islanders talk all the time in daily conversation. Outsiders who become a part of the community, even for a short time, seem to find it infectious. Even so, when they speak, they stand out.

In sum, the most prominent aspect of Tangier speech is its vowels, which are often pronounced so that one hears several vowels in a continuum and a Cockney-like drawling and whining. It thus shares features with the Middle Atlantic states to the north, the southern Coastal Plain, and the outermost

Atlantic communities, but it has a combination of features different from all three regions as well as from Tidewater Virginia.

DAVID L. SHORES
Old Dominion University

Susie Ames, *Studies of the Virginia Eastern Shore in the Seventeenth Century* (1940); William Cabell Greet, *American Speech* (vol. 8, 1933); Anne Hughes Jander, *Crab's Hole: A Family Story of Tangier Island* (1994); David L. Shores, *Journal of English Linguistics* (vol. 18, 1984), *Tangier: Place, People, and Talk* (2000).

Conch

The term *Conch* refers both to a subset of the population of the Florida Keys and to the distinctive speech of this group. Unlike many other groups in the United States, the Conchs are characterized not by ethnicity or the use of a non-English language but by settlement history and regional and social insularity. The Conchs originated with the formation in 1649 of a company of Cockney Englishmen, the Eleutheran Adventurers, who migrated to Bermuda seeking religious and political freedom. During the next century the group migrated again, this time to the Bahamas. From there, many of them settled in Key West after its acquisition by the United States from Spain in 1819, and by the middle of the century they had moved into the upper keys as well. The absence of direct transportation routes and the economic activities of the Conchs isolated them from the U.S. mainland and favored continued cultural and commercial relations with the Bahamas, which provided a steady stream of new settlers, and later with Cuba. Initially, their economic activity revolved around the ocean, with salvaging, sponging, and fishing (the conch was a major source of food as well as the source of the name for the people) the primary commercial activities.

During the last quarter of the 19th century, however, Key West became the world's most important center for manufacturing cigars. In spite of the infusion of new people from the U.S. mainland and Cuba, the Conchs associated primarily with their own people and often educated their children separately. The demise of the cigar industry and subsequent decline in population after 1910 reinforced their isolation. Although tourism and military installations brought a new flow of people from the mainland after World War II, the Conchs continue to maintain a strong sense of their distinctiveness as a group.

The linguistic consequence of their history is a dialect that is clearly different from any other spoken on the U.S. mainland. To outsiders it sounds much like the speech of the Bahamas, and it shares some features with British English, especially Cockney. Although the Conch vocabulary includes a number of unique words, such as *locker* 'closet,' *grits box* 'stove,' and *natural sponge* 'dish-cloth,' the dialect is more remarkable for its distinctive pronunciation. As often in British and southern American speech, Conch speakers do not pronounce the *r* after vowels, producing, for example, *fahthuh* 'farther.' More importantly, the vowels in words like *coat* and *hot* are closer to the British than the American pronunciation. Initial *h* is sometimes dropped in words like *happy* and *hand*, and initial *v* and *w* are sometimes interchanged, resulting in *wery* 'very' and *vorth* 'worth.' The combination of these features, along with others, results in a speech that is unique, like the social history of the Conchs.

GUY H. BAILEY
University of Missouri–Kansas City

Veronica Huss and Evelyn Werner, *Southern Folklore Quarterly* (vol. 4, 1940); Frank K. La Ban, in *A Various Language: Perspectives on American Dialects*, ed. Juanita V. Williamson and Virginia M. Burke (1971); Lee A. Pederson et al., eds., *Linguistic Atlas of the Gulf States: The Basic Materials* (1981); Work Projects Administration, *Florida: A Guide to the Southernmost State* (1939).

Confederate English in Brazil

A little-known chapter in southern history following the Civil War was the exodus of unreconstructed Confederates from the reunited United States, mainly from Texas and Alabama. The largest number, possibly 5,000, went to Brazil, lured by favorable terms for land and the hope of reestablishing a former way of life (other, much smaller groups moved to Mexico, Japan, or elsewhere). The food, customs, and speechways of the American South went with them and have survived in close-knit communities along the Amazon River near Santarém and in Americana, a town 100 miles northwest of São Paulo, where the largest group of "Confederados" (also called "Americanos") now lives. Psychologically attached to but geographically separated from the United States, they maintain a strong sense of pride in their southern heritage, celebrated especially in quarterly reunions.

As Protestant English speakers in a Catholic country whose national language was Portuguese, the Confederados established their own schools and churches. For several generations they married within the community and depended on teachers and ministers from the United States. In gradually assimilating into Brazilian society, they have been shifting to Portuguese, though the older generation still speaks English natively (with the cadence of Portuguese and a number of terms borrowed from that language). Their speech is of interest for two reasons. Not only does it preserve some pronunciations and vocabulary items that are distinctive to the American South (and sometimes recessive there today), but it lacks others that are now strongly associated with the region's speech. In giving insights into what the speech of the Deep South must have been like nearly a century and a half ago, Confederados English reveals that the modern speech of the region is both conservative and innovative.

Among vocabulary that is preserved more strongly in Brazil are *lot* 'barn yard,' *snap bean* 'green bean,' and *light bread* 'white bread.' Other well-known southernisms in Confederados speech include *fritter* 'pancake'; *carry* 'take, escort'; *Christmas Gift* 'Merry Christmas'; *chittlins* 'hog intestines'; *cornpone* 'cornbread'; *goober* 'peanut'; *harp* 'harmonica'; *mushmelon* 'cantaloupe'; *peckerwood* 'woodpecker'; *dinner* 'midday meal'; and *pulley bone* 'wishbone.' Brazilians also know and use *you all* 'you' (plural) and *fixin' to* 'getting ready to.' In a similar fashion, their pronunciation exhibits such traditional southern features as the lack of *r* in words like *car*, *bear*, and *father* (pronounced like *cah*, *bay-uh*, and *fahthuh*). Like older speakers in the Deep South today, they pronounce the first syllable of words like *hellish* and *Elliott* without an *l* sound following the vowel.

However, Confederados English shows little evidence of the southern long *i* in words like *my*, *ride*, and *right* (i.e., they are not pronounced *mah*, *rahd*, and *raht*) or the pronunciation of *pen* and *hem* as *pin* and *him*. Nor do the Confederados show any evidence of the southern drawl, whereby vowels in words like *bid* are stretched to two syllables (*bi-yud*). These features are common and well established throughout the South today among all social classes, so they must have arisen and spread rapidly since the mid-19th century. It is very unlikely that all of these and other features now associated with the South were taken to Brazil and subsequently lost.

The pronunciation of the Confederados suggests that Southern English has undergone considerable change since the Civil War and that, as a result, it may be more distinctive today than it was in the 19th century. Though it has also diverged from its 19th-century ancestor through contact with Portuguese, Confederados English is in other ways both a time capsule and a lost cousin that can help us understand the history of Lower South speech in new ways.

MICHAEL MONTGOMERY
University of South Carolina

Guy Bailey and Clyde Smith, SECOL *Review* (vol. 13, 1989); Cyrus B. Dawsey and James M. Dawsey, eds., *Confederados: Old South Immigrants in Brazil* (1995); Eugene C. Harter, *The Lost Colony of the Confederacy* (1985); Michael Montgomery and Cecil A. Melo, *English World-Wide* (vol. 11, 1990).

French

Francophone populations, though usually neglected in the recounting of the history and development of the South, have nonetheless played a prominent role. The very first settlers in North America seeking refuge for religious reasons were not the Pilgrims at Plymouth Rock in 1620 but French Huguenots in 1562 at coastal Charlefort (sometimes also called Charlesfort), located in what is now South Carolina. Because of privation and Spanish aggression, the settlement at Charlefort did not last long, but toward the end of the 17th century hundreds more Huguenots became part of the founding population of South Carolina, especially in Charleston. Many of their progeny grew wealthy, and indeed for a time Charleston rivaled every other colonial city on the Atlantic Coast for affluence, because of the extensive development of slave-based rice plantations. Despite sporadic testimonies of the subsequent survival of French, it appears that these prominent Huguenots (the most famous among them being "Swamp Fox" Francis Marion) assimilated rather quickly to the English language that predominated in the surrounding colonial setting. Much more for the sake of tradition than for linguistic necessity, the Huguenot church at the corner of Church and Queen streets in Charleston still conducts an occasional service in French according to the 18th-century liturgy of *les Eglises de la Principauté de Neuchâtel et Valangin*.

Though Charleston is unrivaled in Old South tradition, its French Quarter cannot contend with the French Quarter of New Orleans as the leading French-related cultural icon of the South. Indeed, the best-known and longest-surviving Francophone population in the South—and, until recently, the largest—has been located in Louisiana and its environs since the early 18th century. Robert Cavelier de la Salle descended the Mississippi River from New France to its mouth in 1682 and claimed the entire Mississippi Valley and its tributaries for Louis XIV of France (hence, *la Louisiane*). Soon after, French settlements, or posts, were founded at Biloxi (1699), Mobile (1701), Natchitoches (1714), and La Nouvelle Orléans (1718). The varieties of French from the founding of Louisiana until the present form a complex picture, much of which is still speculative. Records clearly attest that French was the language of the colonial administrators, and some form of "popular French" was certainly in wide use. However, French was probably not the first language of many early colonists, who would have spoken a regional patois of France or who were often recruited from Germany or Switzerland. Moreover, communication with early indigenous peoples took place through a regional lingua franca, Mobilian Jargon, which served as a trade language and the language of diplomacy rather than French. It is noteworthy that very few French borrowings penetrated into

HISTOIRE
DE LA
LOUISIANE,
Contenant la Découverte de ce vaste Pays ;
sa Description géographique ; un Voyage
dans les Terres ; l'Histoire Naturelle ; les
Mœurs, Coûtumes & Religion des Natu-
rels, avec leurs Origines ; deux Voyages
dans le Nord du nouveau Mexique, dont
un jusqu'à la Mer de Sud ; ornée de deux
Cartes & de 40 Planches en Taille-douce.

Par M. LE PAGE DU PRATZ.

TOME TROISIEME.

A PARIS,

Chez {
DE BURE, l'Aîné, sur le Quai des Augustins,
à S. Paul.
La Veuve DELAGUETTE, rue S. Jacques, à
l'Olivier.
LAMBERT, rue de la Comédie-Françoise.
}

M. DCC. LVIII.

French book circulated in Louisiana (Historic
New Orleans Collection [1980.205.35], New
Orleans, La.)

the indigenous languages of the Southeast such as the language of the Choc-taw, with whom the French had a strong and long-standing military alliance.

The largest single population of French speakers to arrive in Louisiana dur-ing the colonial period did not come directly from France. French colonists who left the west-central provinces of France and arrived in the early 17th cen-tury in Acadia (modern Nova Scotia and New Brunswick) were expelled from there by the British in 1755. Between 1765 and 1785 approximately 3,000 of them migrated to Louisiana (under Spanish administration from 1763) and occupied arable land principally along the bayous of southeastern Louisiana and the prai-ries of south-central Louisiana. This prolific population was destined to become the standard-bearer for maintaining French in Louisiana to the present day.

During the Spanish administration, the plantation economy of Louisiana began to blossom, dramatically affecting the French language there. On one hand, the massive importation of slaves, coming directly from West Africa for the most part, apparently led to the formation of a French-based creole lan-guage. Theories vary as to the genesis of Louisiana Creole, as it is usually re-ferred to by scholars. The debate surrounding the origin of creole languages is complex, but, at the risk of oversimplifying, the two poles of opposition can be summed up here. Some scholars contend that creole languages were spontaneously generated on (large) plantations where slaves were linguistically heterogeneous and did not share a common tongue. According to this view, the structural parallels among creole languages occur because of either linguistic universals or the interaction of a particular set of African and European languages. Others contend that most creole languages are simply daughter dialects of a pidgin associated with the slave trade, and though the lexicon can vary from one site to another due to different vocabulary replacement, their basic structure remains the same. Regardless, Louisiana Creole became the native mode of communication within the slave population of Louisiana. Very frequently it was also the first language of the slave-masters' children, who were typically raised by domestic bondservants.

In tandem with this, the wealth of what was then known as the Creole society grew. Creole society is not to be confused with the population of Louisiana Creole speakers but is composed, rather, of the affluent planter class of European origin and also of mostly biracial Creole persons of color who held considerable social standing during the Spanish administration, sometimes being plantation owners themselves. Their considerable resources allowed for widespread schooling among Creoles and the resultant acquisition of the evolving prestige French of France, by virtue of boarding schools in France and Louisiana or by private tutoring. Referred to as Plantation Society French in recent scholarship, this brand of French has all but disappeared, in part because of the ruin of Creole society in the aftermath of the Civil War and the resultant severing of ties with France and in part because of the rather swift acquisition of English (even before the Civil War) by members of Creole society. English became economically and socially important under the new American administration, which brought a massive influx of Anglophones, both free and slave, into Louisiana after the Louisiana Purchase of 1803. Not all newcomers after 1803 were English speakers, however. Prior to the Civil War, the affluence of Louisiana attracted additional Francophone immigrants, often educated, whose ranks were swelled by defeated Bonapartistes banished from France and by planters (with their creolophone slaves in tow) fleeing the successful slave revolt in Saint Domingue (modern Haiti). Not all of the 19th-century newcomers settled in Louisiana: a group of Bonapartiste exiles founded Demopolis (in Alabama) in 1817, just prior to statehood.

Dependent on wealth generated by the plantation system and vulnerable to competition with English for maintaining socioeconomic standing, once-prestigious Plantation Society French disappeared from use rather quickly. The vast majority of the agrarian, lower-class Acadian (or Cajun) population worked small farms and did not operate plantations (though some Acadians did gentrify and merge with Creole society). Their autonomy and relative iso-

lation led to a greater longevity for Cajun French. Significant numbers of immigrants (German, Irish, Italian, etc.) in some places even assimilated to the
use of Cajun French for a time. Meanwhile, Louisiana Creole was undergoing
demise, ultimately because of the breakup of the plantation system itself, but
even before that because of the immense influx of Anglophone slaves during
the 19th century, when the importation of foreign slaves was prohibited, leading to massive importation of slaves from states farther east to meet the de-
mand in booming Louisiana. Nevertheless, the social isolation of its speakers
led Louisiana Creole to fare better than Plantation Society French, and today
approximately 4,500 mostly elderly speakers remain, with the largest concentrations in Point Coupee and St. Martin parishes.

Acadiana, the 22-parish area where most Cajun French speakers still live,
can be roughly described as a triangle whose apex is in Avoyelles Parish in the
center of the state and whose base extends along the coast from eastern Texas to
the Mississippi border. The Cajun French spoken there did not begin its demise
until the 20th century, with the advent of compulsory schooling in English in
1916. This factor, coupled with better state infrastructure and accelerated exposure to mass media, eroded the social isolation of the Cajun population and led
inexorably to assimilation to the English standard by younger ethnic Cajuns.
Despite an important resurgence in Cajun pride since the late 1960s (the "Cajun
Renaissance") and attempts to bolster French in Louisiana, only the smallest
fraction of children are now acquiring fluency in any variety of the language.
The few thousand who do so are not acquiring it in natural linguistic communities but primarily in French immersion programs in the public schools
(introduced in 1968 when the state created the Council for the Development
of French in Louisiana to reclaim French and promote bilingualism). Nevertheless, the Cajun Renaissance has spawned preservationist tendencies in some
households; has resulted in a modicum of literary production by Cajun poets,
playwrights, and storytellers; and is linked to the resurgence in popularity of
Cajun music. Authenticity demands that Cajun musicians perform pieces in
French and that even young songsmiths compose a portion of their newest
lyrics in Cajun French.

Census figures for 2000 indicate a Francophone population of 194,100 for
Louisiana. Even adding the creolophone population (4,685 in 2000) to that
figure, the total fell far short of the combined French-speaking and creolophone
populations of Florida in 2000 (125,650 + 211,950 = 337,600). Though European
immigrants must also be taken into consideration, Florida is the new front-
runner in the South, primarily because of its large number of French Canadian
"snowbirds" and recent Haitian refugees. The Canadians, though elderly, repre-

sent a sustainable population as long as Florida remains an attractive retirement location, whereas the mostly elderly Francophone population of Louisiana is not self-replacing, except in a very small minority of cases where grandchildren are being reintroduced to French in a conscious attempt to preserve a linguistic legacy.

A description of the salient features of Cajun French and Louisiana Creole must take into account archaisms hearkening back to the French of the colonizers as well as innovations resulting from isolation and contact with other languages, especially English. For example, in various vocabulary items such as *haut* 'high' and *happer* 'to seize,' both Cajun French and Louisiana Creole preserve the archaic pronunciation of initial *h*, whereas initial *h* has fallen silent in the contemporary French of France. At the grammatical level, both Cajun French and Louisiana Creole preserve the progressive modal *après* (sometimes *apé* or *ap*) of western regional France, denoting an ongoing action, for example, *Je sus après jongler* 'I'm thinking' (Cajun French), or *M'apé fatigué* 'I'm getting tired' (Louisiana Creole). This usage is entirely absent in the standard French of France. Concerning innovations, historic contact with indigenous languages has enriched the vocabularies of French dialects in Louisiana with words such as *chaoui* 'raccoon' and *bayou* (subsequently borrowed into English). Contact with dominant English has had a profound impact on both Cajun French and Louisiana Creole. Assimilated borrowings are easy to find (*récorder* 'to record'), but because of near-universal bilingualism among Cajun French speakers and creolophones in Louisiana, it is even more common to hear the insertion of English vocabulary items into French or creole conversation: *j'ai* ride *dessus le* bike 'I rode the bike.' Imitative calques of English phrasing are also common, as in the case of a Cajun radio announcer reciting the standard expression *apporté à vous-aut' par* 'brought to you by.'

Though overlapping vocabularies are extensive, Louisiana Creole is distinct from Cajun French in a variety of ways. Of particular note in Louisiana Creole are a different system of pronouns, more frequent use of nouns that have permanently incorporated part or all of what were once preceding French articles, placement of the definite article after its noun, absence of linking verbs, absence of inflection on main verbs, and use of various particles to indicate tense. Compare the Louisiana Creole sentence *Yé té lavé zonyon-yé* 'They washed the onions' with *Ils ont lavé les oignons* in Cajun French.

English in Louisiana dethroned Plantation Society French as the most highly valued idiom and may have temporarily protected nonstandard Louisiana Creole and Cajun French from absorption by prestigious standard French (such was the demise of patois and regional French in France). However, today English has become a formidable competitor, with the imminent prospect of supplanting all traditional varieties of Louisiana French and Louisiana Creole in the region where both thrived for more than two and a half centuries. Yet, despite the demise of French as a first language in Louisiana, its influence remains noticeable in the spoken English of the region. Even in New Orleans, where the transition from French to English as the language of everyday communication has long been complete, vestiges of French can be found in colloquial calques such as *get down* 'get out' (of a vehicle) and borrowings such as *banquette* 'sidewalk,' *parrain* 'godfather,' and *beignet* (type of fried dough). This phenomenon is even more common in rural Cajun communities, where one hears French borrowings in remarks such as *We were so honte* (i.e., 'embarrassed') and *I have the envie* (i.e., 'desire') *for rice and gravy*. Less common but still used are structural calques from French: *Your hair's too long. You need to cut 'em* (*hair* as plural, corresponding in use to *les cheveux*) or *That makes forty years we married* (calqued from *Ça fait quarante ans qu'on est marié*).

English is not the only force arrayed against the survival of French in Louisiana. In 2005 in Plaquemines Parish, Hurricane Katrina decimated one of the few remaining non-Cajun Francophone enclaves, and ecological degradation, such as that which augmented the devastating effects of the storm, is contributing to the breakup of some of the more isolated Francophone communities (who mostly self-identify as Houma Indians) in Terrebonne Parish, where French has been best preserved among younger speakers.

MICHAEL D. PICONE
University of Alabama

AMANDA LAFLEUR
Louisiana State University

Barry Jean Ancelet, *Cajun and Creole Folktales: The French Oral Tradition of South Louisiana* (1994); Carl A. Brasseaux, *French, Cajun, Creole, Houma: A Primer on Francophone Louisiana* (2005); Marilyn J. Conwell and Alphonse Juilland, *Louisiana French Grammar* (1963); Thomas A. Klingler, *If I Could Turn My Tongue Like That: The Creole Language of Pointe Coupee, Louisiana* (2003); Kevin J. Rottet, *Language Shift in the Coastal Marshes of Louisiana* (2001); Albert Valdman, ed., *French and Creole in Louisiana* (1997).

German

The presence of the German language in the South today is largely due to immigration from German-speaking countries to Texas and secondary and tertiary settlements in southern states from German language communities in Pennsyl-

German restaurant in Fredericksburg, Tex. (Fredericksburg Chamber of Commerce)

vania. However, it should also be recognized that smaller groups of German-speaking immigrants settled elsewhere in the region but have not maintained the language. Settlers in Louisiana were once numerous enough to warrant an area called the *Côte des Allemands* ('German coast,' upriver from New Orleans), which was settled in 1731. In central and western North Carolina, there were an estimated 8,000 German-speaking settlers after the arrival of the Moravians in 1753. They maintained a strong presence there until the mid-1800s.

By the early 1730s Germans had begun settling in South Carolina, especially in townships established in the interior, such as Orangeburg. The largest settlement, from the 1740s, was Saxe Gotha Township (the modern-day Dutch Fork area of Lexington and Newberry counties), to which came an estimated 12,000 German speakers from Germany, Austria, and Switzerland, most of them Lutherans, by 1760. Although the German language is no longer spoken there, a strong pride in German ancestry has been maintained.

Unlike settlements in the Carolinas, in which the German language had died out by the 20th century, German dialects spoken in the South by speakers whose ancestors first settled in eastern Pennsylvania are alive and well today. The original immigrants brought German dialects from southern Germany (especially the Palatinate), Switzerland, and Alsace. In 1776 one-third of Pennsylvanians were German speakers, numbering between 150,000 and 200,000. They increased to 600,000 by the end of the 19th century.

Speakers of German first came to Pennsylvania in 1683 and in substantial numbers beginning in the early 1700s. Thus, German dialects in the United States have had time to develop unique traits, some of which are due to contact with English. These are considerably more likely to be maintained by future generations than other varieties of German, largely because of the social situations in which they are spoken, namely, religious enclaves.

The German dialect originating in Pennsylvania is called Pennsylvania German or Pennsylvania Dutch (since the word for *German* in the dialect is *Deitsch*, it was misunderstood to be *Dutch* by some English speakers, and the name stuck, as it did in the aforementioned district of South Carolina). There were two types of Pennsylvania German speakers: members of Anabaptist sects (the so-called Plain speakers) and secular or non-Plain speakers, usually of Lutheran or (German) Reformed religious affiliation. The non-Plain were numerically by far the majority of the German settlers; but among them today the language survives only among elderly speakers, and it is on the verge of dying out. However, Pennsylvania German is alive and well among Plain (Amish and Mennonite) speakers, for whom its survival is generally attributed to the values of in-group solidarity and separation from the mainstream of the Plain speakers. It is estimated that there are more than 200,000 Plain speakers of Pennsylvania German in the United States today. While most of them live in Pennsylvania, Ohio, and Indiana, settlements in the South continue to develop.

By 1730 German speakers had begun moving from Pennsylvania to parts of the South. The most prominent and well-documented area of settlement was Virginia's Shenandoah Valley (Rockingham, Augusta, Frederick, and other counties), where settlers continued to arrive, as well as to present-day West Virginia's Pendleton and Hardy counties, throughout the 18th century. In colonial Virginia German was used in newspapers and in both churches and schools, but by the mid-19th century, English had replaced it everywhere but in the home. Today only a few elderly non-Plain speakers remain. Similarly, some Pennsylvania Germans came to the Charlotte/Mecklenburg County area of North Carolina and neighboring South Carolina counties in the late 1700s. The loss of German in these settlements occurred by the mid-19th century, however, probably because they contained members of different religious backgrounds and thus were not isolated from the English-speaking mainstream in the same way in which Plain Pennsylvania German speakers have been.

In the 20th century, Plain Pennsylvania German-speaking communities in Sarasota, Fla., the Staunton/Stuart's Draft area of Virginia, and small towns in Georgia, Texas, and South Carolina were formed by speakers who have migrated either directly from Pennsylvania or via Old Order settlements in Ohio and Indiana. The Pennsylvania German heard in the South today is largely the result of these more recent settlements.

Salient linguistic features of this dialect include frequent use of a progressive construction (see example 1); use of an auxiliary verb *duh* 'do' that functions primarily as a habitual marker (example 2); and the loss of dative case (e.g., the grammatical marking of indirect objects [example 3]). In addition to these structural features, Pennsylvania German, like Texas German, contains many loanwords from English; note *bark* and *carry on* in example 1, *just about* in example 2, and *friends* and *introduced* in example 3.

1. *De Hund war an barke un on-carrye* 'The dog was barking and carrying on.'
2. *Ich glaub sie duhn just about all Englisch schwetzte* 'I think they speak just about all English.'
3. *Eins von sei friends hat ihn introduced zu mich* 'One of his friends introduced him to me.'

In Texas, there is also a history of German language maintenance. The ancestors of these speakers left central and northern Germany and settled in significant numbers in central Texas, especially around New Braunfels, during the 19th century. By 1850 there were more than 15,000 Germans living in the area. Maintenance of the German language was fostered by three main factors: the isolation of German language enclaves on ranches and farmsteads; relatively poor schooling, which did not enforce English monolingualism; and the presence of other languages in the area (most notably Spanish), which increased the tolerance toward bilingualism in the area.

The varieties of Texas German reflect the relatively standard dialects spoken by the ancestors of today's German Americans in the state. Because they did not all speak the same dialect upon arrival, a colonial koiné developed, as the product of the leveling of distinctive features of individual dialects to form a more uniform, mutually intelligible, German variety. Features of Texas German that developed after emigration include the loss of the dative case (as in Pennsylvania German), phonological changes in the vowel system that indicate American English influence, and a multitude of loanwords from English and Spanish. Along with names for the new animals and plants of Texas, such as armadillos and cacti, which were unknown in Germany, English words that reflect cultural and technological changes have also been adopted, for example, *Der sonic boom, der war gar nicht laut* 'The sonic boom, it wasn't loud at all.'

Despite its vibrant past, the future of Texas German communities seems to be language shift to English. While some speakers can still be found, they are largely elderly individuals who have not passed the language on to the next generation.

JANET M. FULLER
Southern Illinois University

Janet M. Fuller, "'Pennsylvania Dutch with a Southern Touch': A Theoretical Model of Language Contact and Change" (Ph.D. dissertation, University of South Carolina, 1997); Glenn G. Gilbert, in *Zeitschrift für Mundartforschung* (vol. 31, 1964), *The Linguistic Atlas of Texas German* (1971); Kurt Kehr, in *Zeitschrift für Dialektologie und Linguistik* (vol. 46, 1979); Raven I. McDavid Jr. and Theodore Lerud, in *Dialectology, Linguistics, Literature: Festschrift for Carroll E. Reed*, ed. Wolfgang W. Moelleken (1984); Silke Van Ness, *American Speech* (vol. 67, 1992).

Gullah

Gullah (also known as Geechee or Sea Island Creole) is spoken today primarily along the South Atlantic coastline, from as far north as Sandy Island, near Georgetown, S.C., to as far south as St. Simons and St. Marys in Georgia, and possibly from lower North Carolina to upper Florida. Although *Gullah* and *Geechee* are not always used interchangeably in coastal areas, from a linguistic point of view they refer to a single language variety. Gullah and other contact varieties of language known as creoles trace their roots to the Atlantic slave trade of the 17th and 18th centuries, as African slaves who spoke mutually nonintelligible languages found an urgent need to communicate with one another and the traders and masters who enslaved them. Gullah drew its vocabulary primarily from the English of British slave traders, plantation owners, and workers (hence it is an English-based creole), while its grammatical structure and pronunciation were heavily influenced by the West African languages brought by slaves to U.S. plantations. Similar creoles emerged in Jamaica, Barbados, and elsewhere in the Caribbean under similar conditions. Gullah is the only English-based creole spoken on the U.S. mainland today.

Scholars have proposed several theories for the origin of Gullah. One of these traces Gullah's beginnings to West African Pidgin English, an English-based maritime variety possibly transported by slaves to North American plantations, there to be passed on to succeeding generations and eventually becoming the creole Gullah. In the creolization process the original pidgin, a variety having a simplified structure and used solely for communication between people without a common language, underwent nativization, by which it developed into a full-fledged creole that was the first language of a group of people. A second theory, based on the fact that South Carolina, Jamaica, and Surinam were all first colonized by settlers from Barbados, is that a 17th-century Barbadian creole, spoken by slaves brought from Barbados, was the source of Gullah as well as Jamaican Creole and Sranan. A third theory dates the period of creolization back to 16th-century Africa and argues that Gullah (and all English-based Caribbean creoles) originated from Guinea Coast Creole English, presumed to have been spoken along the Upper Guinea Coast. These three theories have been disputed at one time or another by those doubting the existence of West African Pidgin English, Barbadian Creole, or Guinea Coast Creole English. A fourth theory traces the roots of Gullah to the Carolina colony itself, to the period 1720–50, which was characterized by rapid growth of the rice industry, institutionalized segregation, and a large African majority on plantations. The physical, social, and psychological isolation of African slaves might have prompted formation of a creole, as these factors would have made full acquisition of English unlikely.

Likewise there are several theories regarding the African element in Gullah. Some scholars have pointed to significant influence from the Kwa languages of southern Nigeria and the African Gold Coast, but others have argued the linguistic prominence of Kru and Mande languages of the coasts of Senegambia, Sierra Leone, and Liberia. The most plausible source for the name *Gullah* is the name of either a Sierra Leonean tribe, the Gola, or an Angolan one, the Ngola. *Geechee* most plausibly comes from either Kissi (pronounced *GEE-zee*), the name of a tribe along the Sierra Leonean/Liberian border, or the Ogeechee River in Georgia. From a demographic perspective, it appears that most Africans brought into the South Carolina colony came from trading stations in four areas: the Guinea Coast–Congo-Angola, Gambia, the Windward Coast (Sierra Leone and Liberia), and the Gold Coast (Ghana). Therefore, at least four primary African language families likely contributed to Gullah's development: Bantu from the Congo-Angola region, Kru and Mande from Gambia and the Windward Coast, and Kwa from the Gold Coast.

Several grammatical features distinguish Gullah from mainstream varieties of English. In Gullah the marking of tense on verbs is optional. In the sentence *Yesterday we clean up*, past time is indicated by the adverb *yesterday* rather than by the verb. Gullah speakers also sometimes indicate past time through use of the auxiliary verb *been*. The sentences in Table 1 illustrate the use of this and other auxiliaries for marking time distinctions in Gullah.

Gullah pronouns also exhibit distinctive characteristics. For example, *e* may be used where mainstream English requires the subject pronoun *he*, *she*, or *it*

TABLE 1. *Comparison of Time Distinctions in Gullah and English*

Time Reference	Gullah	English
Past	I been work	I worked
Continuous	I da work(ing)	I am working
Completed	I done work	I have worked
Habitual	I does work	I usually work

or the possessive pronoun *his*, *her*, or *its* (thus, *E hit e head* can mean "He hit his head," "She hit her head," "She hit his head," etc.). Gullah *um* corresponds to the English object pronoun *him*, *her*, or *it* (thus, *E see um* 'She saw it,' etc.). Other grammatical features that differ from mainstream English include use of the verb *say* to introduce a quotation, as in *E tell me, say, "We ain't in the church."* And *for* or *fuh* may be used in place of *to* to introduce infinitives, as in *E come for get some meat*. Many of Gullah's grammatical features are shared with Caribbean creoles and may come directly or indirectly from West African languages. African influences are also found in the vocabulary of Gullah, in words such as *buckra* 'white man' and *gumbo* 'okra.' It is believed that many of the "basket names" (or nicknames) given to Gullah speakers derive from African sources as well.

Some scholars believe that Gullah, or a Gullah-like creole, played a significant role in forming mainland varieties of African American English, either through contact with speakers of these varieties or via a process known as decreolization. Increased mobility along with more educational opportunities for African Americans following the breakdown of the plantation system may have resulted in the speech of ex-slaves and their descendants becoming more like English, thus producing modern African American English. One type of Gullah was preserved by the Afro-Seminoles, descended from escaped slaves and renegade Indians who left South Carolina and Georgia during the 18th century to establish free settlements in Florida, only to be later exiled in the 1830s to Oklahoma.

On the Sea Islands themselves, limited travel to and from the mainland preserved the distinctiveness of Gullah for many years following the end of the plantation system. Today, however, the building of bridges and the growth of the tourism industry have significantly increased mobility and in-migration, which many believe is causing Gullah to merge with mainland dialects. Some argue that Gullah is dying out. Negative stereotypes and misconceptions have discouraged some older speakers from passing Gullah on to their descendants, for fear that outsiders will ridicule them. However, in recent years there has been a concerted effort to preserve and promote the language and culture of the Gullahs through storytelling, Bible translations, heritage tours, music festivals, and other initiatives. Furthermore, Gullah functions as a significant marker of culture, history, and identity in the communities where it is spoken. Such factors will likely ensure its survival in some form for many years to come.

TRACEY L. WELDON
University of South Carolina

Frederick Cassidy, *American Speech* (vol. 55, 1980); Ian Hancock, *American Speech* (vol. 55, 1980); Patricia Jones-Jackson, *When Roots Die: Endangered Traditions on the Sea Islands* (1987); Salikoko Mufwene, in *Language Variety in the South Revisited*, ed. Cynthia Bernstein, Thomas Nunnally, and Robin Sabino (1997); Joseph Opala, *The Gullah: Rice, Slavery, and the Sierra Leone–American Connection* (1987); Lorenzo Dow Turner, *Africanisms in the Gullah Dialect* (1949; 2002).

Immigrant Languages, Recent

During the last two decades of the 20th century and the early years of the 21st, the United States experienced growth in immigration not seen since the first decades of the 20th century. Moreover, unlike the people who arrived during the great waves of immigration that ended with World War I, most recent immigrants come not from Europe but from Asia and Latin America. The majority of new immigrants to the United States in general and to the South in particular speak Spanish, and this fact is reflected in the growth of the U.S. Spanish-speaking population by more than 10 million during the 1990s as well as in Census Bureau statistics for people who speak a language other than English at home in most southern states. However, while Spanish is unquestionably the most common language other than English in the United States and in most southern states, other languages have also experienced robust growth. Thus, in the United States generally, the number of Vietnamese speakers nearly doubled in the 1990s, increasing by 99.1 percent, and the number of Chinese speakers increased by nearly 62 percent. Nationally, the number of Russian speakers increased by slightly more than 192 percent, and speakers of French Creole, mostly Haitians, increased by 132 percent. Table 2, based on data from the Census Bureau, shows the most common languages other than English spoken in the United States as well as the increase or decrease in the number of speakers between 1990 and 2000.

Like the rest of the country, the modern South is characterized by increasing linguistic diversity. According to the 2000 census, 15.7 percent of the resi-

TABLE 2. *Languages Other Than English Most Commonly Spoken in the United States (by 2000 rank order)*

Language	1990	2000	Change 1990–2000 %	Change 1990–2000 N
Spanish	17,862,477	28,101,052	+57.3	+10,238,575
Chinese*	1,249,213	2,022,143	+61.9	+772,930
French, incl. Patois, Cajun	1,702,176	1,643,838	−3.4	−58,338
German	1,547,099	1,383,442	−10.6	−163,657
Tagalog	843,251	1,224,241	+45.2	+380,990
Vietnamese	507,069	1,009,627	+99.1	+502,558
Italian	1,308,648	1,008,370	−23.0	−300,278
Korean	626,478	894,063	+42.7	+267,585
Russian	241,798	706,242	+192.1	+464,444
Polish	723,483	667,414	−7.8	−56,069
Arabic	355,150	614,582	+73.1	+259,432
Hindi and Urdu	331,484	579,957	+75.0	+248,473
Portuguese or Portuguese Creole	429,860	564,630	+31.4	+134,770
Japanese	427,657	477,997	+11.8	+50,340
French Creole	187,658	435,368	+132.0	+247,710
Greek	388,260	365,436	−5.9	−22,824

*Includes speakers of a variety of Chinese dialects, many of which are mutually unintelligible.
Source: U.S. Census Bureau, 1993, 2003

dents of 12 southern states from Virginia to Texas reported speaking a language other than English at home. Percentages ranged from 3.6 in Mississippi to 31.2 in Texas. Spanish speakers in Florida and Texas constituted the largest groups of southern residents who used a language other than English at home. In addition, nearly 200,000 residents of Louisiana, or 4.7 percent of the population aged 5 years and older, reported using French at home. However, other immigrant languages also figure prominently in the 2000 census reports on individual southern states. In Florida, for example, more than 208,000 people aged 5 years and older reported using French Creole at home, while in Texas, more than 122,000 people claimed to speak Vietnamese at home. Table 3 shows the number of speakers aged 5 years and older of languages other than English in 12 southern states, the number of Spanish speakers, and the number of speakers of Asian and Indo-European languages other than Spanish or English.

A look at the foreign-born population provides an indication of the linguis-

TABLE 3. *Languages Other Than English Spoken by Persons Aged 5 Years and Older in 12 Southern States*

State	Population 5 Years and Older	Number Who Speak Other Languages	% of Population	Spanish or Spanish Creole	Other Indo-European Languages	Asian and Pacific Island Languages	Other Languages
Alabama	4,152,278	162,483	3.9	89,729	43,812	22,122	6,820
Arkansas	2,492,205	123,755	5.0	82,465	22,695	15,238	3,357
Florida	15,043,603	3,473,864	23.1	2,476,528	755,214	164,516	77,606
Georgia	7,594,476	751,438	9.9	426,115	168,629	116,456	40,238
Kentucky	3,776,230	148,473	3.9	70,061	51,025	21,031	6,356
Louisiana	4,153,367	382,364	9.2	105,189	225,750	41,963	9,462
Mississippi	2,641,453	95,522	3.6	50,515	23,700	13,558	7,749
North Carolina	7,513,165	603,517	8.0	378,942	119,961	78,246	26,368
South Carolina	3,748,669	196,961	5.3	110,030	55,116	25,534	5,749
Tennessee	5,315,920	256,516	4.8	133,931	68,879	39,701	14,005
Texas	19,241,518	6,010,753	31.2	5,195,182	358,019	374,330	83,222
Virginia	6,619,266	735,191	11.1	316,274	195,846	170,136	52,935
Total	82,292,150	12,940,837	15.7	9,434,961	2,088,646	1,082,831	333,867

Source: U.S. Census Bureau, 1993, 2003

tic diversity represented in the South today. In 2003 Steven Camarota and Nora McArdle of the Center for Immigration Studies in Washington, D.C., prepared a report on the residence of the U.S. foreign-born population by state, with a focus on the changes from the 1990 to the 2000 census. People from Mexico constituted the largest number of foreign-born residents in all except three southern states. In Florida, Cuban-born residents formed the largest group of the foreign-born. In Louisiana, people from Vietnam constituted the largest foreign-born group. In Virginia, people from El Salvador were the largest group. These results are not surprising. However, a look at the top 15 countries of origin of the foreign-born population of each southern state does reveal a surprising amount of diversity as well as the presence of a number of unexpected groups. In addition to Mexico, Brazil, China (including Hong Kong and Taiwan), Iran, Iraq (in Tennessee), Kenya, Korea, Laos, Mongolia, Nigeria, Pakistan, the Philippines, Thailand, the former USSR, and Vietnam, as well as a number of other Spanish-speaking countries in Latin America, are among the top 15 countries of origin for at least one southern state. Among European countries, only Germany (in 11 states), France (in Kentucky), and Italy (in Alabama) were on the list of the top 15 countries of origin of the foreign-born population in any southern state. Among the more unusual groups is the community of Marshall Islanders, who speak English and Marshallese, an Austronesian language related to other languages of the Pacific. The largest community of Marshall Islanders, numbering more than 2,500, resides in and around Springdale in northwest Arkansas. Starting in 1985 many Marshall Islanders moved there to seek jobs in the poultry industry.

Schools throughout the South, especially in the urban areas where many immigrants settle, have felt the impact of increasing linguistic diversity. In Atlanta, for example, in 2004 the Emma Hutchinson Elementary School reported that 26 percent of the 550 children enrolled spoke English as a second language. Students came from Somalia, the Sudan, Vietnam, Mexico, Cuba, and Venezuela, among other countries.

Space does not permit a full discussion of all of the issues surrounding the changing linguistic landscape of the South. Therefore, the remainder of this article presents several sketches dealing with Asians, particularly Vietnamese in Houston; Chinese in Houston and San Antonio, Tex., and Chapel Hill, N.C.; and Haitians in south Florida.

ASIANS IN TEXAS AND NORTH CAROLINA. Houston, the nation's fourth largest city, like most Texas cities, is home to a large and growing Latino population, numbering more than 730,000 in 2000. However, the city is also home to a substantial and rapidly growing Asian population, including more than 20,000 East Indians, 24,000 Chinese, and 32,000 Vietnamese as well as numerous other Asians in the surrounding communities. In early 2003 the *Houston Chronicle*, the city's major daily newspaper, responded to the increasing influence of Asians in the Houston metropolitan area by launching *Asian Focus*, a special advertising section. By September 2004 distribution had reached 41,000. Because *Asian Focus* is directed to a broad audience of speakers of many different languages, most articles are in English. However, some stories, particularly those likely to interest first-generation immigrants, are presented in both English and the relevant Asian language.

In addition to publications like *Asian Focus*, Houston is home to several Asian radio stations that broadcast in both English and Asian languages. For example, vovn Radio, the "Voice of Vietnam in Houston," broadcasts in Vietnamese on the am dial for seven hours from Monday through Friday and is also available 24 hours a day every day on the Internet. In its publicity material, vovn claims that the Vietnamese listening audience is 150,000. Like vovn, station kgol, "Houston Chinese Radio," whose coverage extends to Austin in the west, Victoria in the south, and Beaumont and Port Arthur in the east, also claims a large potential audience consisting of Chinese from the People's Republic, Taiwan, Hong Kong, and southeast Asia. Interestingly, in its publicity material, kgol claims that many of its 200,000 potential listeners prefer to buy products advertised in Chinese.

As suggested by the example of Atlanta's Emma Hutchinson Elementary School mentioned earlier, the growth of linguistic diversity in the South can be seen especially in the educational arena, both public and private. In Houston, for example, the Chinese Community Center began offering classes in Chinese and calligraphy to children in 1979. At that time, there were only two language classes, with approximately 35 students. In 2003–4 more than 800 students were enrolled in Chinese and extracurricular courses. The center employed 35 teachers and offered Chinese language classes for children from ages 3 to 18 as well as to adults. Similar programs are found in other cities. For example, San Antonio, with a relatively small Chinese population of 3,500, has four Chinese heritage language schools: one organized by parents from the People's Republic of China; another, which uses a different writing system and has a different method of teaching initial literacy, organized by parents from Taiwan; a third organized by a local church; and a fourth, which offers instruction in Cantonese, organized by parents from Hong Kong.

The increased Asian presence in many areas of the South, as well as the growing importance of China in the world economy, has had important consequences in public education. For example, the Houston suburb of Sugar Land, Tex., home to a substantial number of Chinese Americans, now offers Chinese language classes beginning in the eighth grade. While many of the students taking these classes are of Chinese heritage, many others are not. Chapel Hill, N.C., where Asians make up about 5 percent of the population, has adopted a different approach. The Chapel Hill–Carrboro City School District offers one of the relatively few Chinese-English dual language immersion programs in the United States. In the Chapel Hill–Carrboro program, which began in 2002, children from kindergarten through fifth grade spend half of the school day in English and half in Mandarin Chinese. Half of the students are native speakers of English, usually from families that are monolingual in English, while the other half come from Chinese families. The goal is for students to be fully bilingual and biliterate, with the ability to read and write in both languages, by the end of the fifth grade.

Chinese heritage language schools are not limited to Houston and San Antonio, nor are Chinese language programs limited to public schools in Sugar Land and Chapel Hill. Indeed, Chinese heritage language schools are found in every southern state, and many states have schools in all the major cities. The southern sites listed by the Chinese School Association of the United States include the following: Birmingham and Huntsville, Ala.; Baton Rouge, La.; Starkville, Miss.; Fayetteville, Ark.; Athens, Atlanta, and Savannah, Ga.; Cary, Charlotte, and Chapel Hill, N.C.; Clemson, S.C.; and Chattanooga, Memphis, and Nashville, Tenn. Numerous Chinese heritage language schools have been established in Florida, Texas, and Virginia. Although the Chinese constitute only a small percentage of the population of the South, parents and community organizations are putting enormous efforts into transmitting the Chinese language to the next generation.

HAITIANS IN FLORIDA. According to the 2000 census, Florida is the state with the largest number of residents born in Haiti. Numbering 182,224, Haitians constituted 7 percent of Florida's foreign-born population. The language situation of immigrants from Haiti and their U.S.-born children, combined with U.S. racial classifications, presents a number of problems that are particular to this substantial group of immigrants. The first concerns the status of Haitian Creole, the native language of most immigrants. Haitian Creole developed out of the contact between African languages and French on the plantations of Haiti during the colonial period. As a language long associated with rural labor and the urban poor, Haitian Creole enjoyed very little status and for many years was regarded as a corrupted form of French. As might be expected of a language spoken mostly by poor and often nonliterate people, relatively few resources exist for teaching children academic content in their language. The second issue concerns the U.S. system of racial classification, which may ignore important distinctions within groups. According to Flore Zéphir, who has conducted extensive research on the education of Haitian American students in Florida and elsewhere, students of Haitian origin are sometimes classified as African Americans rather than as members of a distinct linguistic and cultural group. As a consequence, Zéphir claims, Haitian immigrants and the children of immigrants are often grouped with native-English-speaking African American students, and little attention is paid to their particular linguistic needs.

Traditionally, linguistic issues in the South have been conceived of primarily in terms of varieties of English or, in the cases of Florida and Texas, of Spanish. However, as the data from the 2000 census makes clear, the modern South is attracting immigrants from numerous parts of the world. Although Spanish is the most common language in all southern states aside from Louisiana, in 2000 more than 3.5 million southerners reported speaking a language other than English or Spanish at home. Given recent trends in immigration, that number can only be expected to increase.

ROBERT BAYLEY
University of California at Davis

Steven A. Camarota and Nora McArdle, *Where Immigrants Live: An Examination of State Residency of the Foreign Born by Country of Origin in 1990 and 2000* (2003); Hyon B. Shin and Rosalind Bruno, *Language Use and English-Speaking Ability: 2000* (2003); U.S. Census Bureau, *1990 Census of Population: The Foreign-born Population in the United States* (1993).

Indian Trade Languages

At the time of contact with Europeans, the South was home to languages belonging to at least five separate families: Algonquian, Iroquoian, Siouan, Muskogean, and Caddoan, plus several distantly related and unrelated languages. Our understanding of the aboriginal linguistic situation of the Ohio River Valley, the Carolinas, and much of the Gulf of Mexico is poor, and there were likely other undocumented languages. This immense linguistic diversity, surpassed in North America only on the Northwest Coast and in native California, set the stage for language convergence in the form of various intertribal linguistic media, including trade languages, some of which were pidginized (i.e., lexically intermixed and grammatically simplified).

Our ideas of the existence and geographic distribution of these languages may in part reflect colonial record keeping, specifically what early European settlers did or did not observe and record. By current indications, most trade languages extended along the Atlantic and Gulf coasts and along major rivers, since waterways served as a major infrastructure for long-distance travel that brought together peoples of distant, diverse linguistic backgrounds and that required linguistic compromises. Whether or not pre-Columbian in origin, such lingua francas grew in significance with the arrival of Europeans in North America and the spread of the fur and hide trade. The latter became the context for their colonial use, hence the name *trade languages*.

Around Chesapeake Bay, the once-powerful Powhatan Indians (Algonquians), their linguistically diverse (or alloglossic) neighbors, and English settlers employed a reduced or pidginized Powhatan. Few linguistic details are available about it, but Pidgin Powhatan apparently served as the medium for more Algonquian loans in English (such as *hominy*, *moccasin*, *opossum*, *persimmon*, *raccoon*, and *tomahawk*) than any other source. In the early 18th century, linguistically diverse Indians of south-central Virginia apparently spoke a common intertribal language associated with the Occaneechi (Siouans) and consisting of elements of Tutelo and Saponi (Siouan), Virginia Algonquian, and Tuscarora (Iroquoian). They used the medium as a trade language with Europeans. Tuscarora likewise functioned as an intertribal medium with neighboring Pamlico (Algonquians) and Woccon (Siouans), serving as a trade language with Europeans. Farther southeast, the language of the once-powerful Catawba (related to proto-Siouan) reportedly functioned as a lingua franca with their alloglossic neighbors in the Piedmont of the upper Carolinas in the mid-18th century. In the interior, Shawnee (Algonquian) operated as an intertribal medium among linguistically diverse tribes from Canada to Georgia, including Algonquians, Iroquoians, Siouans, and probably others, when the Shawnee under the leadership of Tecumseh organized intertribal resistance against American expansion in the early 19th century. Reliable linguistic data have remained elusive for these latter instances, however. What appear as distinct contact media may have been a group of interlocked, interrelated varieties drawing on the same pool of Algonquian, Iroquoian, and Siouan sources with fundamentally similar grammars. Its geographic range extended from the Carolinas along the Atlantic Coast as far north as New England.

Some Spanish historical sources refer to Timucua of northeastern Florida as an indigenous lingua franca through much of the peninsula in the early 17th century, but they ultimately offer little supportive documentation of this medium.

In the 18th century the Creek Confederacy of Georgia, consisting of Muskogee Indians plus various other Eastern Muskogean and non-Muskogean allies, used a reduced form of Muskogee as an interlingual medium. The Seminole, descendants of the Muskogee in Florida, spoke it in contact with non-Indians throughout the 19th century and later. A variety of this lingua franca form of Creek apparently took on much English vocabulary and grammar, perhaps under the influence of English-speaking runaway African slaves, to become an English-based creole language known as Afro-Seminole Creole and to survive in Oklahoma and Texas. Whether this model extended to other Native American communities with reference to a so-called American Indian Pidgin English remains questionable; most supporting data may prove no more than Anglophone-Anglophile transliterations to render native people's actual speech in their own languages or lingua francas easily intelligible to the reader for literary purposes.

The best, most widely documented indigenous case of a trade language in southeastern North America was the Chickasaw-Choctaw trade language, or Mobilian Jargon, a Western Muskogean relative of the lingua franca Creek. Not to be confused with Mobilian proper of southern Alabama (whose historical classification remains in doubt today), Mobilian Jargon reflected some historical association with Mobile as the first French outpost of the area, named after the Mobilian Indians. However, it developed from the pidginization of Muskogean languages, a linguistic process through which speakers of quite diverse indigenous languages of southeastern North America learned Choctaw, Chickasaw, or possibly some related Muskogean tongue incompletely as a second language. In contact with Muskogeans, speakers of Caddoan, Siouan, Algonquian, and probably other indigenous American languages adopted a reduced variety of Muskogean with a compromise grammar and a mixed lexicon, reflecting influences from their first languages. Alloglossic southeastern Indians of the lower Mississippi River Valley also used it with one another, providing the context by which the interlingual medium developed a life of its own and a distinctive grammar, but little morphological complexity. The presence of several "exotic" loans from Algonquian languages of the Great Lakes area and only a few from European sources suggests that Mobilian Jargon's range extended into Algonquian territories of southern Illinois, while remaining comparatively immune to European influences. With the establishment of Louisiana as a French colony in 1699, the pidgin became a major interlingual medium between native peoples of the area, on one hand, and European colonists and African immigrants, on the other.

What sociohistorical circumstances led to the development of Mobilian Jargon is debatable. According to a conventional argument, the pidgin had come about from contact with French colonizers in 18th-century Louisiana. A recent proposal had Mobilian Jargon already in existence before the arrival of Europeans in North America, by drawing on three major considerations: (1) it had an indigenous grammar with a characteristic word order of object-subject-verb and a predominantly Muskogean lexicon with only a few European loanwords, (2) its use did not concentrate solely on European trade and colonization but expanded to diverse indigenous contexts of interlingual contact, and (3) its geographic distribution overlapped closely with that of linguistically diverse but socioculturally quite uniform southeastern Indian groups formerly associated in multilingual chiefdoms of the pre-Columbian Mississippian Complex.

Without replacing the neighboring languages in *local* bilingual situations, Mobilian Jargon remained restricted to multilingual contexts and contact with distant alloglossic peoples, as might have been the case between Muskogeans of the lower Mississippi River Valley and Osage or possibly Oto (Siouans) on the Missouri River. However, it exhibited few, if any, other functional limitations. Mobilian Jargon could be used in any contact situation that required a widely understood medium: long-distance travels on a network of trails and waterways across much of eastern North America; hunting and foraging expeditions into faraway territories; intertribal and colonial trade; intertribal and interethnic marriages; raids on hostile groups and bondage of captives; diplomatic missions; pantribal alliances and multilingual chiefdoms; gambling, ballgames, and dances; ritual gatherings and the practice of native medicine; and employment of native peoples outside one's own community. By the early 19th century at the latest, Mobilian Jargon no longer operated solely as a contact language. For the area's linguistically and culturally conservative Indians, it also became a sociolinguistic buffer against unwanted intrusions from the outside. Fluency in Mobilian Jargon helped confirm their native identity, a safeguard against the continuing threat of enslavement that Indians had to worry about by being mistaken for blacks; use of the pidgin moreover diverted the attention of prying strangers such as traders, missionaries, immigrant settlers, government officials, and anthropologists from the Indians' inner circles. The pidgin survived as a viable medium until the late 1940s or possibly into the 1950s. The last speakers, most of them elderly Native Americans of Louisiana, recalled single words and phrases of what in their mind was a truly cosmopolitan institution, and they did so with uncommon pride as recently as the 1980s. This fact still permitted a fairly inclusive study that relied on linguistic and ethnographic memory fieldwork and drew on philological and ethnohistorical reconstructions.

Farther west of Mobilian Jargon, Caddo likewise served as a contact medium among alloglossic Caddoans and with their neighbors in the early 19th century. No details are available about its grammar, use, or social history.

EMANUEL J. DRECHSEL
University of Hawai'i at Mānoa

James Crawford, *The Mobilian Trade Language* (1978); Emanuel J. Drechsel, *Anthropological Linguistics* (vol. 38, 1996), *Mobilian Jargon: Linguistic and Sociohistorical Aspects of Native American Pidgin* (1997); Ives Goddard, in *The Language Encounter in the Americas, 1492–1800*, ed. Edward G. Gray and Norman Fiering (2000); Michael Silverstein, in *Handbook of North American Indians*, vol. 17, *Languages*, ed. Ives Goddard (1996); Sarah Grey Thomason, *Language in Society* (vol. 9, 1980).

Indigenous Languages, Other

In the 18th and 19th centuries the American South was home to several important language families. The Algonquian and Iroquoian families extended southward from Canada as far as Virginia and North Carolina. Catawba, Woccon, and the distantly related Siouan languages were spoken in Virginia, North Carolina, Tennessee, and Mississippi. The Muskogean family filled the central portion of the South in present Mississippi, Alabama, Georgia, northern Florida, and eastern Tennessee, and Caddo, the southern representative of the Caddoan family, was spoken in east Texas, Arkansas, and Louisiana. Scattered among these families were a number of languages with no known relatives: Timucua was spoken in northern Florida and southern Georgia; Yuchi is thought to have been spoken in central Tennessee; Natchez, Tunica, Chitimacha, and Atakapa were spoken in Louisiana and Mississippi. The area of the lower Mississippi was particularly diverse linguistically, a situation that led in part to the use of Mobilian Jargon, a trade language based on Muskogean vocabulary.

An unusual feature of the South is the very large number of bands or small tribes with distinct names. Many of these small tribes shared common languages: there were approximately 60 Cherokee-speaking towns, for example, and 40 to 60 named Creek-speaking settlements. Some of these small tribes had their own languages, however, and since we lack vocabularies for each, we cannot know their linguistic affiliation. Important groups whose linguistic classification is unknown include Yamasee, Guale, Cusabo, Tequesta, Chacato, Sawokli, Chakchiuma, Mobila, Pascagoula, and Houma. Finally, the languages of a few groups are very poorly documented, so that not enough material is available to establish an affiliation. Only a handful of words survive from the

Calusa language of southern Florida, for example, and the Adai language of western Louisiana may or may not be related to the Caddoan languages. Faced with these uncertainties, some scholars have resorted to piecing together different types of evidence to determine language affiliations. In Georgia, for example, groups like the Yamacraw had Creek personal names and used Creek titles (e.g., *mí·kko* 'chief'), but we are still uncertain what language the Yamacraw spoke. Koasati and Mikasuki speakers also used Creek names and titles and are known to have spoken distinct languages. Others have suggested that language affiliation could be determined based on the origin of tribal names or place-names. This evidence is also of little value. The Cherokee self-designation *tsalaki* is possibly Creek in origin, yet Cherokee and Creek are unrelated. A third type of evidence derives from statements by visitors about the intelligibility of different languages. These statements are sometimes accurate and sometimes unreliable.

Timucua, Atakapa, Chitimacha, and Tunica are described below. Table 6 provides a few words from these four languages.

TIMUCUA. Although the last speakers died in the 18th century, Timucua is one of the best-documented languages of the South, in large part because of the early efforts of Father Francisco Pareja. Pareja journeyed to northern Florida from Mexico in 1595 and introduced the Spanish tradition of language description to North America. He developed a Spanish-based writing system for the language and completed a catechism by 1612, a confessional by 1613, and a grammar by 1614. A great deal can be gained from the study of these documents. The structure of Timucua is typical of southeastern languages, for example, in having subject-object-verb word order and numerous affixes on verbs (Table 4). Pareja's studies are the earliest of their type for any North American language and provide the main sources for subsequent work on the language. Some have speculated that Timucua might be related to the Muskogean languages or even to languages in South America or the Caribbean, but so far no strong evidence has emerged. The only language plausibly linked to Timucua is Tawasa, a short vocabulary of which was obtained from an escaped slave in 1707 or 1708.

ATAKAPA. Atakapa was spoken in the coastal area between Louisiana and Texas. Primary sources on the language include a vocabulary of 45 words collected by Jean Béranger in 1721, a vocabulary of 287 words collected in 1802 by Martin Duralde, and a more substantial collection of words, sentences, and nine short texts collected in 1885 by Albert S. Gatschet. In 1929 John R. Swanton com-

TABLE 4. *Structure of Timucua*

Pedroma	Maria	cachusinta	alihotela
Pedro-ma	Maria	cachu-sin-ta	aliho-te-la
Pedro-TOPIC	Maria	be.in.love-RECIPROCAL-NONFINAL	go.about-PRESENT-INDICATIVE

Pedro anda enamorado de Maria. ('Pedro is in love with Maria.')

TABLE 5. *Structure of Atakapa*

wi'c	kaukau'	me'lc
wi'-c	kaukau'	me'l-c
I-EMPHATIC	water	black-MAKE

'I blacken the water.'

piled the Béranger, Duralde, and Gatschet vocabularies and published a dictionary and sketch. Like the other languages described here, Atakapa has subject-object-verb word order (Table 5).

CHITIMACHA. Chitimacha was formerly spoken in Louisiana. Martin Duralde collected a vocabulary in 1802. In 1881–82 Albert S. Gatschet gathered material for a manuscript dictionary and text collection. John R. Swanton visited in 1907 to check some of Gatschet's work. Morris Swadesh, the only modern linguist to work on the language, worked with the last speakers in 1932–34 to complete a manuscript dictionary, grammar, and text collection. Benjamin Paul, a Chitimacha who served as a consultant for Gatschet, Swanton, and Swadesh, died in 1934. Delphine Ducloux, the last fluent speaker, died in 1940. Swadesh believed that Chitimacha was distantly related to Atakapa, but the relationship has yet to be proven.

TUNICA. Tunica was poorly described until Mary R. Haas began work with Sesostrie Youchigant, the last speaker, in the 1930s. Haas completed a grammar for her dissertation and went on to publish a text collection and dictionary. Tunica is unusual among southeastern languages in having a grammatical distinction between masculine and feminine nouns. In all, the South was home to several dozen distinct languages. None of the languages in Table 6 is now spoken; but 10 native languages were still spoken in 2005, and efforts to document and maintain these continue.

JACK MARTIN
College of William and Mary

TABLE 6. *Comparison of Basic Terms in Four Unrelated Languages of the South*

English	Timucua	Atakapa	Tunica	Chitimacha
Mouth	nipita	ka't	-šóhu	šaʔ, šaʔa
River	ibi	ta'-i	títihtʔɛ	čaʔa·d
Road	eye	wa'ñne	téti	miš
Rock	yobo	wai'	šíhkali	nuš
Child	aruqui	no'mc	ʔśka	yaʔa
Eye	mucu	wō'l	-štósu	kani

Karen M. Booker, *Languages of the Aboriginal Southeast: An Annotated Bibliography* (1991); Heather K. Hardy and Janine Scancarelli, eds., *Native Languages of the South-eastern United States* (2005); Jack B. Martin, in *Handbook of North American Indians*, vol. 14, *Southeast*, ed. Raymond D. Fogelson (2004).

Iroquoian Languages

The southern branch of the Iroquoian language family is related to Mohawk, Seneca, and other northern Iroquoian languages in New York and Ontario. It has three known members, including Cherokee, but almost certainly included others at the time of initial contact with Europeans. Nottoway, spoken in southeastern Virginia, became extinct in the 19th century and is known from word lists. The Tuscarora, the dominant indigenous tribe in eastern North Carolina when English speakers arrived there in the mid-17th century, were decimated by the Tuscarora War of 1711–13. Thereafter remnants of the tribe moved to western New York, where they were welcomed by their kindred and were made the sixth nation of the Iroquoian League in 1722. At present a handful of older speakers of the language remain there.

The Cherokee, who have long dominated southern Appalachia and nearby areas, have always been the largest of the southern Iroquoian tribes. Contact between them and Europeans began with the Spanish under Hernando de Soto (possibly earlier), who called them the Chalaque. By the early 1700s, English traders first from Virginia and then from South Carolina developed extensive bartering networks with them for furs and hides, and they eventually adopted many Cherokee place-names, for example, Nantahala (N.C.), Etowah (Ga.), and Tellico (Tenn.). When white settlers began moving into the southern Appalachians by the middle of the century, the Cherokee nation occupied much of western North Carolina, eastern Tennessee, and northern Georgia; sometimes it ranged as far north as Virginia and Kentucky. The Cherokee were the largest

Ꭰ	a	Ꭱ	e	Ꭲ	i	Ꭳ	o	Ꭴ	u	Ꭵ	v
Ꭶ	ga	Ꭷ	ka	Ꭸ	ge	Ꭹ	gi	Ꭺ	go	Ꭻ	gu
Ꭼ	gv	Ꭽ	ha	Ꭾ	he	Ꭿ	hi	Ꮀ	ho	Ꮁ	hu
Ꮂ	hv	Ꮃ	la	Ꮄ	le	Ꮅ	li	Ꮆ	lo	Ꮇ	lu
Ꮈ	lv	Ꮉ	ma	Ꮊ	me	Ꮋ	mi	Ꮌ	mo	Ꮍ	mu
Ꮎ	na	Ꮏ	hna	Ꮑ	ne	Ꮒ	ni	Ꮓ	no	Ꮔ	nu
Ꮕ	nv	Ꮖ	qua	Ꮗ	que	Ꮘ	qui	Ꮙ	quo	Ꮚ	quu
Ꮛ	quv	Ꮜ	sa	Ꮝ	s	Ꮞ	se	Ꮟ	si	Ꮠ	so
Ꮡ	su	Ꮢ	sv	Ꮣ	da	Ꮤ	ta	Ꮥ	de	Ꮦ	te
Ꮧ	di	Ꮨ	ti	Ꮩ	do	Ꮪ	du	Ꮫ	dv	Ꮬ	dla
Ꮭ	tla	Ꮮ	tle	Ꮯ	tli	Ꮰ	tlo	Ꮱ	tlu	Ꮲ	tlv
Ꮳ	tsa	Ꮴ	tse	Ꮵ	tsi	Ꮶ	tso	Ꮷ	tsu	Ꮸ	tsv
Ꮹ	wa	Ꮺ	we	Ꮻ	wi	Ꮼ	wo	Ꮽ	wu	Ꮾ	wv
Ꮿ	ya	Ᏸ	ye	Ᏹ	yi	Ᏺ	yo	Ᏻ	yu	Ᏼ	yv

The Cherokee syllabary. The Cherokee have always been the largest of the southern Iroquoian tribes, and many place-names in Georgia, North Carolina, and Tennessee are derived from the Cherokee branch of the Iroquoian language family. (Apostolos Syropoulos and Tonia Williams)

tribe occupying the strategic zone between coastal settlements and the vast interior, and their relations with whites were always a factor, first, in British imperial and, later, in American domestic, political, military, and commercial life. Through extensive contact and assimilation, a shift from Cherokee monolingualism to Cherokee/English bilingualism had begun by the early 1800s in their native areas. Since the early 20th century a radical shift to English monolingualism has taken place, though about 10,000 Cherokee speakers still reside in Oklahoma, descendants of those forcibly marched west during the tragic Trail of Tears in 1838.

By the beginning of the 21st century, fewer than 10 percent of North Carolina Cherokee, primarily middle-aged and older members, spoke the language, which is now considered endangered. Major dialects are still found in areas of North Carolina reserved for the Cherokee by the federal government. There are about 1,000 speakers of the Kituwha dialect of the Qualla Cherokee of Swain and Jackson counties and close to 150 who speak the Atali dialect of the Snowbird Cherokee of Graham County. Much of this decline of the language is attributable to prejudices of the dominant American culture. Into the 1950s Cherokee children could be beaten or punished severely if they spoke their ancestral language in federally run boarding schools, which had active policies designed to eradicate Cherokee language and culture. This treatment discouraged many

Cherokee parents from teaching the language to their own children for fear that they, too, would be punished and humiliated.

Written Cherokee uses a syllabary that is remarkable among written languages, in that it was apparently developed by a single person, Sequoyah. Also known as George Guess, Sequoyah was born in 1760 west of Chilhowee Mountain in southeastern Tennessee. Though illiterate himself, Sequoyah was inspired to devise a system for writing Cherokee through his fascination for the "talking leaves" used by white traders communicating in English. Using both invented and borrowed characters, he experimented for many years and by 1821 had assigned symbols to the 85 sounds and sound combinations still used in Cherokee.

Within a year thereafter, the Cherokee Nation adopted the syllabary as its official writing system. According to 19th-century ethnologist James Mooney, a Cherokee speaker could learn to read and write the language in a few months, and thousands quickly became literate. By 1828 a Cherokee press had been established that published the *Cherokee Phoenix*, a newspaper using the syllabary, as well as translations of the Bible and other books in the language. Although a majority of Cherokee speakers use the syllabary, the language can also be written in English letters. Today, there are still bilingual newspapers published in English and Cherokee (using the syllabary).

The syllabary consists of six vowel sounds, the consonant *s*, and 78 combinations of consonants and vowels. Every syllable ends with a vowel sound. Vowel pronunciations include *a* as in *father*, *e* as in *hey*, *o* as in *goat*, *i* as in *machine*, *u* as in *rule*, and a nasally produced /ə/ (spelled with *v*) as the vowel sound in *tug*. Each vowel can have either long or short duration or strong or weak stress. Long vowels require about twice as much time to pronounce as short vowels, as in the example of the short vowel of *ama* 'salt' and the long vowel of *aama* 'water.' There are also pitch differences in the pronunciation of vowels, with the last vowel of each word being nasalized.

Cherokee has consonants similar to English *j*, *s*, *t*, *d*, *k*, *g*, *m*, *n*, *l*, *y*, *w*, and *h*, but it differs in having no sounds resembling *p* and *b*. Cherokee has a glottal sound, which resembles a catch in the throat (as the middle sound in English *uh-oh*), a voiceless *l* (sounded like the English *l* preceded by *h*), *tl* (like English *l* but with the tip of the tongue in position to make a *t* sound), *ts* (as in the end of the English word *eats*), *ch* (as in English *church*), *kw* (as in English *queen*), and *gw* (as in English *Gwen*).

Cherokee grammar is highly complex. Nouns are similar to those of English in representing a person, place, or thing, but Cherokee nouns are divided into two classes: animate and inanimate. Prefixes or suffixes added to nouns are equivalent to articles and adjectives in English.

The verb is the most important part of every Cherokee sentence and can be either active or stative. Active verbs refer to a definite action performed by someone, for example, *jiwoniha* 'I am talking.' Stative verbs refer to passive states or to actions performed by someone other than by the speaker on a recipient individual or group. Each verb must have one or more prefixes followed by a root and at least one suffix. Additional prefixes and suffixes can alter the meanings further. One example is the verb *da-ga-wo-ni-hi-se-li* 'he will speak for him.'

Verbs in Cherokee show great attention to details of the physical world and reflect a way of seeing and interpreting the world that is different from that expressed by English. For example, the Cherokee way of expressing "to hand something to someone" depends on the nature of the object being handed: *gvnea* means "I hand you something nondescript" (probably solid); *gvdea* 'I hand you something long and inflexible'; *gvnvnea* 'I hand you something floppy or flexible' (such as a cloth); and *gvnevsi* 'I hand you something liquid.'

The Cherokee are attempting to preserve and revitalize their rich and fascinating language, and it is now recognized and taught in the schools of Cherokee, N.C. The arrival of casino gambling in recent years has enabled the Qualla Cherokee to invest funds in teaching and reviving the language and culture. The future of the language in the South may therefore not be as dire as it was a few short years ago, but since many Cherokee still do not speak the language at home or on a regular basis, its future is by no means secure.

BRIDGET ANDERSON
Old Dominion University

Margaret Bender, *Signs of Culture: Sequoyah's Syllabary in Eastern Cherokee Life* (2002); Blair Rudes, *Tuscarora-English/English-Tuscarora Dictionary* (1999); Janine Scancarelli, in *Native Languages of the Southeastern United States*, ed. Heather K. Hardy and Janine Scancarelli (2005).

Jewish Language

Language varieties used by Jews in the American South stem from distinctive traditions of settlers who arrived in three waves of immigration from different parts of the world. Although all of these groups used Hebrew as the language of prayer, they brought with them other languages used in both speech and ritual.

Beginning in the 17th century, Sephardic Jews (of Spanish and Portuguese origin) brought a Jewish variety of Spanish called Ladino, which was often tran-

Store sign for Noshville, a Jewish delicatessen in Nashville, Tenn., and a good example of the spread of Yiddish into general American usage (Marcia Montgomery)

scribed in Hebrew lettering. Fleeing the inquisitions of Spain, Portugal, and the New World, Sephardic Jews organized congregations in Savannah, Ga. (1733), Charleston, S.C. (1749), and Richmond, Va. (1789). Later groups established synagogues in New Orleans, Montgomery, and Atlanta. Ladino was common as a language of prayer in these congregations. Although English has largely replaced Ladino in many congregations today, efforts are being made to revive its use.

The second wave of Jewish immigration, from Germany, began in the early 18th century. By the early 19th century, German Jewish congregations had been founded in New Orleans (1828) and Baltimore (1829). Fleeing poverty, persecution, and political upheaval, German Jews brought with them the liberal democratic traditions of the Reform Movement, which had originated in Hamburg. Southern Jews quickly embraced Reform Judaism. Among its tenets was the integration of Jews into local culture. In Germany, this meant that many Jews had abandoned Yiddish before the period of American emigration, even though Yiddish had developed in Germany as a language unifying Jews of all nationalities. In prayers and sermons, Hebrew was replaced by the local language. In Charleston, the issue of replacing Hebrew with English caused a split in the congregation that had begun as an Orthodox, Sephardic community, producing in 1841 the first continuing Reform Jewish congregation in America. In the same year in Richmond, Ashkenazic German Jews established their own congregation. In Memphis, although the congregation was Orthodox, the synagogue was dedicated in 1858 by Dr. Isaac Mayer Wise, the founder of Reform Judaism in America. In Savannah, the once Sephardic Orthodox congregation adopted the Reform prayer book in 1902, and few traces remain of its Sephardic origins.

The third wave of Jewish immigration to America was from Eastern Europe in the late 19th through early 20th centuries. Until restrictive immigration policies were instituted in the United States in 1924, Jews arrived in great numbers, fleeing pogroms and persecution in Russia, Poland, Austria-Hungary, and Romania. Economically, they were generally less well-off than Sephardic or German Ashkenazic Jews. Many embraced more traditional practices of Orthodox and Conservative Judaism. In addition to their native languages, these Ashkenazic Jews brought with them a common language, Yiddish. Although most Ashkenazim settled in the Northeast, and thus Yiddish is closely associated with New York City, many came to southern cities and brought Yiddish with them. As with most immigrant languages in the United States, the use of Yiddish largely died out by the third generation, though its influence is evident in Jewish English today.

Large numbers of words have spread from Yiddish into Jewish English and into general American usage: *bagel, chutzpah, glitch, kibitz, klutz, kosher, kvetch, maven, mensch, nebbish, schlock, schmooze, schmuck, shalom,* and *tchotchke.* Hebrew names for popular holidays and celebrations, such as *Chanukah* and *bar mitzvah,* are used among Jews and non-Jews alike. Compounds with English words are readily formed, as in *Chanukah card* or *matzo ball soup.* Southern Jewish culture merges traditions and words from both worlds. Photographer Bill Aron blends "lox, bagels, and grits" with "magnolias and menorahs." Novelist Tova Mirvis describes meals with "challahs, a fried chicken, two kugels, and . . . hush puppies" and "honey mustard chicken, barbecue beef ribs, sliced kishka, noodle kugel." In Natchez, Miss., the menu of a Passover seder includes matzo balls with gravy. The expression that best summarizes the experience of southern Jews is one that has appeared as the title of books and movies and as a slogan on coffee mugs, T-shirts, and other souvenirs: *shalom y'all.*

CYNTHIA BERNSTEIN
University of Memphis

Sarah Bunin Benor, *Jewish Language Research Website,* <http://www.jewish-languages.org>; Eli Evans, *The Lonely Days Were Sundays: Reflections of a Jewish Southerner* (1993); Marcie Cohen Ferris, *Matzoh Ball Gumbo: Culinary Tales of the Jewish South* (2005); Theodore Rosengarten and Dale Rosengarten, eds., *A Portion of the People: Three Hundred Years of Southern Jewish Life* (2002).

Liberian Settler English

Liberian Settler English (LSE) is the language of the descendants of the 16,000 African Americans who immigrated to Liberia in the 19th century. Its modern character reflects the origins of the original African American settlers and the history of the immigrants and their descendants up to the present day. The term *Settler* refers to a current Liberian ethnic group whose members belong either by descent or by assimilation.

The American Colonization Society (ACS), founded in Washington, D.C., in 1816, had envisioned a settlement in West Africa where free African Americans could have a country of their own, without the discrimination they faced in the United States. Such a proposal appealed to southern slave owners, who saw the presence of free people of color as a threat to the status quo and who therefore provided most of the financial backing for the venture. However, the ACS proved unable to convince a sufficiently large number of free people to go, and most of those who immigrated were individuals who were emancipated upon condition of their immigration to Liberia. The latter group deemed relocation to an unknown land preferable to continued enslavement in the United States.

The initial settlement took place in 1821 to what is now Monrovia. Most of these first Settlers came from Virginia, Maryland, and North Carolina, and subsequently large numbers from Georgia and South Carolina joined them. During the 19th century these five states provided two-thirds of all immigrants to Liberia, with Virginia by far the largest source. For the most part, the Settlers came from small holdings and from fringe agricultural areas rather than from large plantations. In addition to the ACS's colony, Liberia, two state societies established their own colonies as a consequence of disputes with the national society's head office in Washington. Maryland in Africa was founded at Cape Palmas 250 miles southeast of Monrovia in 1834, and Mississippi in Africa was established at the mouth of the Sinoe River 150 miles southeast of Monrovia in 1838. In time, each of these was absorbed into Liberia as a constituent county.

At the time of the Settlers' arrival in Liberia, a pidginized variety of English was already in wide use for trade along the West African coast. Once ACS agents took control of the region, the Settlers' English became the language of power. Accordingly, it influenced the pidgin spoken by the indigenous majority (the Settlers or their descendants have never become more than 3 percent of the total population of the country). For example, elsewhere in pidginized varieties of English along the West African coast, the second-person-plural pronoun is *unu* or *una*, but in Liberia's pidgin, Vernacular Liberian English (VLE), it is *yaw*, from *y'all*. There has been some influence in the other direction (i.e., from VLE to the Settlers' English), but it has been far less pervasive. Any influence from such coastal Niger-Congo languages as Klao, Bassa, and Grebo on LSE has been transmitted via VLE. Education in Liberia served an integrative function, so as a general rule, the modern descendants of Settlers who sound the most distinctively American are those with the least formal education.

In general, the local features that the Settlers' language acquired in West Africa are readily identifiable. At its least integrated, the variety remains fundamentally North American. This is especially true for the LSE of Sinoe County. The Settlers to Sinoe (née Mississippi in Africa) differed from those in the rest of Liberia in that most came from a five-state swath of the Lower South, many from large plantations in Mississippi and Georgia, rather than from smaller farms in Virginia and the Carolinas. Sinoe County received little assistance from the central government and — unlike the other settlements — had virtually no missionary presence prior to the mid-20th century. Finally, from the outset the level of hostility between the Sinoe Settlers and the indigenous population was greater than virtually anywhere else in Liberia. All of these factors contributed to an isolation that has made Sinoe more of a linguistic relic area. As such, it is a valuable source of information about the speech of African American agricultural workers in the mid-19th century in the Lower South. It attests to the long-standing use of individual features in modern-day African American Vernacular English (AAVE): for example, the auxiliaries *be done* (*No goat be in Louisiana because the leopard* be done *carry* [i.e., would have carried] *them all* [away]); *steady* (*She* steady *jumping rope* [i.e., jumped rope continuously]); and stressed *been* (*That boy* BEEN *gone Monrovia* [i.e., went to Monrovia long ago]). It also points to features that have disappeared from AAVE in the United States: for example, the auxiliary *duh* (*Some people* duh *eat palm kernel grease, but I don't like it*) for actions that occur habitually or repeatedly, and the copula *suh* (*But still we* suh [i.e., are] *hard up*). Other features of LSE were shared by AAVE and Southern White Vernacular English: for example, the possessive pronoun *hisn* and the quasimodal *liketa* 'almost' (used especially with verbs involving death). LSE, especially that spoken in Sinoe, is a rich source of information about the language of African Americans in the 19th-century South.

JOHN VICTOR SINGLER
New York University

Alan Huffman, *Mississippi in Africa: The Saga of the Slaves of Prospect Hill Plantation and Their Legacy in Liberia Today* (2004); John Victor Singler, *American Speech* (vol. 64, 1989), in *A Handbook of Varieties of English*, vol. 1, *Phonology*, ed. Bernd Kortmann et al. (2004), in *A Handbook of Varieties of English*, vol. 2, *Morphology and Syntax*, ed. Bernd Kortmann et al. (2004), *World Englishes* (vol. 16, July 1997).

Lumbee English

The language of the Lumbee people is a distinguishing variety of English that weaves together influences from an array of historical and contemporary contact varieties, including those spoken by Highland Scots, Ulster Scots, British, Anglo-Americans, and African Americans. The Lumbee Indians live in a multiethnic community with nearly equal numbers of Anglo-Americans, African Americans, and American Indians and a growing Hispanic population in Robeson County in the southeast corner of North Carolina along Interstate 95 about 20 miles north of the South Carolina border. They comprise the largest American Indian group east of the Mississippi, with more than 45,000 members on their tribal registry. Robeson County has been the home of the Lumbee for at least three centuries. By the early 18th century the Lumbee were speaking a type of English, at least in contact with outside groups; their ancestral language or languages are unlikely to be recovered. However, the strong cultural cohesion of the Lumbee people has nurtured and maintained Lumbee English in the face of language loss and encroachment.

Lumbee English has few features that have not been documented in other varieties of English, but its distinctiveness lies not in its exclusive dialect features but in its unique combination of lexical, phonological, and syntactic structures that set it apart from other dialects of English. Vocabulary items, such as *Lum* 'Lumbee,' *on the swamp* 'in the neighborhood,' *juvember* 'slingshot,' and *ellick* 'a cup of coffee,' are used exclusively within the Lumbee speech community, while other lexical items, such as *gaum* and *mommuck* 'mess,' are related to earlier forms of English that are shared by the Lumbee, Appalachian, and Outer Banks speakers within North Carolina. Phonological forms, such as the raising and backing of /ai/ as in *toide* for *tide* and *h*-retention as in *hit* for *it*, are also shared features related to older versions of English. With respect to grammar, however, a distinctive form that sets Lumbee English apart from other vernacular dialects in the immediate area is the use of *be* as a type of perfect form. That is, Lumbee English may use constructions such as *I'm been there* or *We're got it already* where other dialects would use *have* as in *I've been there* or *We've got it already*. Other grammatical features include *weren't* regularization, as in *I/you/(s)he/we/y'all/they weren't* and *be(s)*, as in *That train bes running every time I get out of class*, which show mixed alignment with immediate and regional contact groups, including Robeson County African and Anglo-Americans.

The story of Lumbee language identity is not simply a matter of speculation about the indigenous American languages that were once spoken by the ancestors of the Lumbee. Instead, it is about the flexibility and resiliency of a

cultural group in shaping a dynamic identity through available language resources. Thus, although the Lumbee have lost traces of their ancestral language
or languages, they have nevertheless carved out a distinctive, systematic dialect of English that reflects their peoplehood as an American Indian group.

CLARE DANNENBERG
Virginia Tech University

Clare Dannenberg, *Sociolinguistic Constructs of Ethnic Identity: The Syntactic Delineation of a Native American English Variety* (2003); Walt Wolfram, Clare Dannenberg, Stanley Knick, and Linda Oxendine, *Fine in the World: Lumbee Language in
Time and Place* (2002).

Muskogean Languages

When the first European explorers penetrated the Southeast, they encountered
a linguistic melting pot. The indigenous tribes spoke languages representing
no fewer than five different language families (the languages within each family
being as diverse as the modern Romance or Germanic languages) and several
isolates, those languages that bear no known linguistic affiliation to any other.
While four of these families had related languages spoken outside the Southeast, speakers of the Muskogean languages resided entirely within the boundaries of the Old South. It was the speakers of these languages who constituted
the politically and socially dominant tribes of the region.

Of the nine languages known to belong to the Muskogean family, seven
are still spoken. Choctaw and Chickasaw are considered to be closely related
dialects even though they have some lexical and grammatical differences. Alabama and Koasati, though mutually unintelligible, bear a closer relationship to
each other than to any other of their sister languages. Mikasuki makes up the
third major branch of the family, and Creek and Seminole together make up
the fourth. The latter two encompass three mutually intelligible dialects: Oklahoma Creek (also called Muskogee), Oklahoma Seminole, and Florida Seminole. Hitchiti, a dialect of Mikasuki, was spoken until the mid-20th century,
while Appalachee, a language originally spoken in the Florida panhandle, became extinct in the early 19th century. Because of the linguistic diversity in the
area, Creek was adopted as a second language and used as a lingua franca by
many of the eastern tribes. In the west, Mobilian Jargon (sometimes called the
Chickasaw Trade Language), a contact language based on Choctaw, was used to
conduct commerce. By the early 20th century it had been replaced by English.

With European expansion, the Muskogean-speaking tribes were system-
atically pushed from their ancestral lands. Earliest documentation places the

Choctaw in what is now east-central Mississippi. During the 1830s most were forcibly removed to Indian Territory, the present state of Oklahoma (from Choctaw *oklah hómma*, literally "people red"), where they established the Choctaw Nation. Descendants of the Choctaw who resisted deportation became the Choctaw tribe headquartered near Philadelphia, Miss. Today there are approximately 6,000 Choctaw speakers in Oklahoma and another 4,500 in Mississippi. The Chickasaw originally resided northeast of the Choctaw. They were sent to Indian Territory along with the Choctaw and founded the Chickasaw Nation. There are perhaps fewer than 1,000 Chickasaw speakers in Oklahoma today.

The Alabama were situated northeast of the Chickasaw, in northeastern Mississippi, during the time of the de Soto expedition, 1539–42. At the advent of the 18th century they were located at the junction of the Coosa and Tallapoosa rivers in central Alabama. A portion of the tribe then moved westward and settled in Spanish Texas near present-day Livingston. The area became the Alabama-Coushatta Indian Reservation in 1854. A few hundred residents there still speak the language. Those who remained in Alabama were moved to Indian Territory and were absorbed into the Creek Nation. The Koasati (or Coushatta) populated an island in the Tennessee River in eastern Tennessee when encountered by the de Soto expedition. In the late 17th century they formed part of the Creek Confederacy and resided in central Alabama. Many followed the Alabama into Texas and western Louisiana in the late 18th century. Today Koasati is spoken by a few hundred members of the Coushatta tribe living on the Alabama-Coushatta Indian Reservation in Texas and another group of 300 to 400 residing near Elton, La.

In 1799 the Mikasuki (or Miccosukee) were located in the area around present-day Tallahassee but soon fled into the Florida peninsula to escape the advancing army of Andrew Jackson. As a result of the three Seminole Wars (1817–18, 1835–42, 1855–58), many were relocated to Indian Territory and became part of the Creek Nation. The remainder secluded themselves in the Everglades and Big Cypress Swamp to avoid deportation. The Miccosukee tribe of Indians of Florida was recognized by the U.S. government in 1962. Mikasuki is spoken by some 1,500 members of the Miccosukee and Seminole tribes living primarily on the Big Cypress, Hollywood, and Miccosukee reservations in southern Florida.

In the 18th century the Upper Creek lived along the Coosa and Tallapoosa rivers in Alabama, and the Lower Creek (or Seminole) populated the banks of the Chattahoochee in Alabama and Georgia. During the removal period some groups were deported to Indian Territory, where they formed the Creek (Muskogee) Nation. The Seminole (from Spanish *cimarrón* 'wild, runaway') fled to Florida. Many were captured after the Second Seminole War and sent to Indian Territory, where they founded the Seminole Nation. Today there are perhaps 4,000 Creek and Seminole speakers in east-central Oklahoma and fewer than 500 Seminole speakers on the Brighton Reservation in south Florida. The Seminole tribe of Florida, federally recognized in 1957, is comprised of both Mikasuki and Seminole (Creek) speakers.

The Muskogean languages all include the distinctive consonants *p, t, c* (which sounds like the initial consonant in English *church* and is sometimes written *ch*, as in English), *k, f, s, ł* (a sound close to the English combination *thl* in *fifthly*; in some languages this sound is written *lh* or *r*), *h, l, w, y, m*, and *n*. All but Creek and Seminole have *b*. Choctaw and Chickasaw have *sh* (similar to the first sound in English *shack*) and a glottal stop (the sound in the middle of the English expression *uh-uh* 'no'). There are three vowels, *i, a*, and *o*, that can be either long or short: for example, Creek *póósi* 'cat' and *pósi* 'grandmother.' Choctaw and Chickasaw also have nasalized vowels, sometimes written with a superscript *n*. Each language uses pitch primarily to indicate certain grammatical processes: for example, Creek *Leykis* (both vowels have the same, level pitch) 'He sits' and *Lêykis* (the pitch of the first vowel starts high, then immediately falls) 'He is seated.'

Sentence word order is subject-object-verb, as in Creek *Honanwa hoktii poohis* 'The man hears the woman' (literally, "man woman hears"). Certain verb final suffixes track clause participants as being the same or different from those of a following clause. In Creek *Híhcin híhcis*, the *-n* on the first verb indicates that the subject of the following verb is different from that of the first: "He saw it and then he (someone else) saw it." Whereas nouns are rarely marked for number, certain verbs of position and motion indicate the plural subject of an intransitive verb and the plural object of a transitive verb by using a different word: for example, Creek *Ifat leykis* 'A dog sits,' *Ifat kaakis* '(Two) dogs sit,' *Ifat apookis* '(Three or more) dogs sit,' and *Íhsis* 'He took it,' *Cáhwis* 'He took them.'

Verb morphology is extensive. The languages are primarily agglutinating, having prefixes, suffixes, and infixes that convey various grammatical meanings. Personal affixes include subject, indirect and direct objects, reflexive, and reciprocal. Other affixes mark tense, voice, causation, modality, instrumentation, position, direction, negation, and interrogation. An unusual feature of the Muskogean languages is that aspect is marked by internal modifications of the verb that involve combinations of infixation, pitch change, and vowel lengthening. Compare the changes in the Creek verb root *nafk-* 'hit' in the following: *Naafkis* (with lengthening of the first vowel) 'He is hitting it'; *Nafêykis* (with an infixed *ey* and concomitant falling pitch) 'He hit it'; *Năaⁿfkeys* (with lengthening of the first vowel, nasal infixation, and extra high pitch) 'He kept hitting it.'

Each of the Muskogean languages has a rich oral literature that includes myths and folktales passed on through the generations. Some explain natural phenomena, while others are designed to instruct and amuse. Many are of the Brer Rabbit genre with Rabbit as the trickster. Highly stylized ritual speech and dance songs are part of the annual Green Corn ceremony still celebrated by many southeastern tribes.

Both the Choctaw and Creek have a long tradition of literacy. Missionaries were sent to these tribes in the early 19th century with the intent of converting them to Christianity. Assisted by dedicated and able native speakers, they studied the language, developed an alphabet, and translated the Bible and other religious and pedagogical works into the native languages. After removal, the constitution and laws of both the Choctaw and Creek nations were published along with newspapers, magazines, and instructional materials. It is estimated that as many as 90 percent of Creek speakers could read and write their language at the beginning of the 20th century. The Choctaw, Chickasaw, Creek, and Seminole nations, along with the Cherokee, became known as the Five Civilized Tribes of Oklahoma partly because of this high rate of literacy. Today the traditional Creek alphabet as developed in the 19th century is still used to write the language. The traditional Choctaw alphabet is employed by speakers in Oklahoma, while a new alphabet was adopted by the Mississippi Choctaw in 1977. The other Muskogean languages remained unwritten until late in the 20th century.

As the number of speakers declines, language revitalization efforts have increased. Various learning opportunities are offered through the tribal organizations, such as the Seminole Bilingual Project in Florida, the Bilingual Education Program of the Mississippi Choctaw, the language committees of the Creek and Seminole nations, and workshops sponsored by the Alabama Culture Committee. Other programs have been instituted at the university level. The Choctaw Bilingual Education Program at Southeastern Oklahoma State University began in the 1970s. Choctaw and Creek classes have been taught at the University of Oklahoma since the early 1990s. Many linguists are currently studying the languages, and some native speakers, concerned that their languages may face extinction, offer language instruction. The success of these programs will determine if the Muskogean languages survive as an integral and vital part of these Native American cultures.

KAREN M. BOOKER
University of Kansas

Marcia Haag and Henry Willis, *Choctaw Language and Culture: Chahta Anumpa* (2001); Heather K. Hardy and Janine Scancarelli, eds., *Native Languages of the Southeastern United States* (2005); Pamela Innes, Linda Alexander, and Bertha Tilkens, *Beginning Creek: Mvskoke Emponavkv* (2004); Geoffrey D. Kimball, *Koasati Grammar* (1991); Jack B. Martin, Margaret McKane Mauldin, and Juanita McGirt, eds. and trans., *Totkv Mocvse/New Fire: Creek Folktales by Earnest Gouge* (2004); Pamela Munro and Catherine Willmond, *Chickasaw: An Analytical Dictionary* (1994); Cora Sylestine, Heather K. Hardy, and Timothy Montler, *Dictionary of the Alabama Language* (1993).

Natchez Language

At the time of intensive European exploration in the Southeast, the Natchez language was spoken in what is now Mississippi, east of the present-day city of Natchez, by the only Mississippian society to survive into the 17th and 18th centuries. After an initial period of friendship with the settlers of Louisiana, hostilities arose between the French and the Natchez, culminating in three wars. The last of these, ending in 1731, almost destroyed the Natchez as a people, with the French selling the captives as slaves in the Caribbean. Two surviving groups fled to the east. One settled among the Cherokee in what is now Tennessee, and the other joined the Creek town of Abihka in what is now Georgia. Both groups were forced to move to Indian Territory (now Oklahoma) during the removal in the 1830s and rapidly acculturated linguistically to the dominant Cherokee and Creek there. By 1907, when John R. Swanton first encountered the Natchez community at Braggs, Okla., there were only five or six fluent speakers of the language. In the late 1930s, when Mary Haas studied the language, only two elderly speakers remained, Watt Sam and Nancy Raven. Haas collected thousands of pages of field notes and was told dozens of traditional stories, for although the language was near extinction, the two speakers still lived in vital Indian communities; thus one does not note the impoverishment found, for example, in the language and narratives of the last speaker of Tunica, who lived in a French-speaking community in Louisiana. The Natchez language in its last years was preserved matrilineally, that is, only children of Natchez-speaking mothers learned to speak it. As the children of Watt Sam, by custom, did not learn Natchez, and as Nancy Raven had no living children, on their deaths (Nancy Raven around 1940, Watt Sam in July 1944) it became extinct.

Linguists consider Natchez to be a language isolate, meaning that there are no closely related languages known. Haas in 1956 postulated a historical relationship between the Muskogean family of languages (Creek, Chickasaw, etc.) and Natchez. Although this relationship has been disputed, it is possible to find regular sound correspondences between Natchez and Proto-Muskogean. For example, Natchez /W/ (a voiceless resonant sound) corresponds to Proto-Muskogean *xʷ* as in Proto-Muskogean *kaxʷ-ka* 'of a fox: to bark' (Choctaw *kawa*; Koasati *kafka*) corresponds to Natchez *kaW-kup* 'fox.'

The syntactic structure of Natchez is typical of the indigenous languages of the southeastern United States. Verbs are either active or stative. In active verbs, subject affixes usually indicate the actors, while in stative verbs the actor is indicated by those affixes that usually mark direct or indirect objects: for example, *·iqM-i-n-uqk* 'I am tired of it' versus *ceq-·i-n-uqk* 'he had sex with me.' The normal Natchez word order is subject-object-verb, and there is a simple system of reference indexing, which cues the listener to a change in subject or topic in a story. Noun and verb modifiers (which serve the functions of English adjectives and adverbs) follow the words that they govern. There is an ergative-absolutive case system for nouns, with the ergative case marking the subjects of transitive verbs (for example, *atawah-ca* 'the wolf' [ergative]) and the absolutive case marking either the objects of transitive verbs or the subjects of intransitive verbs (for example, *atawah-an* 'the wolf' [absolutive]). In addition, there are several locative cases (*cuA tolokop-ic* 'into a hollow log,' *k ahtoLa-k* 'in the canoe,' *k ahtoLa-kuqš* 'toward the canoe').

The most striking feature of Natchez is its system of verbal inflection. Independent verbs take prefixes and suffixes and have an invariant root: for example, *ta-ht-aq* 'I go' (root *-ht-*). Dependent verbs do not take prefixes or suffixes but, rather, are inflected by means of auxiliary elements: for example, *toL-ta-l-aA* 'I weave it' (root *toL-*). Most auxiliary elements, although structurally identical to independent verbs, do not occur alone, and they contribute semantically to the roots to which they are attached: for example, *ceAk-ta-k-aA* 'I cry,' *ceAk-ta-l-aA* 'I make him cry,' and *cak-ta-k-aA* 'I stick him,' *cak-ta-hšal-aA* 'I stick myself.' At times the auxiliary elements indicate great semantic differences among otherwise identical roots: for example, *pa-hal·iš* 'to make red,' *paq-haw·iš* 'to wear a necklace,' *paq-helahci·iš* 'to harness something,' and *paq-heluq·iš* 'to plant something.' Natchez is linguistically important because it is one of the few attested language isolates in the Southeast, an area of great linguistic diversity at the time of first contact with Europeans, and because of its unique classification of action to overtly link the number of a subject, object, or indirect object with repetition of the action.

GEOFFREY KIMBALL

Mary R. Haas, *Kansas Working Papers in Linguistics* (no. 7, 1982), *Language* (vol. 32, 1956), *Proceedings of the Fifth Annual Meeting of the Berkeley Linguistics Society*

(1979); Geoffrey Kimball, in *Native Languages of the Southeastern United States*, ed. Heather K. Hardy and Janine Scancarelli (2005).

New Orleans English

Greater New Orleans—where precincts, wards, major streets, levees, bridges, expressways, rivers, lakes, swamps, and bayous are physical boundaries linguistically dividing a populace of 1.3 million—includes 10 south Louisiana parishes: Orleans, Jefferson, St. Bernard, Plaquemines, St. Tammany, St. Charles, St. John the Baptist, St. James, Tangipahoa, and Washington.

It is imprecise to speak of "white" English or "black" English as discrete varieties in the South, but these rubrics are particularly inappropriate for the New Orleans area. For example, outside Orleans Parish, there are black speakers of Louisiana French Creole and white speakers of Louisiana Cajun French, as well as whites who know Creole and blacks who perceive themselves as being culturally more Cajun than Creole. These groups are also native speakers of English. Commingling has always been the key to the cultural and linguistic development of New Orleans. In south Louisiana spoken English has been enriched by the river, bayou, and prairie vernaculars of the Coushatta, Houma, Tangipahoa, and Tunica-Biloxi south Louisiana native nations; the accents of the city's enslaved Africans as well as of postcolonial rural and city freed or free people of color of African descent; the accents of the city, country, and upriver vernaculars of Creole and Cajun French; and the accents of the bayou and river Isleños, descendants of Canary Islanders who arrived from 1778 to 1783. Many ethnic groups have contributed to the distinctive public culture of present-day New Orleans: not only Europeans from Ireland, Germany, Croatia, Hungary, Italy, France, and Spain, or Sephardic Jews from Turkey, Syria, and Morocco, but also blacks from West Africa, Haiti, Belize, Virginia, and South Carolina, and both whites and blacks from Cuba. The creation continues in the city's Garifuna social clubs; Honduran, Vietnamese, Cajun Kosher, and Arab grocery stores and restaurants; Greek festivals; Filipino social organizations; and spiritualist churches of Mississippi blacks. One of the most recognizable types of New Orleans English is Yat (from *Where y'at?* 'How are you?'). Yat originated among the Irish, German, and Slavic workers who settled in the downtown Ninth Ward, and it is sometimes mistaken for Brooklynese.

New Orleans has always been famous for its cuisine, but the city also has special "house names" for its *cuisine de maison*, a cuisine peculiar to the home and to the ritualized days of the week: Red Monday (beans and rice with chops or sausage), Cabbage Tuesday (cabbage and ham), Meatball Wednesday (meatballs and spaghetti), White Thursday (white beans or butter beans with chops),

New Orleans French Quarter, also known as the Vieux Carré in French,
the oldest neighborhood in the city (pdphoto.org)

Seafood Friday (gumbo, fish, "mudbugs" or crayfish, and crabs), Leftover Satur-
day (whatever was still in the refrigerator), and Deep Fried Sunday (deep-fried
chicken and pork roast).

Though there are linguistic differences to be found within New Orleans English, common elements and idiomatic expressions do exist. One can hear the
end-of-the-day *Good Night!* meaning "Hello," "How do you do?" or "Good
Evening," as a standard two-way greeting in New Orleans neighborhoods as
neighbors stroll past one another's doors. Either the porch sitter or the stroller
could be the first to use the greeting. Some adult speakers retain a subtle distinction first learned as youngsters with the street verb *duck* by using *duck off*
'to walk away quickly and furtively (from a scene or event)' versus *duck out* 'to
walk away obediently and silently (from one's parent or teacher).' *To just rat the
streets* means "to have the reputation of spending at least one evening a week
plus the weekend frequenting night clubs and bars," as in *If you need to find
me, just call my momma, and she'll tell you, You know her—she's just rattin' the
streets! Leave go* is replacing *let go*, as in *Well, leave me go, I've got to get back to
work* or *Leave go of my satchel (book bag) before I get angry!*

Idioms in New Orleans English with *make* abound: *make groceries* 'to shop for groceries,' *make menage* 'to clean house,' *make dodo* 'to take a nap.' *Save* is also a frequent verb form, meaning "to put away," as in *save the groceries, save the dishes, save the clothes, save the jewelry*. Just as *ya hear* is used in many varieties of southern English as a tag at the end of a sentence, *hear, yeah*, and *no* or an objective pronoun are often used in New Orleans English, as in *She's gonna have another cup of coffee, hear?* or *I don't like that, no* or *She's smart, her*. Some phrases are known by both males and females but are more often used by males because they describe activities in which men more frequently participate: for example, *shine* 'to hunt with lanterns at night' during duck season, or *chunk* 'to throw a ball extremely hard.'

A double subject is frequently encountered in southern speech, as in *My brother, he went to the store*; however, in New Orleans one will hear, for emphasis, a triple subject with three pronouns, as in *Me myself, I don't like to drive over that bridge*. Where another person can be part of two conjoined subjects, the pronoun precedes the second subject (*Me and my daddy* or *Myself and Mr. Frank* or *I and Helen*). Doublets also occur in expressions such as *yet and still* 'however' or *feel to believe* 'believe beyond all doubt,' as in *I feel to believe that she'll get better*. There is also the newly emerging *Can you feel me?* among teenagers and young adults to mean "Can you understand me?"

Various semantic changes seem to be taking place in New Orleans English. For example, *still* has taken on the implied meaning of "all the same" or "nonetheless," as in *I thought I was picking up the white wine instead of this red; it's still good (though)*. As for verb forms, *had* plus the past participle of a verb is replacing the simple past-tense form. Teachers not originally from New Orleans report its frequent appearance in the essays of university students. Thus, the following kind of narrative is not uncommon: *Yesterday afternoon I had run into Sylvia. I had told her we're thinking about going to Dauphin Island for the weekend. And she had said that she'd get in touch with us tonight*. One way to interpret this usage is to say that *had* plus the past participle conveys a notion of past plus present (i.e., when the speaker is narrating the events).

Shop signs provide a rich source of linguistic data, innovation, and play, demonstrating how spoken forms can emerge in written language. One can spot a fish market sign announcing "Live Crab" or "Catfish Clean Free for You," or a grocery store sign admonishing "No Bicycle Allowed Inside" or announcing "Ripen Cantlopes 2 for $3.00," or a natural foods deli sign introducing a new verb to catch customers' attention, as in "Smoothie on over Here."

Also providing examples of speech change in progress is local talk radio, where one can commonly hear the *-th* of *both* becoming *-d*, as in *both of them* (pronounced *bode*) or the final *j* sound becoming a very pronounced *-che* syllable, as in *orange* (*o-ran-che*) or *Baton Rouge* (*rou-che*). The name *New Orleans* itself also has different pronunciations according to social class and the formality of social context. There is the upper-crust, Garden District form (*New OR-lee-yans*), the form pronounced by locals for outsiders or foreigners (*New Or-LEANS*), the working-class and middle-class pronunciation (*Nu AW-lans*), and the self-mocking form that New Orleanians use to poke fun at their own varied speech habits (*N'Awlins*). In these and other ways, the rich heritage of New Orleans English continues to flourish and evolve.

In late August 2005 Greater Metropolitan New Orleans and other parts of the Gulf South were damaged or destroyed by Hurricane Katrina and its attendant storm gusts and ensuing tornadoes. Within hours the devastation caused surrounding lakes to breach six levee systems and to flood the 10 parishes of Greater New Orleans, resulting in nearly 2,000 deaths and rendering close to 300,000 people homeless. Yet remaining or returning residents continue to prove to be a people affirming life. The hub of this coastal area is Orleans Parish, what local people and tourists mean by New Orleans. New Orleans is known as the Crescent City because it rims a crescent-shaped bay or port along the Mississippi River. Disasters of Katrina's magnitude remind us of another name: the City that Care Forgot, suggesting the insouciance of daily life of a coastal people. The City that Care Forgot is also the Big Easy, because of its traditional artful celebration and affirmation of life in literature, song, art, and tourism. The appellation of the Big Easy absorbs all the ways in which *New Orleans* might be pronounced, as it also absorbs and embraces the Crescent City and the City that Care Forgot.

MACKIE J. V. BLANTON
University of New Orleans

Madeline Aubert-Gex, "A Lexical Study of the English of New Orleans Creoles" (M.A. thesis, University of New Orleans, 1983); John Cooke and Mackie J. V. Blanton, eds., *Perspectives on Ethnicity in New Orleans* (1981); Greater New Orleans Community Data Center, <http://www.gnocdc.org/>; Sybil Kein, ed., *Creole: The History and Legacy of Louisiana's Free People of Color* (2000); Joseph Logsdon, *Perspectives on Ethnicity in New Orleans*, ed. John Cooke (1979); Los Isleños Heritage and Cultural Society, <www.losislenos.org>; Margaret M. Marshall, *Anthropological Linguistics* (vol. 24, 1982); Gwendolyn Midlo Hall, *Africans in Colonial Louisiana: The Development of Afro-Creole Culture in the Eighteenth Century* (1992); Dorice Tentchoff, *The Culture of Acadiana: Tradition and Change in South Louisiana*, ed. Steven L. Del Sesto and Jon L. Gibson (1975).

Outer Banks English

The Outer Banks, a shifting 200-mile-long chain of barrier islands off the coast of North Carolina sheltering the largest series of sounds in the eastern United States, are replete with history. This legacy includes the ill-fated Lost Colony settlement on Roanoke Island in the 1580s, the demise of the infamous pirate Blackbeard off the island of Ocracoke in the early 1700s, and the first successful flight of a power-driven airplane by the Wright brothers at Kitty Hawk in 1903. The Outer Banks are also home to one of the most distinctive dialects of American English, the so-called Outer Banks Brogue or Hoi Toider dialect. The latter name is an imitation of the traditional pronunciation of the vowels in *high* and *tide* and is indicative of the linguistic separation of the Outer Banks from the mainland, where *tide* usually sounds like *tahd* rather than *toid*.

The permanent settlement of English speakers on the Outer Banks began in the early 1700s, largely via eastern Virginia by way of the elaborate coastal waterways. The dialect of the Outer Banks still shows greater affinity with the Eastern Shores of Virginia and Maryland than with mainland North Carolina just a few miles across the Pamlico, Albemarle, and Currituck sounds. The original English-speaking inhabitants came predominantly from southwestern and southeastern England, along with some from Ireland, and this linguistic heritage is still evident. In fact, this is one of the rare American dialects still mistakenly identified as British or even Australian by outsiders, including by native speakers of British English. Though sometimes romanticized as a location where Elizabethan English has been preserved intact, the Outer Banks have a dynamic dialect that combines conservative with innovative forms.

The most prominent Outer Banks dialect traits are the vowel sounds, which include, of course, the pronunciation of *tide* and *time* as *toid* and *toim*. The pronunciation of the vowel in words like *sound* and *brown* is probably even more unusual among American English dialects. *Brown* sounds close to *brain*, and outsiders have been known to confuse these words or *round* and *rained*. Also distinctive is the vowel in words like *caught* and *bought*, which sounds close (but not identical) to that of words like *put* or *book* and is thus more similar to present-day British dialects than to other American English ones.

Distinctive grammatical traits include *weren't* (but not *were*) with singular subjects, as *I weren't there* or *She weren't here*, a pattern found in the United States only among coastal dialects from the Outer Banks to the islands of the Chesapeake Bay. There are a number of distinguishing vocabulary items related to physical location or to topography, such as *slick cam* 'calm water,' *camel-back* 'a mound of sand on the beach,' and *creek* 'small salt-water inlet between islands.' One also finds creative labels that contrast ancestral islanders with outsiders (called, e.g., *dingbatter*, *did-dot*, and *touron*, a blend of *tourist* and *moron*). These terms reflect the ambivalent reactions of residents to the ever-escalating tourist industry that has dominated the local economy since the emergence of paved roads and the public ferry system after World War II. The inundation of the Outer Banks with outsiders has had a dramatic effect on the traditional dialect. Older and some middle-aged speakers born on the islands may routinely use "the Brogue," but only the handful of younger islanders who have a strong affinity for traditional island ways of life maintain the older speech.

WALT WOLFRAM
North Carolina State University

David Stick, *The Outer Banks of North Carolina* (1958); Walt Wolfram and Natalie Schilling-Estes, *Hoi Toide on the Sound Side: The Story of the Ocracoke Brogue* (1997); Walt Wolfram, Kirk Hazen, and Natalie Schilling-Estes, *Dialect Change and Maintenance on the Outer Banks*, Publication of the American Dialect Society, no. 81 (1999).

Ozark English

The English of the Ozark Mountains of northwest Arkansas and southwest Missouri has been recognized for more than a century as one of America's quintessential backwoods dialects. It is closely related historically and structurally to the English of Appalachia, from where many of the early settlers of the Ozarks came in the 19th century. It has been similarly subject to conflicting and contradictory value judgments, being both romanticized and stigmatized. Popular stereotypes about Ozark English preserving Elizabethan or Shakespearean English abound, just as do caricatures of Ozark hayseeds and hillbillies (images that locals sometimes exploit, as they did for years at the now-defunct Dogpatch USA amusement park between Jasper and Harrison, Ark.).

There is some validity to the view that Ozark English preserves more archaic words and usages than most other types of American English, but linguists have shown that it is in most ways like all other American varieties and that, although popular writers stress the relic usages to be found, it has a complex mixture of the old and the new. Among older usages are *join* and *boil* pronounced with long *i* (*jine* and *bile*), *afeard* 'afraid,' *hit* 'it,' the prefix a- on present participles (*He come a-tearin' up that hill*), and past-tense verb forms used as past participles (*We have took them up* and *He has swam across the river*). While these and similar forms can be found in Renaissance-era writers of England, others (e.g., *chimley* 'chimney') are of Scottish heritage. Equally noteworthy are usages that are apparently innovations in the hills, such as *everwhat* 'whatever' (*Everwhat you do, don't blame me*); *everwho* 'whoever' (*Everwho took the money left in a hurry*); and *baking powders* 'baking powder.' All the terms cited so far are shared with Appalachia, but novel forms that are Ozarkisms include *noodle* 'to catch fish with bare hands'; *antic* 'irresponsible, ungovernable'; *auger* 'to look around surreptitiously or go about aimlessly'; and *bush up* 'to hide in shrubbery.'

The leading authority on Ozark speech, folklorist Vance Randolph, spent much of the first half of the 20th century collecting material from throughout the region and presented it in his volume *Down in the Holler: A Gallery of Ozark Folkspeech* (1953). While he documented many archaisms, he took a special interest in the colorful and unusual usages of Ozark speech (e.g., *fox-head* 'moonshine whiskey,' *kingdoodle* 'an imaginary monster') and in the plentiful euphemisms for taboo vocabulary that seemed at odds with "less-refined" lives of hillfolk. He found that *bull* was avoided in favor of *male, cow-critter, gentleman cow*, and similar locutions, especially in mixed company. *Dam, sow, buck*, and many other terms designating the sex of an animal were also considered indelicate. *Roger* and *piece* are, or at least were, taboo because they refer to sexual intercourse. No doubt such usages, noted by Randolph mainly in the 1920s and 1930s, have declined markedly, but they throw interesting light on the traditional mores of backwoods culture.

Such exotic usages aside, Ozark English is for the most part typical of the speech of the Upper South (e.g., in the use of *is* with subjects that are plural nouns but not plural pronouns — thus, *The children is misbehaving* vs. *They are misbehaving*) or the South as a whole (pronouncing both *pen* and *pin* like the latter word and using *done* as a helping verb, as in *I done told him not to do that*). However, Ozark English will continue to be perceived as different for reasons that have as much to do with beliefs about life in the hills as with actual speech patterns themselves.

MICHAEL MONTGOMERY
University of South Carolina

Donna Christian, Walt Wolfram, and Nanjo Dube, *Variation and Change in Geographically Isolated Communities: Appalachian English and Ozark English* (1988); Bethany Dumas, *Mid-South Folklore* (vol. 3, 1975); Vance Randolph, *The Ozarks: A Bibliography* (1972); Vance Randolph and George P. Wilson, *Down in the Holler: A Gallery of Folkspeech* (1953; 1979).

Siouan Languages

The Siouan-speaking peoples are often thought to represent the quintessential mounted warriors, hunters, and tipi-dwelling Plains Indian, and it comes as a surprise to many that Siouan tribes were native to the Southeast and that the

The Quapaw are another Siouan tribe, otherwise known as Akansa, from which the Arkansas river and state derive their name. (Edward S. Curtis, Library of Congress, Washington, D.C.)

language family may have originated there. The Siouan languages of the Southeast come from two distinct branches of the language family. The Quapaw tribe, originally of Arkansas, has as its closest relatives the Osage, Kansa, Omaha, and Ponca tribes of the eastern plains. The other Siouan languages of the Southeast form the Ohio Valley linguistic subgroup, named for their probable original location along that river, and are quite distinct from Quapaw. These include the Biloxi, Ofo, Tutelo, Saponi, Moneton, and Occaneechi tribes. The Catawban and Yuchi (Euchee) tribes, originally of the Carolinas and eastern Tennessee, are separate language families but are distantly related to Siouan.

The Quapaws lived in several villages near the mouth of the Arkansas River when first encountered by the Marquette and Jolliet expedition in 1673. They were called Akansa by Algonquian-speaking tribes of the Illinois Country, and that is the source of the state name, Arkansas. The Quapaws now live in northeast Oklahoma around the town of Miami. Quapaw no longer has fluent speakers, but recorded materials from the 1960s and 1970s along with archival material collected in the 19th century have made possible Robert Rankin's manuscript dictionary and short published grammar.

When first encountered by d'Iberville in 1699, the Biloxi lived near Biloxi Bay along the present-day Alabama-Mississippi border. Today they live with the Tunica tribe near Marksville, La. The Biloxi language was the subject of field investigation by Smithsonian ethnographers and linguists Albert S. Gatschet and James Owen Dorsey, whose text collection and dictionary were later published by Dorsey and Swanton. Versions of several Brer Rabbit stories can be found in the Biloxi text collection. Some of these are apparently of Native American origin, and some evidently entered Biloxi by way of African slaves and originated in West Africa. Dorsey's field notes provided data for a grammar of the language by Einaudi.

The Ofo tribe is likely the group referred to as the Mosopelea in early colonial documents. The Mosopelea lived in the eastern Ohio Valley and moved down that river and the Mississippi, probably in colonial times, ultimately settling in Mississippi and then Louisiana. People of Ofo ancestry live among the Biloxi and Tunica today at Marksville. In 1907 the Smithsonian ethnographer John R. Swanton located a single remaining speaker of Ofo living among the Tunicas and recorded a vocabulary of more than 600 words, which is all we have of the language. This vocabulary was published by Dorsey and Swanton and provided data for a grammar sketch by Rankin. *The Last of the Ofos*, a novelette by Quapaw author Geary Hobson, is a fictional account of a last speaker of the Ofo language, including his experiences with Smithsonian anthropologists.

The other Ohio Valley Siouan languages were spoken in what are now Virginia and West Virginia. Moneton, spoken along the Kanawha River in West Virginia, is attested with only two words, *mani* and *it^{h}ą́*, which are said to have meant *water* and *great*, respectively, in the language of the tribe. These correspond to nearly identical words for the same concepts in other Virginia Siouan languages, so we know the Monetons spoke a related language. One language, Occaneechi, is not attested at all but was said by several explorers to have been a lingua franca used for trade and based on a language very similar to Tutelo. We must take them at their word that the language was Siouan.

As far as it is possible to tell from the short vocabulary available, Saponi was essentially the same as Tutelo. These tribes and the Occaneechis occupied several villages in the Virginia piedmont between 1650 and 1670, when the Tutelos were first visited by John Lederer. The Tutelo and Saponi moved north with the Iroquoian-speaking Tuscaroras. The Saponis disappear from history after this, and the Tutelos, loyalists during the American Revolution, moved to Canada, where they live today near Brantford, Ontario. Fieldwork by J. N. B. Hewitt, James Owen Dorsey, Horatio Hale, and a few others made it possible for Oliverio to produce a grammatical survey and a dictionary of Tutelo. Working with Iroquoian speakers at the Six Nations Reserve in Ontario in the early 1980s, Marianne Mithun encountered three remaining Tutelo speakers and made a short recording. Apparently there are no remaining speakers now.

Table 7 contains a short comparative vocabulary illustrating the relationship of the Siouan languages of the Southeast to other languages in the family.

TABLE 7. *Comparison of Words in Siouan languages*

English	dog	water	great	flint point	spirit
Proto-Siouan	*wišųke	*wiŕį	*ihtáka	*wą·he	*warą·xi
Dakota	šúka	mni	tʰáka	wą	wanáai
Quapaw	šóke	ni	ttáka	mą	wanáye
Biloxi	čóki	ani	nitą-	ąksí	anáčci
Ofo	ačʰúki	áni	itʰá	ąfhí	-nąči
Tutelo	čʰógo	mani	itʰá	mąksi·	wanáči·
Saponi	čʰúki	mani		mąki·	
Moneton		mani	itʰą		

ROBERT L. RANKIN
University of Kansas

Raymond J. DeMallie, in *Handbook of North American Indians*, vol. 14, *Southeast*, ed. William Sturtevant (2004); James Owen Dorsey and John R. Swanton, *A Dictionary of the Biloxi and Ofo Languages: Accompanied with Thirty-One Biloxi Texts and Numerous Biloxi Phrases* (1912); Paula F. Einaudi, *A Grammar of Biloxi* (1976); Geary Hobson, *The Last of the Ofos* (2000); Giulia R. M. Oliverio, "Grammar and Dictionary of Tutelo" (Ph.D. dissertation, University of Kansas, 1996); Robert L. Rankin, in *The Native Languages of the Southeastern United States*, ed. Heather K. Hardy and Janine Scancarelli (2005); Robert L. Rankin and Giulia Oliverio, in *Festschrift in Memory of Frank Siebert*, ed. David Costa and Blair Rudes (2003).

Spanish

Spanish is by far the most commonly spoken language other than English in the United States. Primarily as a result of large-scale immigration in recent decades, the Latino population now numbers more than 35 million, 80 percent of whom claim to speak at least some Spanish at home. The United States is now the world's fifth most populous Spanish-speaking country, trailing only Mexico, Spain, Colombia, and Argentina. Spanish speakers tend to be concentrated in the Southwest, California, Florida, and a number of metropolitan areas such as New York and Chicago. In Florida, where the Spanish-speaking population has traditionally been dominated by Cuban Americans, numerous other groups from Central America and Colombia have settled in recent years. In addition, southern states other than the traditional areas of settlement in Florida and Texas have recently experienced remarkable increases in the Latino population. Figures from the 2000 census show that between 1990 and 2000, the number of people in North Carolina who claimed to speak Spanish in-

TABLE 8. *Spanish-Speaking Population of the United States, Florida, Texas, and Six New Settlement States, 1990–2000*

	1990	2000	Increase (n)	Speak English Less Than "Very Well," 2000 (n)
Alabama	42,653	89,729	47,076	40,299
Arkansas	27,351	82,465	55,114	43,530
Georgia	122,295	426,115	303,820	246,270
North Carolina	105,963	378,942	272,979	218,795
South Carolina	44,427	110,030	44,427	53,605
Tennessee	49,661	133,931	84,270	64,375
Florida	1,447,747	2,476,528	1,028,781	1,187,335
Texas	3,443,106	5,195,182	1,752,076	2,369,035
United States	17,339,172	28,101,055	10,761,883	13,751,260

Source: U.S. Census Bureau

creased by 258 percent, a higher percentage than in any other state. In Arkansas, the increase amounted to 202 percent, while in Georgia the number of Spanish speakers increased by 248 percent. In Tennessee, the Spanish-speaking population grew by 170 percent during the 1990s; in South Carolina, by 148 percent; and in Alabama, by 110 percent.

Table 8, based on data from the U.S. Census Bureau, shows the increase in the Spanish-speaking population between 1990 and 2000 in Alabama, Arkansas, Georgia, North Carolina, South Carolina, and Tennessee—six states where Latinos have settled in large numbers—as well in Florida and Texas, the two southern states with traditionally large Latino populations. The table also includes information about the number of Latinos in each state who reported that they spoke English less than "very well."

As shown by a comparison of the six "new settlement" states with Florida and Texas, the absolute numbers of Spanish speakers in the new settlement states are not great. In fact, they are dwarfed by the numbers of Spanish speakers in Florida and Texas. However, Spanish speakers in the new settlement states tend to be concentrated in particular areas and consequently to have a more substantial impact on education and other public services at the county or city level than at the state level. In the carpet manufacturing center of Dalton, in northwest Georgia, for example, the population is more than 40 percent Latino, and the city's newsletter, the *Dalton Messenger*, is published in English and Spanish. In addition, because the immigration of Spanish speakers to most of

TABLE 9. *Latino Population Growth in New Settlement Counties*

County	State	Latino Population 1990	2000	Increase (n)	Increase (%)
Gordon	Georgia	200	3,268	3,068	1,534
Murray	Georgia	136	2,006	1,870	1,375
Cabarrus	North Carolina	483	6,620	6,137	1,271
Alamance	North Carolina	736	8,835	8,099	1,100
Randolph	North Carolina	734	8,646	7,912	1,078
Union	North Carolina	675	7,637	6,962	1,031
Benton	Arkansas	1,359	13,469	12,110	891
Sampson	North Carolina	727	6,477	5,720	791
Catawba	North Carolina	921	7,886	6,965	756
Robeson	North Carolina	704	5,994	5,290	751
Washington	Arkansas	1,546	12,932	11,406	747
Durham	North Carolina	2,054	17,039	14,985	730
Rowan	North Carolina	651	5,369	4,718	725
DeSoto	Mississippi	306	2,516	2,210	722

Source: U.S. Census Bureau

the South is a recent phenomenon, in a number of states people who report speaking Spanish at home are less likely to be fully proficient in English than Spanish speakers in more established communities. For example, according to the 2000 census, 57.8 percent of the people nationwide who claimed to speak Spanish at home reported that they spoke English very well. In North Carolina, only 42.3 percent did so.

While the growth of the Latino population was dramatic in all southern states, it was even more so in individual counties. For example, in Mecklenburg County, N.C., which includes Charlotte, the Latino population increased from less than 7,000 in 1990 to nearly 45,000 in 2000. Gordon County, Ga., had 200 Latinos in 1990 but more than 3,200 in 2000. Table 9, based on data from the 2000 census, shows the changes in the Latino population in the counties in the South with the greatest percentage increases.

The growth in the Latino population throughout the South has numerous consequences in education and language contact, including language maintenance and shift, borrowing of English words into Spanish, and code-switching (the alternate use of English and Spanish in the same discourse and often in the same sentence). The remainder of this article briefly explores those topics, with emphasis on the states with the greatest increases in the Latino population and the two states with traditionally large Latino communities.

EDUCATION. The rapid increase in the number of children who enter U.S. schools without the proficiency in English to compete successfully in all-English classrooms has led to contentious debates for many years over whether children should be taught in the native language, how long children should be enrolled in bilingual classes, and whether schools should strive to develop the native language of children while teaching them English. Aside from Florida and Texas, where both bilingual education and English as a Second Language programs are widespread, these debates have been of relatively little concern to most southern states because the number of English language learners in southern schools was very small until the 1990s. That situation has now changed. According to the Pew Hispanic Center, in 1990 the number of Spanish-speaking children with limited proficiency in English in the six new settlement states whose Spanish-speaking population is shown in Table 8 was only 18,000. By 2000 the number had grown to 64,000. The rapid growth of the number of school-age children without full English proficiency, combined with the new accountability standards under the federal government's No Child Left Behind legislation, has meant that many school districts throughout the South have had to develop new programs to meet the needs of English language learners. For the most part, these programs have involved English as a Second Language instruction. It remains to be seen whether bilingual programs will become widespread, as they are in Texas.

LANGUAGE MAINTENANCE AND SHIFT. Recent years have witnessed attempts to make English the official language at both state and national levels. Proponents of official English argue that new immigrants, particularly Latinos, are less willing to learn English than previous generations of immigrants. However, this belief is not borne out by data from large-scale studies. For example, in 2002 the Pew Hispanic Research Center surveyed a well-stratified sample of the U.S. Latino adult population. The survey results showed that 61 percent of U.S.-born respondents considered themselves to be English-dominant, and 35 percent considered themselves bilingual. Fully 78 percent of third-generation and later respondents considered themselves English-dominant, and only 22 percent considered themselves bilingual.

Information from large-scale surveys is confirmed by ethnographic work in Texas communities. For example, a recent study of language use in Mexican-descent families in Texas and California was able to locate very few children of

U.S.-born mothers who had developed substantial productive ability in Spanish. In the absence of major changes in language policy, particularly language in education policy, bilingualism in most Latino communities in the South, as in other parts of the country, is likely to remain a transitory phenomenon. Indeed, some scholars who advocate providing all children with the opportunity to become bilingual argue that the danger is not that children of immigrants will fail to learn English. Rather, the danger is that they will fail to develop their heritage language and that, as a consequence, communication between parents and children will suffer and the United States as a whole will have lost an important linguistic resource. Middle-class Cuban Americans in Florida, however, appear to be an exception to the general pattern. A 1996 study of Cuban American families in Miami found that middle-class mothers associated their children's success with competence in Spanish, while working-class mothers associated success with ability in English.

CONTACT WITH ENGLISH. The linguistic consequences of Latino settlement in areas of the South aside from Florida and Texas have only begun to attract attention. Researchers at North Carolina State University, for example, have studied whether new Latino immigrants to Siler City and Raleigh, N.C., were adopting features of Southern English. Specifically, they looked at whether Latino immigrants in the two communities had adopted the southern vowel system when speaking English, as well as other features of Southern English such as *fixin' to* and *y'all*. They found that for the most part, the new immigrants were not adopting southern vowels, although use of expressions such as *y'all* was not uncommon. However, whether a speaker adopted southern vowels depended on the extent of the speaker's identification with and participation in the English-speaking local community. To cite just one example, a teenage brother and sister in one immigrant family were oriented differently to the local culture. The brother, who was heavily involved with athletics at his predominantly Anglo school, appeared to have adopted the local vowel system. The sister, however, was not involved with local Anglo youth and had not adopted southern vowels.

In contrast to the states where Latinos have settled recently, Spanish in Texas and Florida exhibits many features that can be attributed to prolonged contact with English. For example, many English words have been borrowed into Texas Spanish and, at least in informal speech, have replaced their Spanish equivalents. Sociolinguist Carmen Silva-Corvalán lists the examples in Table 10.

An even more obvious consequence of language contact, at least in Texas, is widespread code-switching. For example, one young man, when asked whether he preferred speaking Spanish or English, responded: *Prefiero español porque*

TABLE 10. *Changes in Southwest Spanish Due to Contact with English*

Southwest Spanish	Standard Spanish
puchar 'to push'	*empujar*
mapear 'to mop'	*pasar la fregona*
dostear 'to dust'	*sacudir el polvo*
cuitear 'to quit'	*darse por vencido*
liquear 'to leak'	*gotear*
fensa 'fence'	*reja*
pipa 'pipe'	*cañería*
traques 'tracks'	*rieles*
suiche 'switch'	*interruptor*
biles 'bills'	*cuentas*

I'm more used to it 'I prefer Spanish because . . . .' This type of mixed language is not confined to the informal speech of young bilinguals. Rather, it can be heard in the mass media as well. For example, in the early 1990s, KXTN, a popular radio station in San Antonio, Texas, adopted a bilingual format, and disc jockeys and newscasters began to code-switch frequently, as in the following examples, recorded in 1992 and 1993:

> *En sports los tres equipos de Texas perdieron.* 'In sports, the three Texas teams lost.'

> KXTN *Tejano one-o-seven* FM, *the official hit station for Jesse James. Keep it right where it is to win your free tickets to the Jesse James Leija fight . . . December third, huh, mañana ¿verdad? At the Arena? ¡Escuche y gane! Con sus amigos de Tejano one-o-seven* FM. *Good morning!* '. . . tomorrow, right? At the Arena? Listen and win! With your friends from Tejano one-o-seven FM.'

The type of language mixing shown in the examples from KXTN is often stigmatized, especially by Spanish speakers from Mexico or elsewhere in Latin America. However, as its widespread use in the media attests, it clearly serves a function in bilingual communities. In fact, the ability to code-switch seamlessly from Spanish to English and back again serves as a marker of bilingual Latino identity in many communities because it shows a competence possessed only by people who are highly proficient in both languages.

The increase in the Latino population throughout the South has been extremely rapid. As is the case with Latino immigration in the United States generally, the majority of Spanish-speaking immigrants to the South are from Mexico, although substantial numbers of Central Americans and Colombians have joined the traditional Cuban American population in Florida. Despite the large percentage increase, it is important to keep the growth of the Latino population in perspective. Aside from Florida and Texas, percentages of growth are high because the number of Latinos in most southern states was very small before the 1990s. Latinos still constitute a very small percentage of the population of the South. Given the recent nature of Latino immigration, most adults are Spanish-dominant, if not monolingual in Spanish, and they often form distinct communities in cities like Raleigh. The extent to which Spanish is maintained in the areas of new settlement will depend on a large number of factors, including patterns of immigration, language in education policy, and the overall development of the region. However, there can be little doubt that at least in some southern communities, Spanish is now an important part of the linguistic landscape, as it has been in Texas since the original European settlement and in Florida since the 1960s.

ROBERT BAYLEY
University of California at Davis

Robert Bayley and Ruth King, in *Needed Research on American Dialects*, ed. Dennis R. Preston (2003); Robert Bayley and Otto Santa Ana, in *A Handbook of Varieties of English*, vol. 2, ed. Bernd Kortmann and Edgar Schneider (2004); Mollyann Brodie, Annie Steffenson, Jaime Valez, Rebecca Levin, and Roberto Suro, *2002 National Survey of Latinos* (2002); Rakesh Kochhar, Roberto Suro, and Sonya Tafoya, *The New Latino South: The Context and Consequences of Rapid Population Growth* (2005); Wallace E. Lambert and Donald M. Taylor, *Applied Linguistics* (1996); Sandra R. Schecter and Robert Bayley, *Language as Cultural Practice: Mexicanos en el Norte* (2002); Carmen Silva-Corvalán, in *Language in the USA: Themes for the 21st Century*, ed. Edward Finegan and John R. Rickford (2004); Walt Wolfram, Philip Carter, and Beckie Moriello, *Journal of Sociolinguistics* (vol. 7, 2004); Stanton Wortham, Enrique G. Murillo, and Edmund T. Hamann, eds., *Education in the New Latino Diaspora: Policy and the Politics of Identity* (2002).

Texas English

Texas English is a variety of Southern English with a unique twist: English is historically the second language of Texas. Spanish was spoken there for nearly a century before English and has been in continual use since the 18th century. Further, for 75 years after its initial settlement, Texas had significant immigration directly from Europe, especially from Germany, Austria, Czechoslovakia, Italy, and Poland, making it a multilingual state. German and Czech, in particular, were still widely used as late as World War II and are still used by some older speakers. Finally, since 1970, Texas has undergone dramatic demographic changes that have reshaped its population and language.

While the outcome of the Texas Revolution ensured that English would dominate in the new nation/state, the early Hispanic settlement meant that many Spanish words (e.g., *mesa*, *remuda* 'herd of horses,' and *pilón* 'small gift with a purchase') would blend with the language that Anglos brought from the east to form a unique Texas mix. Anglos (and their slaves) from both the Lower and Upper South moved rapidly into Texas after 1840, with Lower southerners dominating in the east and Upper southerners in the north and central regions. There was considerable mixing, however, and the Lower South/Upper South dialect division was blurred in Texas. Upper South words (e.g., *green bean* and *chigger*) and pronunciations (e.g., intrusive /r/ in words like *warsh* for *wash*) coexisted and competed with Lower South words (e.g., *snap bean* and *red bug*) and pronunciations (*r*-lessness in words like *four*). In south and west Texas a substantial number of Spanish words spread into English. Words like *frijoles* 'beans,' *olla* 'earthenware jar,' *arroyo* 'gully,' and *remuda* reflect not only the relatively large numbers of Hispanics but also the importance of Mexican Americans in the development of a distinct Texas culture.

Most Southern English hallmarks occur extensively in Texas. These include both phonological stereotypes such as the *pen/pin* vowel merger (both sound like the latter) and the loss of the off-glide of /ai/ (monophthongal or flat /ai/) in words like *ride* and *right* (so that they sound something like *rahd* and *raht*) and also grammatical features like *y'all*, *fixin to*, and *might could*. In addition, a number of words seem to have originated or have their greatest currency in Texas (e.g., *tank* 'stock pond,' *maverick* 'stray or unbranded calf,' *doggie* 'calf,' and *roughneck* 'oil field worker'). At least one traditional pronunciation, the use of *ar* in words like *horse* and *for* (this makes *lord* sound like *lard*), occurs only in Texas, Utah, and a few other places.

Rapid metropolitanization and massive in-migration since 1970 have had significant linguistic consequences for Texas, with the most important one being an emerging rural-urban linguistic split. The *pen/pin* merger and the *lord/lard* merger are now recessive in metropolitan areas, although both (and especially the former) persist in rural areas and small cities. Even as these traditional pronunciation features are disappearing, new developments are emerging in the cities. The vowels in words like *caught* and *cot* are becoming merged (both sound like *cot*), as are the vowel pairs in words like *pool* and *pull* (both sound like *pull*). The rural-urban split so far is only a phonological one: grammatical features such as *y'all* and *fixin to* are expanding to nonnatives in metropolitan areas and to the Hispanic population. Moreover, some phonological features seem to be gaining strength as markers of a Texas identity. For instance, in the 1989 Texas Poll the single most important correlate to the use of monophthongal or flat /ai/ is whether or not respondents favor Texas as a place to live. The role of a Texas identity in maintaining such items ensures that Texas English will remain a variety of Southern English even as it continues its unique evolution.

JAN TILLERY
University of Missouri at Kansas City

E. Bagby Atwood, *The Regional Vocabulary of Texas* (1962); Guy Bailey et al., in *Sociolinguistic Variation: Data, Theory, and Analysis*, ed. Jennifer Arnold et al. (1996); Fred A. Tarpley, *From Blinky to Blue-John: A Word Atlas of Northeast Texas* (1970); Jan Tillery and Guy Bailey, *Language Magazine* (2003).

Tidewater Virginia Dialect

In the last 75 years, studies of American English have often mentioned Virginia prominently as having a distinctive dialect. This is frequently taken to mean Virginia as a whole. But these studies almost exclusively center on eastern Virginia, specifically on the area called Tidewater. That region includes, but is more than, the Hampton Roads area of the southeastern part of the state, with its harbor formed by the channel through which the James and Elizabeth rivers flow into the Chesapeake Bay and bordered by the cities of Newport News and Hampton to the north and Norfolk, Portsmouth, Virginia Beach, and Chesapeake to the south. Historically and linguistically, Tidewater Virginia (by no means homogeneous) is the entire portion of Virginia east of the fall line, marked by an imaginary line from Alexandria on the Potomac to Fredericksburg on the Rappahannock to West Point on the York to Richmond on the James and southward. Hampton Roads is the cosmopolitan center; but it is only one of three main areas within the Tidewater region, the other two being the Northern Neck (between the Rappahannock and the Potomac), now being influenced from the north and especially by the Washington, D.C., area, and the Eastern Shore, with influences from Washington, D.C., Baltimore, and Philadelphia.

In 1607 the first permanent English settlement was made in the Hampton Roads area in Jamestown, not far from where the College of William and Mary is situated in Williamsburg. By 1675 or so, all the accessible land in this immediate area had been settled and occupied by Europeans, producing one of the first varieties of American English. Though early settlers came from all over the British Isles, the majority came from southern England, especially London, Kent, and Gloucester. It is hard to miss the English origins of Tidewater place-names such as Hampton, Norfolk, Portsmouth, Suffolk, Surrey, Middle-sex, Lancaster, Essex, and York. Present-day Virginians, especially those in the Tidewater having assumed aristocratic forebears, believe that British nobility flocked to the colony. Actually the vast majority of settlers were unschooled, unlettered, and propertyless (often indentured servants), though some were farmers, merchants, lawyers, clergymen, country gentlemen, or the youngest sons of the aristocracy who had fallen victim to primogeniture (whereby only the eldest son could inherit). The most prominent were Cavaliers, nobility and others who had fled England's civil wars in the 1640s, among whom were the Carters, Lees, Randolphs, and Byrds. Their sons were often educated at Oxford or Cambridge, becoming familiar with Shakespeare, Marlowe, and the King James version of the Bible and developing into a nucleus of well-educated men of affairs. The port of Norfolk was a center of trade and cultural life that had close relations with London, and its merchants often became part of London society. All this meant that the Tidewater dialect essentially grew out of south-ern England.

Historically the feature of Tidewater speech attracting most notice is the pronunciation of words like *out*, *house*, and *about*. Outsiders mistakenly try to render them as *oot*, *hoos*, and *aboot*, but they sound rather more like *owt*, *howse*, and *abowt*. These Tidewater pronunciations have general currency at all social levels today.

A conspicuous but now declining feature of Tidewater speech is the so-called broad *a* or Cavalier *a*, as in *dahnce* (*dance*). More associated with eastern New England today, this pronunciation has long had currency among certain "old families" in the Tidewater, as in *pahth*, *lahf*, *cahnt*, *rahther*, and *fahst* for *path*, *laugh*, *can't*, *rather*, and *fast*. However, most Virginians, including in the Tide-water, now pronounce these words with the vowel of *cat*, a practice more or less universal during Shakespeare's time. The broad *a* developed later, and its use has never been uniform. One occasionally hears it in *vahse* (*vase*), *ah-ther* (*either*), and *tomahto* (*tomato*) in the Tidewater, but only generally in one word: *ahnt* for *aunt*. It is more common among women than men and rare at best among young speakers.

A third feature once very prominent in Tidewater speech is the loss of *r* in words such as *cahn* (*corn*), *cah* (*car*), *he-uh* (*here*), *fuh* (*fur*), and *dinnuh* (*din-ner*). Like broad *a*, the lack of *r* has been losing ground and among whites is now rarely heard except among older speakers, though it is general among African Americans. A feature once common among the elite, but relatively rare today, is insertion of *y* after an initial *k* or *g* sound in words like *kyar* (*car*), *kyarter* (*carter*), and *gyarden* (*garden*).

An interesting aspect of Tidewater speech is the pronunciation of family names and place-names. These often differ from what the spellings would suggest; years ago people heard and learned names before they read them. Until not long ago *Harwood* was pronounced *Herod*, especially by the family and their associates. For years the Harwoods of Middlesex County used the latter pronunciation, but now they call themselves *Harwoods*. Similarly one can cite *Burwell* (formerly *Burel*), *Taliaferro* (formerly *Tolliver*), *Beauchamp* (formerly *Bechem*), *Langhorne* (formerly *Langun*), *Callowhill* (formerly *Carol*), *Jordan* (formerly *Jerdun*), and *Camp* (formerly *Kemp*).

Place-names are sometimes more conservative. Today natives of *Warwick*, *Norfolk*, and *Suffolk* pronounce these as *Warik*, *Nawfuk*, and *Suhfuk*. Outsiders and most Virginians now pronounce these as spelled, and all Virginians will probably give way to this practice in time. Another case is *Portsmouth*. Natives of the larger region generally pronounce it as spelled, but others who either live in or are from the city pronounce the first syllable as *Porch*. The old Tidewater crowd considers this to be "a provincial localism," and others scorn it as "lower-class," "uneducated," or a "vulgar local innovation." Actually the pronunciation occurs in the speech of both blacks (who often say *Poachmouth*) and whites, the young and old, the educated and uneducated, and the upper and lower class, and it has a long and dignified history. *Porchmouth* is found in London chronicles and registers and in the State Papers of Henry VIII, indicating its British origin.

Other more current features of speech tend to set Tidewater Virginia apart as a distinct dialect region. A partial listing includes *a-fred* (*afraid*), *nek-ed* (*naked*), *sence* (*since*), *melk* (*milk*), *hum* (*home*), *lang* (*long*), *tyuzdi* (*Tuesday*), *dyu* (*due*), *syuit* (*suit*), *miz* (*Mrs.*), and *nevyu* (*nephew*). Moving from one small town to another, to the coastal fringes like Guinea Neck, or to islands like Tangier, one encounters *feesh* (*fish*), *poosh* (*push*), *extry* (*extra*), and *far* (*fire*).

For many features Tidewater speech reflects that of some of the country's first Europeans and that of a regional coastal center from which other dialects emerged and that played a key role in the development of the American South. However, in numerous regards Tidewater English remains distinctive today, especially in its pronunciation.

DAVID L. SHORES
Old Dominion University

E. Bagby Atwood, in *English Studies for James Southall Wilson*, ed. Fredson Bowers (1951); Virginius Dabney, *Virginia: The New Dominion* (1971); Hans Kurath and Raven I. McDavid Jr., *The Pronunciation of English in the Atlantic States* (1961);

Edwin Francis Shewmake, *English Pronunciation in Virginia* (1927); David L. Shores, in *American Speech* (vol. 61, 1986).

Yuchi Language

The Yuchi language, also spelled Euchee, is spoken south of Tulsa, Okla. At the time of European contact it was spoken west of the Appalachians in what is now central Tennessee. The first record of the language is found alongside drawings in the 1736 sketchbook of Philip Georg Friedrich von Reck, a Swiss religious immigrant in South Carolina. During the 1700s the Yuchi also had several towns in Georgia and Florida. They were forcibly removed to Indian Territory, now Oklahoma, with the Creek Confederacy in the 1830s. Unlike many of the smaller tribes who helped form the Creek Confederacy, the Yuchi retained their identity and language separate from the Muscogee Creek.

Yuchi is considered a language isolate. This means that there are no known languages—living or extinct—related to Yuchi. In 1911 linguist Edward Sapir suggested a possible genetic relationship between the Siouan language family and Yuchi. However, no regular sound correspondences between Yuchi and Proto-Siouan-Catawban have been confirmed, so this claim remains disputed.

Yuchi has regional and gender variations. There were at least three regional dialects spoken through the late 1880s, two of which are still used today. One dialect is shared by speakers of the Polecat (Kellyville-Sapulpa, Okla.) and Duck Creek (Bixby-Hectorville, Okla.) communities; the other, known as Big Pond Dialect, is spoken in the westernmost community of Sand Creek (Bristow-Depew, Okla.). The dialects differ mainly by a higher tongue position for vowels in Big Pond Dialect. Men and women use different pronouns when referring to the opposite sex. Women tend to use more conservative forms, and these are considered to be more polite forms today. For example, men will refer to most women as *sā-* 'she,' but women will refer to men as *s'ā-* 'he' when they are the same age or younger and as *'o-* 'he' if they are older, their husbands, or any man to whom they wish to show respect.

Yuchi shares features common to most of the indigenous languages of North America and the southeastern United States. The basic word order of clauses is subject-object-verb. Subject and object pronouns are prefixed to verbs. Because every verb carries this referential information on it, independent nouns are often dropped from the sentence. Hence, verbs tend to be long and include all the information that would be in an English sentence. Yuchi is also an active-stative language. On active verbs, subject prefixes indicate the actor, and object prefixes indicate the patient (something or someone who receives or is affected by the action). However, on stative verbs the subject is indicated by patient prefixes, reflecting a more passive role. Unlike most of the other languages of the Southeast, however, Yuchi has a large inventory of sounds, which includes an *f*, glottal distinctions for all consonants, and nasal vowels.

One of the most interesting features of Yuchi is its noun class system. In order to make a noun definite, the speaker must know if the noun is able to initiate action (animate) or not (inanimate). If the noun is inanimate, the speaker must know the inherent position of that object: whether it is sitting (*-chē*), standing (*-fa*), or lying (*-'ā*). If the noun is animate, the speaker will mark it as being a Yuchi male, a Yuchi female, or any other living being (*-wā*). In addition, Yuchi shows concepts such as possibility, potential, ability, desire, evidence, and co-operation through auxiliary verbs and particles that can be combined in a staggering number of ways in order to create nuances of meaning.

Only a handful of elders speak Yuchi fluently today. However, an active group of adults is successfully learning the language through intensive work with the elders. These are also teaching the language to children in an effort to rebuild Yuchi as a daily language among dedicated families. This project and others started in the 1990s have produced a large body of literature, including a grammar, traditional stories, personal and tribal histories, Bible and song translations, and teaching materials. The language is being retained in parts of the traditional ceremonies and at the Yuchi church in songs and prayers.

MARY S. LINN
University of Oklahoma

Jason Baird Jackson and Mary S. Linn, *Anthropological Linguistics* (vol. 42, 2000); Kristian Hvidt, *Von Reck's Voyage: Drawing and Journal of Philip Georg Friedrich von Reck* (1990); Mary S. Linn, *Florida Anthropologist* (vol. 50, 1997), *A Reference Grammar of Euchee (Yuchi)* (forthcoming); Mary S. Linn and Jason Baird Jackson, in *Voices from Four Directions*, ed. Brian Swann (2004); Günter Wagner, in *Publications of the American Ethnological Society* (1930; 1974), in *Handbook of American Indian Languages* (1934).

African American Discourse Features

Aside from features of grammar and pronunciation that distinguish African American English from other varieties, African Americans have other distinctive ways of using language and communicating. Some are a legacy from Africa, while others originated in slavery and its aftermath. Naming practices, preaching styles, and ritualized insults are discussed elsewhere in this volume. Other features of discourse and communication linked with African Americans involve changes in volume and pitch of voice, direct and indirect ways of getting a point across, and facial expressions.

The body language of "suck-teeth" and "cut-eye," both used to show annoyance, disapproval, or hostility toward another person, is found among American blacks, among blacks in the West Indies, and in West Africa. Sucking air between the upper teeth and the lower lip may be a stronger put-down than catching the person's eye and then pointedly looking away. Both gestures may have been part of a code used during slavery time to communicate meaning in an indirect way. Cutting the eyes away by looking down would be an insult disguised as ingratiating behavior.

Other forms of indirectness were required for survival in a society where strict rules of behavior dictated the ways African Americans could interact with whites. Blacks had ways of expressing subversive meanings without explicitly violating unspoken rules. Indirectness (for example, speaking to someone within earshot of a third party, who is the real target of the comment) is still a language style among African Americans, particularly when dealing with institutional authorities.

On the other hand, a blatantly direct language style also characterizes African American English. This style of in-group speaking may have developed as a reaction to the repressive language norms for talking to outsiders. It is characterized by "loud talking" and other ways of "reading" or putting down a person in an open verbal attack, such as "marking" or mimicking another.

Language can be used to persuade or manipulate others. Before rap was a genre of music, "rapping" was a form of conversational interaction designed to persuade the listener, whether as a form of logical argument or of flirtation. Listeners, on their part, may use back-channeling comments (e.g., *Tell it!*) extensively to encourage the speaker. This type of feedback can be seen as an extension of the call-and-response style that characterizes many African American church services and may hark back to African rhetorical patterns.

Every culture has developed its own special ways of using language and accompanying gestures. Whether by the use of special handshakes or exaggerated volume of the voice, African Americans have many ways of using language to accomplish social goals that do not depend on word meaning and grammar.

ELLEN JOHNSON
Berry College

Lisa J. Green, *African American English: A Linguistic Introduction* (2002); Thomas Kochman, *Black and White Styles in Conflict* (1981); Thomas Kochman, ed., *Rappin' and Stylin' Out: Communication in Urban Black America* (1972); Marcyliena Morgan, in *African-American English: Structure, History, and Use*, ed. Salikoko Mufwene, John Russell Rickford, Guy Bailey, and John Baugh (1998); John Russell Rickford and Russell John Rickford, *Spoken Soul: The Story of Black English* (2000).

African American Naming Patterns

African American personal names and naming practices represent a double consciousness, the dual but often conflicting realities of being Africans in America: the desire to embrace the culture and language of their rich West African heritage, on one hand, and their continuous struggle for full acceptance as Americans, on the other. Such has been the legacy of the institution of slavery since the first Africans were brought to North America in 1619.

In his novel *Roots: The Saga of an American Family*, Alex Haley describes how his ancestor, Omoro Kinte of the Mandinka tribe, carried out the very old tradition of selecting a name for his first-born child, a son, during the seven days after his birth: "It would have to be a name rich with history and with promise, for the people of his tribe—the Mandinkas—believed that a child would develop seven of the characteristics of whomever or whatever he was named for."

One of the most important principles of the African worldview is the concept of *nommo*—the magical power of the word, an all-encompassing force that serves to shape, influence, and define everything related to humans and their place in the universe. One way in which this force is manifested is in the power of name giving.

Until a child is named, according to West African belief, he or she is not regarded as a human being. Names shape personality, influence fate, and bestow desirable characteristics. Therefore, names must have meaning, be unique and creative, and reflect status and prestige. In many African tribes, a baby's birth name must be kept secret so that it cannot be used to cast a spell on the child. Consequently, the child is given a nickname, known as a "basket name." Basket names often reflect conditions surrounding the birth of the child, such as the weather, physical appearance or condition, and personality. *Morning*, *Lazy*, *Boney*, and *Easter* are examples of English basket names used by Africans during and after slavery.

The custom of secret given names was continued when Africans were brought to the New World as slaves. Slaves often hid their real African names in favor of names given to them by their white slave owners, especially when talking to whites or outsiders. Real names were used among family and close friends.

A very significant aspect of African naming was the tradition of naming children according to the day of the week on which they were born. Table 11 shows 14 West African day names. These come primarily from the Twi language of the Asante people and serve as examples of day names and their variations in spelling. Scholars note

TABLE 11. *West African Day Names*

	Male	Female
Sunday	Quashee	Quasheba
Monday	Cudjo	Juba
Tuesday	Cubbenah	Benaba/Cubena/Benah
Wednesday	Quaco/Kwaco	Cuba
Thursday	Quao	Abba
Friday	Cuffee/Cuffy	Pheba/Phibbi
Saturday	Quame/Kwame	Mimba

that the most popular day names appearing in American slave records were *Quaco* ('Wednesday,' male), *Quashee* ('Sunday,' male), and *Cuba* ('Wednesday,' female). Day names that survived during and after slavery were often those whose sound and meaning could easily be transformed from West African languages to English: for example, *Benaba/Cubena/Benah* ('Tuesday,' female) to *Venus*; *Pheba/Phibbi* ('Friday,' female) to *Phoebe*; and *Cudjo* ('Monday,' male) to *Joe*. Some day names were often translated into English, for example, with *Monday* and *Friday* becoming popular names among slaves. After day names began to take on negative connotations around the beginning of the 19th century, their use gradually declined in favor of more English names.

However, day names in their African forms occurred prominently in the Gullah language of the blacks in the coastal areas of South Carolina and Georgia in the 1930s. Basket names and personal names that indicated circumstances of birth, birth order, place-names, objects in nature, and names of occupations were also widely used by the Gullahs;

many, no doubt, were chosen primarily for their sound.

Though geographical and social isolation preserved many African naming customs among Gullah speakers during and after slavery, such was not the case in other slave communities, where white slave-masters often chose names to dehumanize the enslaved Africans and to strip them of their dignity and individuality. These names ranged from those from classical ancient civilizations (*Cato*, *Pompey*, and *Caesar*) and names identical to those of plantation livestock (*Ned* and *Dolly*) to place-names (*Africa*, *Baltimore*, *Carolina*). After emancipation, many former slaves largely rejected these names in favor of more traditional Anglo-American names such as *William*, *John*, *Elizabeth*, and *Mary*. Religious and biblical names, popular in West Africa, also were common during and after slavery, among them *Abraham*, *Amos*, *Esther*, and *Isaac*.

Basket names and names known as "phrase names" (*Pleasant Times*, *Try and See*, and *Gift of God*) remained popular among many former slaves. However, as blacks were attempting to assimilate into the dominant American society during the late 19th and early 20th centuries, European American names continued to be a major influence on African American names and naming practices, though many remained in shortened forms (from slavery), such as *Willie, Tom, Sam, Jim,* and *Eliza/Liza/Lizzie.*

However, the 1960s Black Nationalism period marked the beginning of a dramatic and deliberate breaking away from this European influence, with African Americans embracing an unprecedented pride in their African heritage, while reclaiming pride in African American culture. This period saw the emergence of African, African-sounding (simulating the structure, sounds, and rhythms of African names), and Afrocentric names that have greatly influenced naming among American blacks for more than three decades now. One of the most popular of these "invented" names, *Keisha/Kisha/LaKeisha*, has apparently become the original model of African American female naming from the mid-1960s through the late 1980s. Other examples of female names are *Tamika/Tameka/Tomika, Tawana, Tisha/LaTisha, Shonda/LaShonda, Shameka, Shaniqua, LaQuisha, Shanté,* and *Kenya.* Comparable male names emerging during this period include *Javon, Devon, Jomar,* and *Jeron* (names with a preference for stress on the second syllable).

A study of the given names of the class of 2002 at Hampton University, a private, historically black college in Hampton, Va., found that the most frequently occurring female name was *Tiffany/Tiffanie/Tiffani*, followed by *Jennifer, Kim/Kimberly, Nicole, Natasha, Tasha,* and *Stacey/Stacy/Stacey Ann.* For males, the most popular were *Michael/Mikal/Mike*, followed by *Robert, Sean/Shaun, Corey/Cory/Korey, Eric/Erik, Jason, Nathan/Nathaniel/Nate,* and *William.* These findings confirm that African Americans continue to select from a core of mainstream names. However, the study also revealed many unique and African-sounding names, as well as Muslim/Arabic-inspired names: *Tameka/Tamika, Jerrita, Nerina, Shawquia, Donniesha, Ashema, Jakita, Delrita, Chiniqua, Caniece, Chifaun, Acquanetta, Ashanti, Jamillah,* and *Rashida.* Male names in this category include *Keon, Tellis, Javid, Jamaal, Jerej, Kamari, Obari, Jevon,* and *Rockearis.* African American naming, therefore, is an extension of the dynamic character of African American language (Black English/Ebonics), whose speakers value creativity of language and verbal superiority.

Thus, the African practice of giving the most unique, unusual, and elegant names possible, where sound is as important as meaning, is an integral part of the African American oral tradition. When asked why she chose the names *Milan, Morocco,* and *Marseilles* for her sons, an African American mother remarked, "I just liked the way they sounded."

A growing trend in contemporary naming practices among African Americans is the distinctive use of capitalization, apostrophes, and prefixes in the construction of names. Representative recent examples of female names include *Kor'Tina*, *Sha'Ronda*, *Shonte're*, *De'reassa*, *Ki'ana*, *Da'Vonna*, and *D'Nai*. *JaMeka*, *K'dija*, *Shay'na*, *Ta'Ja*, *TaTa-nisha*, *Te'On*, *V'Shae*, *Tre'Anna*, and *Deja/De'ja/De'Jah/Dejah* are names for both males and females. Male names include *Da'Quan*, *De'Shanti*, *De'Shawn*, *D'Juan*, *J'ru*, and *YoKel*. These names seem to reflect the desire of African American parents to give their children one-of-a-kind names, even if the uniqueness is merely a variation in spelling.

The history of African American personal names and naming practices in the United States illustrates not only the desires of African Americans to relate to and assimilate into the dominant culture but also their conscious attempts to express cultural and group differences. Undergirding this history has always been the legacy of the oral tradition and its African worldview. Considering the belief in the magical power of the word and the value placed on verbal creativity, a significant number of African American names will, no doubt, continue to reflect the uniqueness, innovation, and creativity demanded by the power of naming.

MARGARET G. LEE
Hampton University

Molefi K. Asante and G. Renee Munta-qim, *The African American Book of Names and Their Meanings* (1999); J. L. Dillard, *Black Names* (1976); Herbert G. Gutman, *The Black Family in Slavery and Free-dom, 1750–1925* (1997); Alex Haley, *Roots* (1976); P. Robert Paustian, *Names* (vol. 26, 1978); Newbell Niles Puckett, in *Black Names in America: Origins and Usage*, ed. Murray Heller (1975); Lorenzo Dow Turner, *Africanisms in the Gullah Dialect* (orig. ed., 1949; with new introduction by Katherine Wyly Mille and Michael B. Montgomery, 2002).

Conversation

Sometimes referred to as talking, chatting, visiting, jawing, small talk, or repartee, conversation involves the oral exchange of ideas, opinions, and sentiments. Loosely structured, it often flows along according to whims and inclinations with little purpose beyond visiting or "passing the time of day." Allen Tate, in an essay titled "A Southern Mode of the Imagination," argued that northern conversation was about ideas, whereas "the typical southern conversation is not going anywhere; it is not about anything. *It is about the people who are talking.*" An aspect of regional manners, Tate wrote, southern conversation is a way "to make everybody happy." Ellen Glasgow in *The Woman Within* insisted that in the South "conversation, not literature, is the pursuit of all classes." In the frontier South with dwellings miles apart and life lonely and often harsh, lengthy visits were common, and hospitality was extended even to strangers. Church meetings, court days, political rallies, funerals, and even hangings became occasions to socialize, to hear the news, and to discuss mutual concerns. At the country store loafers congregated, and in cold weather they clustered around the warm stove to play checkers or cards and swap yarns.

Southerners have long taken pride in being, and listening to, great talkers, making folk heroes of preachers, law-

Swapping stories, Vicksburg, Miss. (William R. Ferris Collection, Southern Folklife Collection, Wilson Library, University of North Carolina at Chapel Hill)

yers, politicians, and storytellers. Whether conversing in a lowly cabin, a white framed house, or a mansion, they reveled in loquaciousness. Young ladies mastered the art of "small talk"; matrons loved to gossip about household matters, child rearing, and sensational happenings. Thomas Nelson

Page commends "the master of the plantation" as a "wonderful talker" who "discoursed of philosophy, politics, and religion." When discussing hospitality Page reports, "The conversation was surprising: it was of crops, the roads, politics, mutual friends, including the entire field of neighborhood matters, related not as gossip, but as affairs of common interest which everyone knew or was expected and entitled to know." In Charleston, New Orleans, Natchez, and other cities planters and professionals met in their social and literary clubs, welcomed distinguished guests, and engaged in enlightened repartee, sometimes over dinner or while sipping old wines.

Blacks, meanwhile, developed distinctive conversational skills. Zora Neale Hurston in *Mules and Men* (1935) recalled from her childhood in Eatonville, Fla., the men who gathered at the country store or on the front porch to exchange tales, and her works are filled with examples of black conversation, including the "lying" sessions when stories were swapped. Writers such as Ralph Ellison and Alice Walker structure their works around conversational lore.

In more recent times, for both blacks and whites, the front porch (the "gallerie" to Cajuns) attracted the family and their friends. Shaded perhaps by tall trees and equipped with rocking chairs and sometimes palm-leaf fans or ceiling fans, it was a place to relax, to watch passersby, and to welcome relatives, neighbors, the postman, a salesman, the minister — whoever happened to stop and "sit a spell." In French Louisiana the visitor might be offered dark-roast coffee; in other areas, iced tea or lemonade. The mint julep sometimes encouraged joviality on plantation verandas. With the advent of radio, television, and air-conditioning, the front porches were enclosed or gave way to cooler interiors out of the heat

and dust, and no longer were people as likely to pass the time with simple conversation.

WALDO W. BRADEN
Louisiana State University

Roger D. Abrahams, *Southern Folklore Quarterly* (vol. 33, 1968); Waldo W. Braden, *The Oral Tradition in the South* (1983); Merrill G. Christophersen, *Southern Speech Journal* (vol. 19, 1954); Everett Dick, *The Dixie Frontier: A Comprehensive Picture of Southern Frontier Life before the Civil War* (1948); Frank L. Owsley, *Plain Folk of the Old South* (1949); Allen Tate, *Essays of Four Decades* (1968).

Creolization

The earliest African slaves in the Lowcountry and on the Sea Islands of South Carolina and Georgia spoke various African languages that were often mutually unintelligible. The common language that they acquired was an English-based pidgin. An analogous situation occurred in southeastern Louisiana, where a French-based pidgin arose. Pidgin languages develop as a means by which speakers of diverse languages may communicate with one another. A pidgin has no native speakers: it is a second language by definition. But it became a native tongue when it was passed on to the American-born children of those enslaved Africans. Once a pidgin acquires native speakers, it is said to be a creole language. As a native tongue it must serve not merely the restricted functions of a pidgin but all the functions of a language. Gullah is a creole language developed by the descendants of enslaved Africans in South Carolina and Georgia. In Louisiana a

French creole usually called Louisiana Creole developed.

The process of linguistic change in which two or more languages converge to form a new native tongue is called by students of linguistic change "creolization." The creole language Gullah continued to evolve — both in inner form and extended use — in a situation of language contact. There was reciprocal influence of African and English features upon both the creole and the regional standard. The English contribution was principally lexical; the African contribution was principally grammatical.

The process of linguistic change provides a model for explaining other aspects of the transformation from African to African American culture. What might be called the "creolization of black culture" involves the unconscious "grammatical" principles of culture, the "deep structure" that generates specific cultural patterns. Such "grammatical" principles survived the Middle Passage and governed the selective adaptation of elements of both African and European culture. Herded together with others with whom they shared a common condition of servitude and some degree of cultural overlap, enslaved Africans were compelled to create a new language, a new religion, and indeed a new culture.

Not only was the structure of the new language a result of the creolization process, but the structure of language use was as well. The African preference for using indirect and highly ambiguous speech — for speaking in parables — was adapted by American-born slaves to a new natural, social, and linguistic environment. This aspect of the creolization process is strikingly evident in their proverbs. By employing the grammar of African proverb usage and the largely English vocabulary of the new creole language, African Americans were able to transform older African proverbs into metaphors of their collective experience in the New World. Some African proverbs were simply translated into the new vocabulary; others underwent minor changes. Still others retained the semantics of the African proverbs but completely transmuted the rhetoric into metaphors more meaningful to the new environment.

Naming patterns exemplify another way in which Gullah-speaking slaves preserved their African linguistic heritage while also combining aspects of it with English. The traditional African custom of "basket naming," or bestowing of private names, continued into the 20th century. As late as the Civil War, all seven West African day names, as well as other African basket names, appeared on slave lists in the South Carolina Lowcountry. But African continuities were not manifested solely in the static retentions of easily recognized African names. On the contrary, behind many of the apparently English names of the slaves were African naming patterns. In many cases African meanings were retained with direct translation of names into English. Day names, in particular, were frequently translated into their English equivalents (e.g., *Monday*). But the creolization process, by which African means of using language were applied to a new tongue, produced such fresh seasonal basket names as *Christmas*. Similarly, black names revealed the adaptation to new places of the African pattern of naming after localities.

The creolization process was vividly exemplified in black storytelling. The folk narrative tradition of African Americans, like that of their African ancestors, was eclectic and creative. They took their sources where they found them, remembered what they found memorable, used what they found usable, and forgot the forgettable. Both inherited aesthetic grammars, and the realities of the new environment played mediating roles in that process. Animal trickster tales constituted the most numerous type of folk narrative among African Americans, as among Africans, but African Americans did not merely retain African trickster tales unchanged. On the contrary, the African narrative tradition was itself creative and innovative both in Africa and in America, where it encountered a strikingly different social and natural environment. The African American trickster tales indicate the black response to that new environment and efforts to manipulate it verbally and symbolically. In addition to animal trickster tales, the slaves narrated a cycle of human trickster tales in which the trickster role was not played by a surrogate slave — the rabbit — but by a real slave, John. Both animal and human trickster tales manifested continuities with African themes and with African traditions of indirect speech.

The study of linguistic creolization is a relatively recent phenomenon; the application of creolization theory to the study of African American culture represents a promising approach to understanding the transformation of diverse African cultures into African American culture.

CHARLES JOYNER
Coastal Carolina University

Melville J. Herskovits, *The Myth of the Negro Past* (1941); Charles Joyner, *Down by the Riverside: A South Carolina Slave Community* (1984); Lawrence W. Levine, *Black Culture and Black Consciousness: Afro-American Folk Thought from Slavery to Freedom* (1978); Robert Farris Thompson, *Flash of the Spirit: African and Afro-American Art and Philosophy* (1982); Lorenzo Dow Turner, *Africanisms in the Gullah Dialect* (1949, 2002); Peter Wood, *Black Majority: Negroes in Colonial South Carolina from 1670 through the Stono Rebellion* (1974).

Dictionary of American Regional English

The *Dictionary of American Regional English* (DARE) seeks not to prescribe how Americans *should* speak or even to describe how people across the country *do* speak in formal or standard contexts. Instead, it documents the varieties of English that are *not* found throughout the country — those words, phrases, pronunciations, and grammatical features that vary from one region to another, that are learned at home rather than at school, or that are part of oral rather than written culture. The plan for the dictionary was devised by Frederic G. Cassidy and Audrey R. Duckert. It was carried out by Cassidy, Joan Houston Hall, and

Frederic G. Cassidy, original editor and co-conceiver of the Dictionary of American Regional English (George E. Hall, photographer)

others. A unique feature of *DARE* is the use of maps in the text (with state sizes adjusted to reflect population density rather than geographic area) to show where particular words were collected during interviews with 2,000 people across the country. Whenever possible, editors assign regional labels that describe where the word or phrase is used. The *DARE* fieldwork, local newspapers, memoirs, and oral evidence provide good indications of both regional and social distributions.

Analysis of the maps and of the regional labels used in *DARE* entries makes it clear that the South (by which *DARE* means southern and eastern Maryland, eastern Virginia, eastern and central North and South Carolina, southern and central Georgia, Florida, central and southern parts of Alabama, Mississippi, and Louisiana, as well as

east Texas) still retains thousands of language features that reflect its distinctive cultural background and history. The region known as the South Midland, extending from the South as far west as Missouri, Arkansas, and eastern Oklahoma, and northward into the southern parts of Ohio, Indiana, and Illinois, is the next most frequent regional label in *DARE*. And when labels referring to subregions such as the Southeast, South Atlantic, and Gulf states are also included, there is no question that the "South," as defined in this *Encyclopedia*, is easily the most distinctive region of the country in its words, phrases, pronunciations, and grammatical constructions.

A very few examples are included here to illustrate some of the distinctively southern terms found in *DARE*: *battercake, corn dodger, hopping John, hush puppy*, and *red-eye gravy* for foods; *cooter, hoppergrass, mosquito hawk, peckerwood*, and *piney-woods rooter* for animals; *cup towel, flying jenny, mourners' bench, play-pretty*, and *rawhead and bloodybones* for aspects of material culture; *fixin' to, for to, hisn/hern, might could*, and *y'all* for grammatical and syntactic features; and *co'cola, hep, janders, nekkid*, and *sallet* for pronunciation variants. The index to the published volumes of *DARE* allows readers to go from the lists of entries labeled "South," "South Midland," and so forth directly to the dictionary's entries.

Based on face-to-face interviews carried out in all 50 states between 1965 and 1970 and on an extensive collection of other materials (diaries, letters, novels, histories, biographies, newspapers, government documents, ephemeral notes, and in recent years, digital resources), *DARE* provides historical documentation for every headword and sense (there are approximately 50,000 senses in the first four volumes), and it dates every quotation used. Quotations from such prominent southern writers as William Faulkner, Eudora Welty, Flannery O'Connor, and Joel Chandler Harris, as well as from many lesser-known southerners, are used to provide illustrations of usage. This excerpt from Faulkner's *Intruder in the Dust*, for instance, is used at the entry for *cup towel* (a dish towel): "The sheriff stood over a sputtering skillet . . . a battercake turner in one hand and a cuptowel in the other."

Four volumes have been published to date: *A–C* (1985), *D–H* (1991), *I–O* (1996), and *P–Sk* (2002). The fifth volume of text (*Sl–Z*) is expected in 2009, to be followed by a volume of ancillary materials (including fieldwork data, contrastive maps, a cumulative index, and the bibliography) and an electronic edition.

JOAN HOUSTON HALL
University of Wisconsin

An Index by Region, Usage, and Etymology to the Dictionary of American Regional English, vols. 1 and 2 (1993) and 3 (1999); Frederic G. Cassidy and Joan Houston Hall, eds., *Dictionary of American Regional English* (1985–); Joan Houston Hall, in *Language in the USA: Themes for the Twenty-first Century* (2004); Allan Metcalf, in *Language Variety in the South Revisited*, ed. Cynthia Bernstein, Thomas Nunnally, and Robin Sabino (1997).

Fixin' to

Fixin' to has developed in Southern American English as a phrase having numerous pronunciations, a complex origin, and a variety of meanings, the most familiar one indicating the immediate futurity of a proposed action. Thus, in *I am fixin' to go* and *She is fixin' to fix supper* the *going* and the *fixing supper* are soon to occur. In grammatical nomenclature *fixin' to* is a phrasal auxiliary verb (it has also been called a "quasimodal," "almost modal," or "semiauxiliary" verb) that precedes and modifies a main verb. It has been well known in southern lore and everyday speech for almost two centuries, its first recorded usage being in 1829, in the *Virginia Literary Museum* (*I'm fixing to go*).

Fixin' to has evolved new forms, functions, and meanings from existing words, following a universal tendency in languages. Its pronunciation often changes to *fixin ta* and may also be heard in the South as *fikin ta, fisin ta, fikin na*, or *fix ta*. During the Great Migrations of the early 20th century, *fixin' to* moved out of the South with African American speakers who developed new forms and new pronunciations, such as *fixin na, fin na, fit'n ta, fin ta, fit na, fi'in*, and *fin*.

Fix maintains its original meaning, "to make firm, stable, or hold steady," as well as meanings that later developed from this ("to fasten or attach," then "to repair," and then "to prepare"). Since *preparing* points toward a future occurrence, the meaning of futurity is applied to *fix* in the South. *She is fixin' to fix supper* thus illustrates two distinct meanings: "She is getting ready to prepare supper."

As a phrasal auxiliary *fixin' to* precedes the main verb in a clause to influence the meaning of the time relationship. For instance, *I'm fixin' to leave* ("I'm about to/getting ready to leave") or *I was fixin' to leave when she arrived* ("I was about to/getting ready to leave when she arrived") signifies an imminent event intended to happen in the immediate future, indicating a psychological readiness as well as a physical one. *I'm fixin' to go home* ("I'm going to go home") gives a sense of future determination and immediate action, but when not intending immediate action, a speaker can use *fixin' to* to convey a false promise or the subtle implication that an action is being (or has been) delayed. A speaker who says *I was just fixin' to do that* may have been only

procrastinating or perhaps did not intend to perform the action at all. Then the use of *fixin' to* approaches irony.

Thus, *fixin' to* may express futurity, immediacy, priority, definiteness, certainty, preparatory activity (psychological or physical), procrastination, or ironic contradiction. A speaker can manipulate these notions, and the interpretation of any given instance is determined by the context of the speaker and audience. *Fixin' to* is therefore a highly complex form unique to the English language, one that cannot always be simply replaced by *getting ready to, about to*, or another phrase. Because of its great usefulness, southerners will probably resist any effort to replace it in their speech.

MARY ZEIGLER
Georgia State University

Frederic G. Cassidy, ed., *Dictionary of American Regional English*, vol. 2 (1991); Marvin K. L. Ching, *American Speech* (vol. 62, 1987); Mary B. Zeigler, *Southern Journal of Linguistics* (vol. 26, 2002).

Folk Speech

Folk speech has two distinct senses. The first refers to popular, vernacular, often local speech that differs from the standard, formal, textbook, and usually more widespread variety of a language. Although some writers have used the label to identify largely nonurban, uneducated speech, and some folklorists have incorporated this definition into their work, even the best-educated and highest-status speakers of a region may use this first sort of folk speech. It includes variation in pronunciation, grammar, and vocabulary.

For pronunciation, linguistic geography profusely documents regional differences in individual words (e.g., *greazy* is more common in the South than *greasy*) as well as in general trends (e.g., the fact that southerners pronounce *e* before *n* or *m* like *i*, so that *ten* and *hem* are identical to *tin* and *him*). There are extensive differences in grammar, as in the past tense of verbs (*I seen him yesterday*), and linguistic studies have also verified the popular perception that southerners' vocabulary often differs from that of other Americans. The southerner's use of *y'all* is perhaps the best example. Even the meanings of words shared with other regions are often distinct. A southerner who offers to *carry you* somewhere means to "give you a lift," not hoist you up in his or her arms and transport you.

The American Dialect Society, which was founded in 1889, has been an institutional focus for the study of this first type of folk speech, and its publications *American Speech* (1925–), *Dialect Notes* (1890–1939), and *Publication of the American Dialect Society* (1944–) are among the most important. The study of folk speech in the South has often focused on the legacy of, or deviations from, British speech patterns in Appalachia or other rural areas. The nature of African American English, the influence of other languages, and the relationship between speech and social class have also been central concerns. Projects such as the *Linguistic Atlas of the Middle and South Atlantic States* and the *Linguistic Atlas of the Gulf States* show the broad distribution of speechways across the region.

The specific vocabulary of the South is being richly documented in the *Dictionary of American Regional English*, and many items there qualify as folk speech in either the first or both of the senses here. Smoky Mountain vocabulary and grammar are thoroughly treated in the *Dictionary of Smoky Mountain English*.

The second type of folk speech is more in keeping with modern folklorists' definition of folklore in general—that it has *artistic* expression. It is not highfalutin, in the most common sense of "artistic," but it is something beyond the ordinary, something that calls attention to itself, making the listener think that the speaker is being playful or creative. While many examples of such speech may be innovative, it is still deeply rooted in the traditions of an area, and the South is perhaps the best-known and best-studied region for such folk expressions, proverbs, euphemisms, similes, metaphors, and the like. For example, *raining like an old cow pissing on a flat rock in Arkansas* gets much more immediate notice than *It's raining very hard*. In short, the first is artistic expression, or folk speech of the second type.

Many expressions, proverbs, and the like are in fact folk speech in both senses of the term. They often differ from more widely distributed language (sense 1), but they also call attention to themselves through audacity, cleverness, subtlety, or other devices associated with folk linguistic artistry (sense 2). Speech that is based in and is uniquely valued by its own community is folk speech; however, that which is regional but is everyday talk is not, in the second sense of the term.

Thus, a southerner who says *He's so high he couldn't hit the floor with his hat* (that is, "drunk") is using folk speech, but one who says *I'm fixin' to leave* 'getting ready' or *I might could go* 'might be able to' is not, since the latter usages are ordinary in most southern speech communities. Nonsoutherners, however, who often take a romantic and/or prejudicial view of everything southern, tend to perceive any talk by the region's natives as artistic folk speech. Many have similar attitudes toward African American English or some foreign-accented speech, varieties that outsiders view as performances rather than the ordinary usage of some speech communities. Such varieties are often the target of imitations, another indication that speakers who believe they use more mainstream varieties often assign folk value to the ordinary usage of others. In short, according to sense 2, well nigh anything a southerner says might be folk speech to a nonsoutherner.

Folk speech can be a word, a phrase, a style of speaking, or even less than a word. "Folk noises" have hardly been studied, though chants, calls, and imitations have figured in a few works, and the "rebel yell" is a famous folk cry. The elongated vowel in *shiiiiit* is clearly an extension of the so-called southern drawl into a specific word, one known and imitated even outside the South, particularly in situations in which the word expresses disbelief.

Also little studied, until recently, is folk speech having to do with stylistic tendencies. For example, the classical tradition in southern education left behind both place-names (*Sparta*, *Athens*) and personal names (*Cato*, *Cicero*). This, combined with a traditional knowledge of the Bible and a desire for "big words," produced a genre known as "fancy talk" in African American speech and influenced southern pulpit styles in general, some examples of which combined learned words with rhythmic cadences and even rhyme:

> Never before had the universe received this annunciation, and never before had any man or woman received the salutation.

In the area of phrases and proverbial phrases, southern folk speech (and the study of it) shines. Vance Randolph, George P. Wilson, Archer Taylor, and Bartlett J. Whiting have compiled noteworthy collections, although not all of these deal only with southern speech. Among proverbial comparisons there is the pattern *as X as a Y* (or *X-er than a Y* and other obviously related forms), as in *busy as a one-armed paperhanger*, and *so X that Y*, as in *so tight [that] he wouldn't give a dime to see the Statue of Liberty piss across New York Bay*. Most collections combine the grammatical forms cited above with the others — *X enough to Y* and *too X to Y* (both related to *so X that Y*), and *to X like a Y* (often interchangeable with some forms of *as X as a Y*). There are other minor comparative forms: *look like a sheep-killing dog, run around like a chicken with its head cut off, make more noise than 99 cows and a bobtailed bull*.

Though comparisons dominate, a few other forms based on nouns (*the straw that broke the camel's back*), verbs (*come a cropper*), and prepositional phrases (*in hot water*) are included in most studies, along with other expressions not so easily classified grammatically. Some might be identified as threats (*I'm going to jerk a knot in your tail*); wisecracks and comebacks (*Your feet don't fit no limb*, said to one who asks *who?*); exclamations and warnings (*Katy bar the door!*); insults (*You don't amount to a hill of beans*); taunts (*Redhead, cabbage-head, 10 cents a pound*, directed to a red-haired person); boasts (*Hooo-eee! I'm half horse and half alligator!*); and miscellaneous sentential items (*Hope in one hand and shit in the other and see which fills up first!*). Such a classification is practical rather than theoretically exhaustive, and many of these items, although collected in southern venues, are surely more widespread.

Although the content of southern folk speech reveals a preoccupation with rural, traditional matters, newer items display changing attitudes and concerns. Growing evidence suggests that southerners more than any other Americans may assign particular importance to folk speech, in response perhaps to the negative image some outsiders have of southern speech in general. Nevertheless, southern folk speech is important to the region, usually has a distinct local flavor, and will likely be around as long as the culture exists.

DENNIS PRESTON
Michigan State University

Cynthia Bernstein, Thomas Nunnally, and Robin Sabino, eds., *Language Variety in the South Revisited* (1997); Frederic G. Cassidy et al., *Dictionary of American Regional English* (1985–); James B. McMillan and Michael B. Montgomery, *Annotated Bibliography of Southern American English* (1989); Michael B. Montgomery and Guy Bailey, *Language Variety in the South: Perspectives in Black and White* (1986); Michael B. Montgomery and Joseph S. Hall, eds., *Dictionary of Smoky Mountain English* (2004); Stephen J. Nagle and Sara L. Sanders, *English in the Southern United States* (2003); Vance Randolph and George P. Wilson, *Down in the Holler: A Gallery of Ozark Folk Speech* (1953).

Grammar, Changes in

The grammar of English in the American South has been evolving since the early 17th century, when the region began to be colonized by immigrants from southern and western England. Some grammatical features of Southern English can be traced to the language of these early settlers; others were introduced by English speakers arriving later from northern England, Scotland, and northern Ireland. Although American English in its early stages had the reputation of being relatively uniform (compared with British English), dialects began to emerge as settlement patterns developed; contact between European immigrants, African slaves, and Native Americans affected the language of different regions; and new grammatical features arose. In the South, distinctive variations became especially evident in such urban focal speech areas as Charleston, Savannah, and New Orleans; in the mountains of the Appalachians and Ozarks; and in isolated coastal areas of the Outer Banks of North Carolina, Chesapeake Islands of Virginia and Maryland, and Sea Islands of South Carolina and Georgia. All these regional varieties have continued to evolve, so that, contrary to popular belief, not even isolated coastal regions or the most remote mountain communities retain intact the English originally brought to them.

Southern English has also been subject to social forces, some of which have reinforced speech differences. Among the consequences of the slave trade and plantation culture were the emergence and the evolution of African American Vernacular English (AAVE) as a means of maintaining black identity. The Civil War and Reconstruction reinforced distinct southern speech varieties. Other forces favored the sharing of linguistic features. Industrialization in the late 19th century led to urbanization and migration from the countryside. World War I and especially World War II brought many southerners out of comparative isolation. The advent of air-conditioning has more recently encouraged migration to the South. The civil rights movement led to greater integration and increased levels of education. As a result of these and other social forces, some stereotypically southern features are expanding, while others are declining or becoming associated with social or ethnic varieties.

Expanding Grammatical Features.
Some of the most salient grammatical features of Southern English remain strong and may even be spreading.

Second-person-plural pronouns. No feature is more closely identified with southern speech than *you all* (with the accent on the first syllable) and *y'all* to refer to more than one person, as in *Are y'all coming over tonight?* Some evidence suggests that *y'all* is being used increasingly by young southerners and by people of all ages in other parts of the United States. At the same time, *you guys*, once restricted to the North, is gaining favor among some southerners as an informal form of addressing multiple listeners. *You'uns*, a form having the same meaning and once common in Appalachian parts of the South, is disappearing rapidly.

Double (or multiple) modal verbs. English generally does not permit two modal auxiliary verbs (*may, might, can, could, shall, should, will, would*) to occur together, but southerners frequently combine them, as in *I might could do it*, to express a degree of tentativeness, indirectness, or politeness. Double modals are holding strong in the South and sometimes show up outside the region as well, especially among African Americans, whose linguistic roots are in the region.

Fixin' to. The expression *fixin' to* means something like *about to* or *preparing to*, as in *I was just fixin' to leave.* Its use is widespread among all regional and social groups in the South, and it is often acquired by nonsoutherners who move to the region.

Declining and Restricted Features.
Some features that are evident in records from earlier centuries have become less common or are now as-

sociated with certain ethnic or social varieties in the southern United States.

Invariant be. In Southern English the uninflected form *be* (occasionally *bes*) may be used as a main verb or an auxiliary, where general usage requires *am*, *are*, *is*, *was*, or *were*. It was common in colonial America, but in modern Southern English its use has declined among whites. In AAVE, where it signifies habitual action, it may be used with singular or plural subjects, especially in the construction *be* plus a verb plus *-ing*, as in *They [or he] be working in Texas*. Along similar lines, omitting the main verb *be*, as in *You ugly*, is declining in usage among whites in the South, though use of the feature is still evident in AAVE.

Third-person zero suffix. English generally requires an *-s* ending for verbs in the present tense when they have a third-person singular subject. In Southern English, the suffix may be omitted, somewhat more often if the subject is a pronoun, as in *She stay in Texas*. Evidence of this feature has been found in written records from 16th-century England and the 19th-century American South. It is now more common in AAVE than in general southern speech.

Zero plural. The English plural is generally formed by adding an *-s* to nouns. When certain nouns are preceded by a number, Southern English allows the *-s* to be deleted, as in *I walked six mile to school every day*. The *Linguistic Atlas of the Gulf States* (LAGS) showed that in the 1970s this feature was more than four times more likely to be used by the oldest speakers than by the youngest speakers in its survey, suggesting that it is disappearing.

Zero possessive. English generally uses *-'s* on nouns to signal possession. Southern English occasionally omits the *-s* suffix, as in *The man hat is on the floor*. Today this is commonly associated with AAVE.

Third-person-plural -s and plural was. General English has no ending for verbs in the present tense when the subject is *you* or a plural noun or pronoun. Southern English sometimes adds an *-s* to the verb if the subject is a noun, as in *My brothers works at night* (but not *They works at night*). The feature was present in the English of Ulster Scots settlers. In addition, past-tense *were* may be replaced by *was*, as in *We was all at home*. Research shows these usages are declining today and are associated with working-class speech.

Liketa *or* liked to. Southern English uses *liketa* preceding a past participle verb to mean *nearly*, as in *I liketa died*. Associated now with rural working-class speech, *liketa* has been declining among younger generations.

A-*prefixing.* The structure *a-* plus a verb plus *-ing*, as in *He come a-runnin'*, was once common in both British and American dialects, but it is declining in general southern speech. LAGS found the feature to be associated with older, less-educated speakers. It may still be heard in the Appalachian region and in other relatively isolated communities, such as the islands of the Outer Banks in North Carolina.

Irregular relative pronouns. Whereas English generally requires a relative pronoun in such expressions as *the people who/that live in the South*, Southern English may omit the *who* or *that*. In addition, *what* is occasionally used as a relative, as in *the people what live in the South*. These features are now declining.

Nonstandard preterits and past participles. Many varieties of English have nonstandard irregular verb forms, as in *I seen him do it*, or *I've knowed them for years*. Verb forms were in flux in the 16th, 17th, and 18th centuries, and some British relic forms, such as *clum* 'climbed,' *holp* 'helped,' *knowed* 'knew/known,' and *riz* 'rose/risen,' may be heard in the South, though their use is declining. LAGS reveals that younger people and those of higher socioeconomic status are less likely to use such past-tense and past-participle forms as *come* 'came,' *growed* 'grew/grown,' *eat* 'ate/eaten,' *drownded* 'drowned,' or *run* 'ran.' In contrast, *dove* 'dive,' is used more often by younger, better-educated speakers, even though it was once considered a nonstandard form.

Perfective done. In Southern English *done* sometimes replaces *have* as an auxiliary verb, as in *I done forgot what he wanted*. Documented in early 19th-century usage, this feature is declining. Like nonstandard preterits, it characterizes the speech of older, working-class southerners.

Other Grammatical Features of Southern English. Some grammatical features are limited to regions within the South; Appalachian English, for example, has possessive forms ending in *-n* at the end of a phrase, as in *Is this*

yourn? Some are limited to AAVE; for example, remote-time *been* (stressed) connotes distant past, as in *She* been *write the letter* (i.e., a long time ago). Some, such as *ain't*, double negatives (*It ain't gonna do no good*), or *them* in place of *those* (*How do you like them apples?*), are common not only in the South but in other regions as well. In spite of the varieties of ways in which southern grammar is changing, there is no evidence that it is disappearing as a distinguishing attribute of southern speech.

CYNTHIA BERNSTEIN
University of Memphis

E. Bagby Atwood, *A Survey of Verb Forms in the Eastern United States* (1953); Cynthia Bernstein, in *English in the Southern United States*, ed. Stephen J. Nagle and Sara L. Sanders (2003); Patricia Cukor-Avila, in *English in the Southern United States* (2003), ed. Stephen J. Nagle and Sara L. Sanders; Crawford Feagin, *Variation and Change in Alabama English: A Sociolinguistic Study of the White Community* (1979); Michael Montgomery, in *From the Gulf States and Beyond: The Legacy of Lee Pederson and LAGS*, ed. Michael B. Montgomery and Thomas E. Nunnally (1998); Lee Pederson et al., eds., *The Linguistic Atlas of the Gulf States*, 7 vols. (1986–92); Edgar W. Schneider, in *English in the Southern United States*, ed. Stephen J. Nagle and Sara L. Sanders (2003); Jan Tillery, in *Language Variety in the South: Historical and Contemporary Perspectives*, ed. Michael Picone and Catherine Evans Davies (forthcoming); Jan Tillery and Guy Bailey, in *English in the Southern United States*, ed. Stephen J. Nagle and Sara L. Sanders (2003).

Illiteracy

Inability to read and write in any language has been the conventional definition of illiteracy and the basis of most illiteracy statistics. The concept of "functional" illiteracy was advanced during World War II as a result of the U.S. Army experience with soldiers who "could not understand written instructions about basic military tasks." The South has exceeded the rest of the nation in illiteracy, whether defined in functional terms or as the inability to read and write in any language. Information from the U.S. census of 1870 illustrated the South's heritage of illiteracy. No area of the region had less than 12 percent illiteracy. The cotton-culture regions, particularly the river valley and delta areas and the Piedmont and Coastal Plain, were 40 percent or more illiterate. The South was agricultural, and agriculture then depended not on science but on traditional practice—learning by doing rather than by reading. The 1870 census found 4.53 million persons 10 years of age and older unable to read in the nation; 73.7 percent of them resided in the South. Four-fifths of blacks were illiterate at that time.

The agricultural economy rested upon a sparsely distributed population, the use of child labor that discouraged school attendance, and a prejudiced and often fatalistic people who lacked the means for upward mobility in the expanding industrial system of the nation. The church was more important as a social institution than the school; word of mouth, song, and story were prominent means of cultural transmission. Under these conditions illiteracy served to conserve tradition and retard cultural change, whereas a more general literacy would have accelerated adaptation and change. Said a Jasper County, Miss., man, "My grandfather—he raised me—figured going to school wouldn't help me pick cotton any better."

When the education of a generation of children is neglected, the deficiency persists throughout a lifetime. Teaching adults to read has not been as effective in eliminating illiteracy as have mortality and out-migration from the South. The neglect of a generation of schoolchildren during the Civil War (those 5 to 14 years of age in 1860) resulted in higher illiteracy rates for the native white population in 1900 (who then were 45 to 54 years of age) than for either the preceding or succeeding generation.

A decline in illiteracy has occurred in the South and the nation. As educational benefits were extended to blacks through both public and private schools (including schools sponsored by religious groups, such as the Congregational Church, and by private foundations, such as the Rosenwald Fund), illiteracy rates dropped.

The change in illiteracy in Georgia from 1960 to 1970 illustrates the source of gains and losses of illiterates in a state. The number of Georgia illiterates in 1960 was reduced by 45 percent by 1970. Some 22,530 were estimated to have died during the decade, and 23,840 were lost through out-migration. The Adult Basic Education Program of the state taught 14,380 to read during the period. However, 6,290 new illiterates, aged 14 to 24 years in 1970, entered the category. This new group testifies to the failure of the family and the school to inculcate literacy skills. The National Center for Education Statistics in 1992 showed that the South still scored lower than any other region on literacy measures.

The 2000 census showed that 9 of the 11 states with less than 78 percent high school graduates are in the South. In 1980 the South had approximately 398,000 illiterates, according to estimates based on the 1980 census and the November 1979 Current Population Survey. The distribution by color was white, 44.9 percent; black, 51.4 percent; other nonwhite, 3.7 percent. By age, illiterates were distributed as follows: 14–24 years, 9.2 percent; 25–44 years, 17.0 percent; 45–64 years, 32.2 percent; and 65 years and older, 41.6 percent. These are individuals unable to read and write, according to census definitions; functional illiterates are more numerous.

In general, illiterates have lower learning capacity, are more likely to be welfare recipients, and have higher rejection rates for military service. If female, they have higher fertility rates, and instances of infant mortality among illiterates are always higher. There is more illiteracy in rural than in urban areas.

ABBOTT L. FERRISS
Emory University

Sterling G. Brinkley, *Journal of Experimental Education* (September 1957); John K.

Folger and Charles B. Nam, *Education of the American Population* (1967); Eli Ginzberg and Douglas W. Bray, *The Uneducated* (1953); *Historical Statistics of the United States to 1970* (1975); Carman St. John Hunter with David Harman, *Adult Illiteracy in the United States: A Report to the Ford Foundation* (1979); U.S. Bureau of the Census, *Current Population Reports*; Sanford Winston, *Illiteracy in the United States* (1930).

Linguistic Atlas of the Gulf States

Directed by Lee Pederson of Emory University, the *Linguistic Atlas of the Gulf States* (LAGS) is a constituent of the American Linguistic Atlas or Linguistic Atlas of the United States and Canada project. It reports the results of an extensive survey of regional and social dialects of English in eight southern states: Tennessee, Georgia, Florida, Alabama, Mississippi, Louisiana, Arkansas, and Texas (as far west as the Balcones Escarpment). It is the most comprehensive source of information available on the English of the South. Fieldwork for LAGS was begun in 1968, and the last of seven interpretive volumes that describe the research and summarize its results was published in 1992. The LAGS basic materials provide primary texts (in the form of responses to questionnaire items) for the study of English in the region and a description of the sociohistorical and sociolinguistic contexts necessary for their interpretation. The LAGS interpretive volumes inventory dominant and recessive patterns of linguistic usage in the Gulf states, identify and characterize the primary regional and social varieties of the region, and identify areas of linguistic complexity that require further study. More generally, LAGS provides a historical baseline for Southern English against which future linguistic developments can be measured and from which earlier varieties can be reconstructed. That baseline encompasses roughly the period between 1880 and 1940, the decades during which most LAGS informants were born (note, however, that the oldest informant was born in 1870 and the youngest in 1965). Both the design and the implementation of LAGS reflect its historical focus.

Tape-recorded interviews (or field records) with 1,121 informants in 699 localities in 451 counties comprise the basic data for LAGS. The informants include 594 men and 527 women, and 239 are African American (blacks were interviewed in all areas where they exceeded 20 percent of the population in 1930, before the effects of the Great Migration were fully realized). Both the average age (62.24) of informants and the overrepresentation of the less-educated (38.62 percent have an eighth-grade education or less) reflect the historical orientation of LAGS.

A series of analogs reduces the 5,300 hours of tape-recorded speech in the LAGS field records to graphic formats at various levels of abstraction. The protocols are the primary and most concrete analog of the field records. Containing phonetic transcriptions both of target items that were elicited by an 800-item questionnaire and of other useful phonological, grammatical, and lexical data that occurred during interviews, the protocols serve as comprehensive

guides to the field records; their 121,000 pages of phonetic transcriptions are a major source of evidence on Southern English as well. Each protocol is conveniently summarized in an idiolect synopsis, a one-page abstract of its phonological, lexical, and grammatical substance, and the entire contents of all of the protocols are captured in the concordance, an alphabetical listing in normal orthography of every phonetically transcribed item and its place of occurrence in the LAGS protocols. University Microfilms published the protocols and idiolect synopses, along with the LAGS questionnaire and guide to phonetics and protocol composition, as LAGS: The Basic Materials on microfiche and microfilm in 1981; The Concordance of Basic Materials followed in 1986.

These microform texts serve as the input to still another analog, a set of computer files that rewrite LAGS data in ASCII format. When the computer files are combined with a series of mapping programs (both available from the Linguistic Atlas Project at the University of Georgia), they allow users to create their own maps and provide a kind of automatic linguistic atlas in electronic form. These files also form the basis of the seven interpretive volumes published by the University of Georgia Press. Those volumes include a handbook, which summarizes the LAGS methodology, informants, and communities; a general index, which summarizes the contents of the concordance; and a technical index, which summarizes the contents of the computer files. The other four volumes, the *Regional Matrix* and the *Regional Pattern* (vols. 4 and 5) and the *Social Matrix* and the *Social Pattern* (vols. 6 and 7) summarize many of the substantive results of LAGS and provide a useful overview of regional and social variation in the English of the Gulf states. The LAGS interpretive volumes (4–7) include information both on the distribution of individual linguistic features and on those combinations of features that produce regional patterns. Map 3, for instance, shows the regional distribution of *chigger* and *red bug*, two synonyms for a tiny bug in the grass that burrows into the skin and causes itching. Map 5 shows how LAGS uses the distribution of *chigger* in combination with three other features (*red worm* [a worm for fishing], an intrusive *uh* between the *b* and *r* in *umbrella*, and a strong *r* pronunciation in *March*) to help identify and delimit a Highlands pattern in the English of the Gulf states, a pattern that is also characterized by the use of such terms as *French harp* 'harmonica,' *tow sack* 'burlap bag,' *barn lot* 'barnyard,' and *green beans* (as opposed to *snap beans*). Using quantitative distributions of similar combinations of lexical, phonological, and grammatical features, LAGS identifies 20 subregional patterns that comprise two basic regional configurations, Interior and Coastal. The Eastern Highlands serves as a focal area (i.e., core or cultural hearth) for the former, and the Central Gulf Coast/Lower Delta serves as the focal area for the latter.

LAGS also identifies 20 types of social markers in the English of the Gulf states; these often interact with re-gional patterns in complex ways. The social markers reflect categories of race (black and white), sex, age, and education either in isolation or in combination. For example, LAGS identifies 31 features as characteristic of African American speech, with about half of these further subcategorized by age and education; 35 features are identified as primarily white. The occurrence of monophthongal or flat /ai/ in *right* (pronounced something like *raht*), a white social marker, illustrates the complex relationship between social markers and regional patterns. While the vast majority of the LAGS informants who have this feature are white (91.66 percent), as Map 6 shows, flat /ai/ also has a complex regional distribution, occurring primarily in the Eastern Highlands and the Ozarks; in the Piney Woods of south Georgia, Alabama, Mississippi, and Louisiana; and in Texas. This kind of interaction between social markers and regional patterns gives southern speech much of its richness and complexity. Among the many virtues of LAGS is its capacity for capturing those interactions. LAGS thus maps and provides the raw material for researchers to chart the almost infinite detail of Southern English, and its data on the social patterning deepens our understanding of language change and variation in the region's speech.

GUY H. BAILEY
University of Missouri–Kansas City

Guy Bailey and Jan Tillery, *American Speech* (vol. 74, 1999); Michael Montgomery, *American Speech* (vol. 68, 1993); Lee Pederson, in *American Dialect Research*, ed. Dennis Preston (1993); Lee Pederson

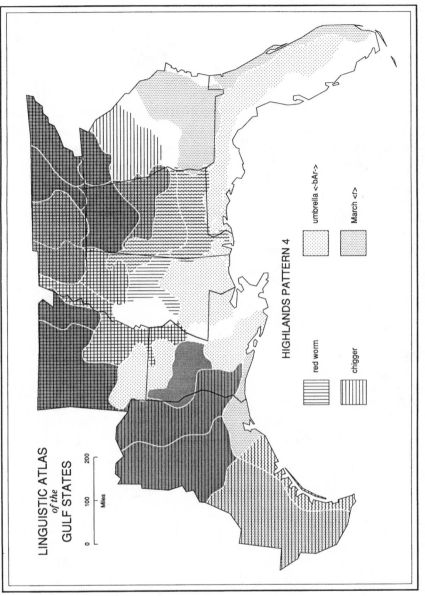

Map 5. Highlands Pattern 4 (Source: Lee Pederson, Susan McDaniel, and Carol Adams, Linguistic Atlas of the Gulf States, vol. 5, Regional Pattern [1991], p. 73; cartography by Borden D. Dent)

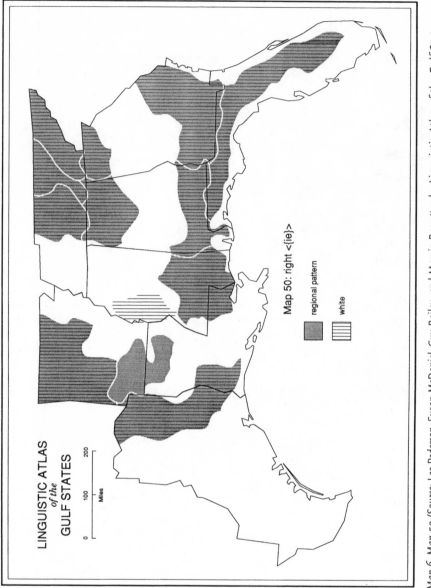

Map 6. Map 50 (*Source: Lee Pederson, Susan McDaniel, Guy Bailey, and Marvin Bassett, eds., Linguistic Atlas of the Gulf States, vol. 7, Social Pattern [1992], p. 151; cartography by Borden D. Dent*)

et al., eds., *Linguistic Atlas of the Gulf States*, 7 vols. (1986–92).

Linguistic Atlas of the Middle and South Atlantic States

The *Linguistic Atlas of the Middle and South Atlantic States* (LAMSAS) is the largest segment of the American Linguistic Atlas or Linguistic Atlas of the United States and Canada project, which was designed to survey the regional and social differences in spoken American English. LAMSAS covers the region from New York state south to Georgia and northeastern Florida, and from the eastern coastline as far west as the borders of Ohio and Kentucky. Along with Hans Kurath's *Linguistic Atlas of New England* (conducted in the early 1930s and published 1939–43), LAMSAS treats the primary settlement areas of the earliest states of the United States. LAMSAS consists of interviews, the transcriptions from which are in fine phonetic notation, with 1,162 selected, native informants from 483 communities (usually counties) within the region. Interviews often required six to eight hours to complete; they were conducted with a questionnaire of 104 pages, averaging seven items per page, designed to reveal regional and social differences in everyday vocabulary, grammar, and pronunciation. Field-workers often avoided asking questions directly, in favor of more conversational interviews rich in local lore. In the days when the primitive machines that were available could record only short segments, phonetically trained field-workers wrote down in fine phonetic notation words and phrases that matched the intentions of the questionnaires. Initial fieldwork was conducted by Guy Lowman, a veteran of the New England survey, beginning in 1933. After Lowman's death in a car crash in 1941, Raven McDavid largely completed the remaining interviews in upstate New York, Georgia, and South Carolina by 1949.

The speakers selected for LAMSAS and other atlas interviews were long-time residents of their communities, generally of middle age through the oldest living generation. They came from three different social strata: folk speakers (with little education or social involvement), common speakers (with a high school education and more social activity), and in about one-fifth of the communities, cultivated speakers (with a college education or its equivalent in experience and with wide exposure to high culture). Forty-one African American speakers were interviewed in the South Atlantic area, which represented forward thinking at the time, though not yet equal representation in numbers. LAMSAS thus records the English spoken along the Atlantic Coast in the second quarter of the 20th century among people of different social positions and degrees of education. It provides a benchmark for varying forms of the English language for a particular region at a particular time, with special reference to the development of the language in the late 1800s, when most of the interviewees were born and grew up. The significance of LAMSAS is thus principally historical. Along with the New England atlas, LAMSAS is also the key to making the best use of all the other regional atlas projects, which document the English spoken in secondary and tertiary American settlement areas (such as the *Linguistic Atlas of the Gulf States*). The *Handbook of the Linguistic Atlas of the Middle and South Atlantic States* describes the methods, speakers, and communities of the project. LAMSAS, therefore, occupies a place beside other major projects in the history of the English language, and its survey data provided the basis for the first truly detailed delineation of southern speech. Unlike the *Dictionary of American Regional English*, a complementary project that seeks to record all identifiable "dialect" forms, LAMSAS seeks to define the typical, everyday language of Americans as that speech differed among the speakers of its region.

Even before LAMSAS interviews were complete, Hans Kurath published his *Word Geography of the Eastern United States* (1949) on the basis of New England and existing LAMSAS data (for the South, this included Virginia, West Virginia, and North Carolina). This volume described the basic pattern of American English dialects in three largely east-to-west bands, Northern, Midland, and Southern, which largely correlated with 18th-century settlement patterns. These dialect regions were confirmed in Kurath and McDavid's *Pronunciation of English in the Atlantic States* (also based on atlas data). Southern dialects were further subdivided into Upland Southern (also known as South Midland or Upper Southern) and Coastal Southern (also known as Plantation Southern or Lower Southern).

Coastal/Plantation Southern was found across the survey area in places where the land could support plantation agriculture, while Upland Southern/South Midland speech was found in areas that generally could not, whether because the land was mountainous or too poor in quality to support large-scale agriculture. Raven McDavid wrote numerous articles using LAMSAS evidence, for example, showing the complex interrelations between the pronunciation of /r/ and South Carolina society and defending the speech of African Americans against popular stereotypes while demonstrating its status as a dialect of American English.

LAMSAS data is now becoming available online, along with information and data from other surveys of the American Linguistic Atlas Project, at <http://www.lap.uga.edu>. Speakers' responses, in standard spelling (for some items also in Atlas phonetic transcriptions), are recorded in separate data tables for each question. Each response is accompanied by coding to identify the speaker, comments by speakers and field-workers, and information when necessary on the special status of a response (i.e., if it was suggested, heard, collected from an auxiliary informant, or otherwise doubtful or noteworthy). It is possible to browse the responses given for different questions, to search for words and phrases across all of the questions so far entered into the database, and to make maps online of where LAMSAS speakers said particular words and phrases. The size and detail of the LAMSAS digital database has enabled new kinds of linguistic analyses, for example, complex statistical processing and implementation of geographical information systems. Both the paper records and digital presence of LAMSAS and the American Linguistic Atlas Project are maintained at the University of Georgia, under the direction of William A. Kretzschmar Jr.

WILLIAM A. KRETZSCHMAR JR.
University of Georgia

William A. Kretzschmar Jr., *American Speech* (vol. 78, 2003); William A. Kretzschmar Jr., ed., *Dialects in Culture: Essays in General Dialectology by Raven I. McDavid Jr.* (1979); William A. Kretzschmar Jr. and Edgar W. Schneider, *Introduction to Quantitative Analysis of Linguistic Survey Data: An Atlas by the Numbers* (1996); William A. Kretzschmar Jr., Virginia McDavid, Theodore Lerud, and Ellen Johnson, eds., *Handbook of the Linguistic Atlas of the Middle and South Atlantic States* (1993); Hans Kurath, *A Word Geography of the Eastern United States* (1949); Hans Kurath and Raven I. McDavid Jr., *The Pronunciation of English in the Atlantic States* (1961).

Linguists and Linguistics

The formal study of language in the South has flourished for three-quarters of a century, led by linguists, academic institutions, projects, and conferences that have documented, analyzed, and mapped the region's languages. In 1989 a book-length bibliography listed nearly 4,000 published books, articles, reviews, and notes on the history, vocabulary, pronunciation, grammar, place-names, personal names, and other aspects of the region's English; the number of items approaches 5,000 today. This literature reveals the English of the American South to have a multiplicity of varieties unmatched by any other region of the country, a far cry from outside perceptions and portrayals of Southern English as uniform.

Shortly after fieldwork for the *Linguistic Atlas of the United States and Canada* commenced in 1928, the project began work in the South Atlantic states of Virginia, North Carolina, and South Carolina interviewing mainly older, less-educated, and less-traveled speakers in an effort to document thousands of individual usages and to employ these both to map regional variations and to outline dialect areas, especially as these reflected settlement history. Fieldwork for the *Linguistic Atlas of the Middle and South Atlantic States* lasted from 1933 to 1974, under the direction of Hans Kurath, first of Brown University and then the University of Michigan, and later of Raven I. McDavid Jr. of the University of Chicago. The *Linguistic Atlas of the Gulf States*, directed by Lee Pederson of Emory University from 1968 to 1992, encompassed eight states from Florida and Georgia to Texas and completed atlas work in the southern states.

Among the more eminent scholars of language of an earlier generation working at southern institutions and making major contributions to scholarship on the region's language have been James B. McMillan (University of Alabama), Norman Eliason (University of North Carolina), Claude Merton Wise (Louisiana State University), Lee Pederson (Emory University), Archibald Hill (University of Texas), and Juanita Williamson (LeMoyne-Owen College). The most prolific and influential linguist to write on the region's English was the South Carolinian Raven I. McDavid Jr. of the University of Chicago. A number of the contributors to this volume are linguists well known for their more recent research into southern language(s). Until very recently nearly all academics studying the South's English have been natives, but this is increasingly less so today. Indeed one of the earliest to document local variations in African American speech (in the 1830s) was the German Francis Lieber, professor of political economy at South Carolina College (now the University of South Carolina) and founding editor of the *Encyclopedia Americana*. While these and other academics have made major scholarly contributions, it is noteworthy that the region's language has always fascinated a wide spectrum of laypeople, who have engaged for decades in collecting, debating, exploring, and speculating about the meanings and origins of words and other usages, both in print and elsewhere.

The earliest universities to offer doctoral-level study in the field were the University of North Carolina and the University of Alabama, both of which established departments of linguistics in the 1940s. They were followed by the University of Texas, Georgetown University, the University of Florida, the University of South Carolina, the University of Georgia, and Louisiana State University. These and other institutions provide advanced training in the complete range of linguistic specialties, theoretical and applied.

A major advance in the region was the creation in 1969 of the Southeastern Conference on Linguistics (SECOL), whose object is the scholarly study of language in all its aspects. SECOL, which for many years held semiannual meetings (now annual), is currently headquartered at Auburn University and publishes a scholarly journal, *Southern Journal of Linguistics*, through the University of Mississippi. The Linguistic Association of the Southwest, whose territory overlaps with that of SECOL, was founded in 1972 and publishes *Southwest Journal of Linguistics*. Three major conferences in the Language Variety in the South series have gathered a wide array of scholars to present current research at the University of South Carolina (1981), Auburn University (1993), and the University of Alabama (2004).

MICHAEL MONTGOMERY
University of South Carolina

William A. Kretzschmar Jr. et al., *Handbook of the Linguistic Atlas of the Middle and South Atlantic States* (1993); James B. McMillan and Michael B. Montgomery, *Annotated Bibliography of Southern American English* (1989); Michael B. Montgomery and Guy Bailey, eds., *Language Variety in the South: Perspectives in Black and White* (1986); Lee Pederson et al., *Handbook of the Linguistic Atlas of the Gulf States* (1986).

Literary Dialect

Serving as comic device, signifier of social status or regional background, and component of literary realism, the tradition of representing dialectal speech in American literature came into its own in the second quarter of the 19th century. Early works drew on several regionally associated varieties of American English but are most strongly and most often connected to depictions of southern speech, black and white. These representations, beginning with the American humor tradition, often functioned as comic tropes or as attempts at realistic speech. Some of them, however, reinforced social distance between the dialect speakers and the presumed standard-speaking author and audience, as a way of poking fun at or condescending to less-educated, lower-class, rural speakers, particularly African Americans and southerners of all races.

The decline of the southern frontier, already taking place a generation before the Civil War, and the resulting nostalgia for disappearing ways of life led to the "old southwestern" humor tradition, with Tennessee, Georgia, Alabama, Mississippi, Louisiana, Arkansas, and Missouri comprising the "southwest" or southern frontier. With this came the first major wave of American dialect writing. Augustus Baldwin Longstreet's *Georgia Scenes* (1835) was among the first and most influential of this genre. The frontier settings and themes of its sketches were supported by the speech of uneducated frontier characters, with characterizations and descriptions that were well received by audiences and critics. One Longstreet character, Billy Curlew, exemplifies the colorful speech used in these frontier characterizations: "Well dang my buttons, if you an't the very boy my daddy used to tell me about," exclaims Billy upon meeting

the narrator of "The Shooting Match." Other writers soon contributed to the genre, including George Washington Harris of Tennessee, William Tappan Thompson of Georgia, Charles F. M. Nolan of Arkansas, William Gilmore Simms of South Carolina, Henry Clay Lewis and Thomas Bangs Thorpe of Louisiana, and Hardin E. Taliaferro and Johnson Jones Hooper of North Carolina, all best known for works that appeared in the 1840s or 1850s. They represented southern frontier characters speaking a nonstandard dialect, which emphasized these characters' lack of sophistication, social status, and education. For example, Thompson's Major Jones character, who appears in many sketches, often finds himself in urban settings where the country-bred Jones stands out in part because of his speech. In one sketch, he visits the "opery," but he "couldn't hardly make out hed nor tail to it, though [he] listened at 'em with all [his] ears, eyes, mouth, and nose." Jones concludes that "a body what never seed a opery before would swar they was evry one either drunk or crazy as loons, if they was to see 'em in one of ther grand lung-tearin, ear-bustin blowouts." The lack of sophistication was further highlighted by the contrast between the dialectal speech of the characters and the standard speech of the narrator. This popular convention of the prewar humor genre highlighted the social distance between the authors, who were generally educated, upper-class members of their communities—Longstreet was a superior court judge, for example, while Thorpe was a newspaper editor and politician—and the "folk" characters who peopled the stories. That distance was echoed within the audience of the literature, who, unlike many featured characters, had access to literacy and reading materials.

After the Civil War, southern speech continued to be well represented in American dialect writing. "Local color" writers focused on the idiosyncrasies, including speech, of particular regions and their inhabitants, contributing to the development of dialect writing as well as to the rise of realism in American fiction, in part through local color writers' attempts to reproduce realistic scenes and speech. The popularity of writers such as George Washington Cable and Kate Chopin of Louisiana, Mary Murfree of Tennessee, Martha Strudwick Young of Alabama, Ruth McEnery Stuart of Arkansas, and Joel Chandler Harris of Georgia (whose *Uncle Remus* stories were known worldwide) resulted in the increasing use of dialect as a mimetic device (a literary device used to imitate reality). For example, Cable's characters speak a variety of English steeped in Louisiana French Creole, as exemplified in the speech of the title character of his 1883 novella *Madame Delphine*, who asks a friend to care for her daughter should any harm befall Madame Delphine: "I wand you teg kyah my lill' girl."

Toward the end of the 19th century and well into the 20th, the American realistic short story and novel evolved, as did the use of literary dialect, with characters and situations that lent themselves to portrayals of realistic speech. Writers associated with the local color movement and the rise of realism, including Cable, Chopin, Charles W. Chesnutt of North Carolina, and Mark Twain, whose native Missouri was part of the "old Southwest," led the late-century use of dialect to enhance realism in fiction, perhaps best exemplified by Twain's *Adventures of Huckleberry Finn* (1884). In the 20th century the work of Jesse Stuart of Kentucky, Lexie Dean Robertson of Texas, and William Faulkner and Eudora Welty (both of Mississippi), among many others, featured realism in southern literary dialect.

Realism was not the only goal of literary dialect in late 19th- and early 20th-century fiction. Some authors used dialect to mark characters as nonstandard or inferior in relation to narrator, author, or audience. One device, "eye dialect," involved the use of alternative spellings that look different on the page but do not represent alternative pronunciations (for example, *wuz* for *was* or *whut* for *what*), which sometimes contributed to negative characterizations. While some writers have used eye dialect in ways that do not necessarily stigmatize the speaker, the device can also function simply to mark a speaker as "other," particularly as a less-educated or socially or racially inferior person, without providing any real information about that person's dialectal pronunciations.

Both black and white authors have frequently represented the speech of southern blacks. The portrayal by whites sometimes had less to do with realism in characterization than with the reaction of white writers and audiences to changes in the social order during and after Reconstruction. This is seen especially in works of the plantation tradition, an offshoot of the local color movement. In this tradition, which capitalized on white nostalgia for an idealized version of the antebellum South, white authors such as Thomas Nelson Page of Virginia and Thomas Dixon of North Carolina used black dialect primarily to differentiate African Americans from whites in the service of glorifying slavery and rationalizing continuing racial inequality. The "frame narration" in such work re-creates and reinforces the distance between a white speaker who introduces, or frames, the tale and the African American narrator who tells it, as well as the distance between the African American narrator and the predominantly white audience. Almost invariably, tales in the plantation tradition portray former slaves as longing for the old plantation days and characterize them as submissive and childlike. The use of black dialect that was endemic to stories of the plantation tradition and in minstrel shows became in many white minds inextricable from reality and accepted as symptomatic of black inferiority. This powerful and persistent image has resulted in serious critiques of African American literary dialect as depicted by white authors, including Twain, Joel Chandler Harris, Ambrose Gonzales of South Carolina, and Faulkner, with some scholars charging these authors with resorting to stereotype to portray black speech, while others defend the authenticity of their dialectal representations.

Associations with minstrelsy and the plantation tradition led many black writers of the late 19th and early 20th centuries to avoid representations of dialectal speech in their work, with Chesnutt being a notable exception. His "conjure tales" of the 1880s and 1890s mimic the formal conventions of the plantation tradition while subverting its goals and themes by indirectly condemning slavery and criticizing southern racial relations, all in the guise of the plantation tradition. Chesnutt's narrator, Julius McAdoo, a former slave, recounts tragic tales of slavery days in a dialect designed to disguise or otherwise make palatable the subversive nature of the stories to their white audience. For example, when Julius's white employer, John, responds skeptically to a story by Julius highlighting the need for white "masters" to be tolerant and fair and asks if he has made it up, Julius responds, "No, suh, I heared dat tale befo' you er Mis' Annie [John's wife] dere wuz bawn, suh. My mammy tol' me dat tale w'en I wa'n't mo'd'n knee-high ter a hopper-grass." A similar exception was Zora Neale Hurston, who re-created the speech and rich oral traditions of close-knit African American communities in Florida in *Their Eyes Were Watching God* (1937). However, several of Hurston's African American contemporaries, most famously Richard Wright, railed against her representations, arguing that her work perpetuated the stereotypes established and maintained by the plantation tradition and minstrelsy.

The tradition of representing southern speech in literature continues into the 21st century. Contemporary writers of fiction and poetry, including Alice Walker of Georgia, Pat Conroy of South Carolina, Lee Smith of Virginia and North Carolina, Sonia Sanchez of Alabama, Denise Giardina of West Virginia, and James Alan McPherson of Georgia, draw from the rich linguistic traditions of their home regions, while playwrights such as Suzan-Lori Parks of Kentucky and Shay Young-blood of Georgia bring contemporary southern speech to the stage and to new audiences. Literary dialect remains important to students of southern language and culture because the attempts by authors, whether to reproduce realistic speech or to differentiate characters by means of their dialect, offer meaningful information about southern life and the artistic representations of it. It can reveal how older forms of speech and language, as well as popularly held attitudes toward southern varieties of American speech, change over time, as reflected in the literary dialect of texts and in how audiences and critics respond to it.

LISA COHEN MINNICK
Western Michigan University

Cynthia Goldin Bernstein, ed., *The Text and Beyond: Essays in Literary Linguistics* (1994); Walter Blair and Raven I. McDavid Jr., eds., *The Mirth of a Nation: America's Great Dialect Humor* (1983); Hennig Cohen and William B. Dillingham, eds., *Humor of the Old Southwest* (3d ed., 1994); Sumner Ives, in *Tulane Studies in English* (1950); Gavin Jones, *Strange Talk: The Politics of Dialect Literature in Gilded Age America* (1999); Lisa Cohen Minnick, *Dialect and Dichotomy: Literary Representations of African American Speech* (2004); Michael North,

The Dialect of Modernism: Race, Language, and Twentieth-Century Literature (1994).

McDavid, Raven I., Jr.

(1911–1984) LINGUIST.

Raven Ioor McDavid Jr. was born and raised in Greenville, S.C. He graduated from Furman University in 1931 and received his Ph.D. in English in 1935 from Duke University, with a dissertation on the political thought of John Milton. In 1937 he attended a summer linguistic institute at the urging of his commandant at the Citadel military academy, his first teaching position. (The commandant thought that McDavid, because of his heavy southern accent, needed remedial training in elocution.) He was selected as a model informant for a dialectology class at the institute, was intrigued with what he heard there, and proceeded to become the foremost student of southern speech—and of American English more generally—of his time.

McDavid entered the field of linguistics just at the point of its rapid development as a modern academic discipline. After his initial spark and further institute training, he embarked on a survey of South Carolina for Hans Kurath's American Linguistic Atlas Project. World War II intervened, but after working in the Army Language Section during the war, McDavid became Kurath's chief field-worker. During the next 15 years he spent a great deal of his time in the field with informants from Ontario to Florida; he eventually completed more than 500 interviews (averaging six to eight hours each), a record unmatched by any other Ameri-

Raven I. McDavid Jr., a groundbreaking dialectologist who believed that contemporary speech was a product of the cultural circumstances of its speakers, of their social and economic life, and of the historical development of that life (Bill Kretzschmar, photographer, archive of the Linguistic Atlas Project, University of Georgia)

can dialectologist. At the same time McDavid wrote prolifically, including landmark articles, his abridgement of H. L. Mencken's *The American Language* (1963), and, with Hans Kurath, a volume that still serves as a standard reference, *The Pronunciation of English in the Atlantic States* (1961).

His first major academic appointment was at Case Western Reserve University in 1952. In 1957 he moved to the University of Chicago, the institution with which he was most closely identified. In 1964 McDavid succeeded Kurath as editor in chief of the *Linguistic Atlas of the Middle and South Atlantic States*, and in 1975 he accepted responsibility for the *Linguistic Atlas of the North-Central States*. He directed editorial work on both projects until his death in 1984. Recognition came late for McDavid, but in time he won major funding for his atlas projects from the National Endowment for the Humanities and received honorary degrees from Furman, Duke, and the Sorbonne. The *Linguistic Atlas of the Middle and South Atlantic States* began appearing in print in 1980 from the University of Chicago Press. The university's Joseph Regenstein Library produced microfilm copies of the *Basic Materials* volumes from the North-Central and Middle and South Atlantic atlas projects.

McDavid's experience in the field shaped his thought. He always insisted on the importance for linguistics of primary data, of real speech by real people, as opposed to rarefied theory. He believed that contemporary speech was a product of the cultural circumstances of its speakers, of their social and economic life, and of the historical development of that life, and that an accurate understanding of our speechways could have a positive effect on the well-being of all members of society.

These ideas made McDavid a primary force in the development of sociolinguistics. His first landmark article, "Postvocalic /-r/ in South Carolina: A Social Analysis" (1948), shows a mature handling of the complex correlations between South Carolina culture and speakers' pronunciation of /r/ after vowels. Another benchmark, "The Relationship of the Speech of American Negroes to the Speech of Whites" (1951; written with Virginia G. McDavid), provided a corrective to common misapprehensions about the speech of African Americans long before Black English became a popular research area in sociolinguistics. McDavid was in the vanguard of those examining the effects of population movements and urbanization upon our speech, and, in an effort to carry benefits from dialectology to a wide audience, McDavid also promoted applications of his research, especially for the public schools. McDavid studied the speech of all regions of the United States but never forgot his roots in the South: his extensive bibliography is studded with both technical and popular essays such

as "The Position of the Charleston Dialect" (1955), "Changing Patterns of Southern Dialects" (1970), and "Prejudice and Pride: Linguistic Acceptability in South Carolina" (1977; written with Raymond K. O'Cain).

WILLIAM A. KRETZSCHMAR JR.
University of Georgia

Anwar Dil, ed., *Varieties of American English: Essays by Raven I. McDavid Jr.* (1980); William A. Kretzschmar Jr., ed., *Dialects in Culture: Essays in General Dialectology by Raven I. McDavid Jr.* (1979); Raven I. McDavid et al., eds., *Linguistic Atlas of the Middle and South Atlantic States*, fascicles 1 and 2 (1980, 1982); H. L. Mencken, *The American Language*, ed. R. McDavid (1963).

Narrative

Narrative and narration are scholarly terms for storytelling. Oral and written narratives abound in the South in a wide range of types, two primary ones being personal experience stories and oral folk narratives. The latter are stories that are passed down from generation to generation or within a community and can focus on a series of events or practices. Narratives may have a limitless variety of topics: occupation, history, belief, recreation (hunting and fishing stories are commonly told throughout the South), process (how to do something or, rather, how I/we do something), scariest experiences, most important events, holiday practices, cultural practices (birth, death and burial traditions), family stories, and gender-related stories.

In the South, narrative still plays a major cultural role. People share stories for a variety of reasons, but whatever their reasons may be, noted southern literature scholar Fred Hobson has written that southerners have a "radical need to explain and interpret the South. . . . The rage to explain is understandable, even inevitable given the South's traditional place in the nation—the poor, defeated, guilt-ridden member, as C. Vann Woodward has written, of a prosperous, victorious, and successful family. The Southerner, more than other Americans, has felt he *had* something to explain, to justify, to defend, to affirm."

The history and culture of the South make narrative important to its people. Narratives of the South maintain a dedication to the sense of place, and cultural landscape and lifeways are generally included in these stories. From southern literature to the daily gatherings of southerners at work, at the grocery store, and elsewhere, narratives circulate, and we expect, need, and appreciate them.

Hearers of narratives expect a story to flow in a way that is usual for their culture; in the Western literary and storytelling tradition, this means that the story has a beginning, a middle, and an end and progresses in a linear fashion. In 1967 William Labov and Joshua Waletzky identified the elements of personal experience narrative: an abstract, orientation, temporal organization of complicating structure, evaluation, validation, explanation, transformation or resolution, and a coda. The abstract provides a way for a speaker to insert a narrative into a conversation in a seamless fashion and is the transition to a story. It usually comes in the form of "Back when I was growing up . . ." or a similar phrase. The orientation of a narrative provides the necessary background of the story—the "who, what, when, where" information; an example from the well-known Tar Baby story would be "One day atter Brer Rabbit fool 'im wid dat calamus root . . ." The complicating action is set forth through the temporal organization of events—one event follows another. After Brer Rabbit happens upon the Tar Baby, a series of mishaps occurs during which he utters the famous line, "Please don't throw me in the briar patch." A narrative also includes an evaluation of actions or events and a validation of the event that enhances its credibility; this validation may include either praise or blame for the reported events. These aspects generally take the form of an utterance about the truth of the story. The explanation considers the event's causes. The narrative can undergo transformation whereby objective events can be deleted and subjective ones inserted. Finally, the story ends when the speaker or writer provides through a coda a bridge back to the place in the conversation where the abstract began. In the Tar Baby story, these are the final lines: " 'I'll speck you'll take dinner wid me dis time, Brer Rabbit. I done laid in some calamus root, en I ain't gwineter take no skuse' sez Bref Fox, sezzee."

Narratives almost always revolve around a central figure or important event or sometimes both of these. The people depicted in folk narratives of the South become characters as much as people in actual life are, and their actions, while rooted in truth, at times are slightly exaggerated—hence what Labov and Waletzky call the transformation. A single narrator might be down-home or folksy or sophisticated or funny or serious, depending upon his or her audience and intention in sharing the story. Personal experience or oral folk narratives are told for a variety of reasons, whether didactic, informative, entertaining, or cautionary, and are shaped by the teller's intent.

In southern narratives, just as in the literature of the American South, sense of place is an important factor. For example, the southern climate is favorable to reptiles, and nearly every southerner has at least one story about the ways in which the teller deals with a snake or repels snakes. In sharing a story, narrators often give the basic information about where a story takes place, but they also share information about other things. Oral historians examine narratives for historical elements, while folklorists investigate narratives to document a cultural practice or a cycle of stories that might circulate in an area or region. Linguists study narratives as pieces of discourse, looking for common patterns or differences. Linguistic markers such as *umm* and *uh*, repetition of words or phrases, hedges (expressions such as *kind of* and *rather*), pronoun shifts (as from first to second person), deixis (words that indicate location and reference), and linguistic evidentials (phrases such as *they say*, which provide evidence or pseudoevidence for a statement) can help linguists understand how and

why certain narratives function as they do. Further, oral narratives can provide much important phonological and lexical data for linguists. A narrator's choice to use Standard American English or to opt for nonstandard dialect elements also conveys important information about a narrative and a narrator—especially if the narrator intentionally chooses a nonstandard form in order to fit in with the audience.

Different forms of narrative are found among different cultural groups in the South. Shirley Brice Heath studied groups in three small communities in the Piedmont Carolinas: working-class whites in a traditional mill village, working-class blacks, and the middle- and upper-middle-class whites who set the community standards. All three groups had different styles of storytelling and different ways of teaching children the rules of storytelling for their particular culture. Narratives of working-class whites always had a moral, were "truthful," and could be told only with the main character (or a family member) present. Working-class blacks valued verbal skills and embellishments in their stories, which were expected to be entertaining, though they might stretch the truth. Other research reveals that, depending upon the region within the South, African Americans and whites have different views of storytelling and narrating and the truth. In rural northern Louisiana, for instance, older white men, when asked to share a story, sometimes begin with a phrase such as "You don't want to hear these lies now, do you?" or "These are just a bunch of lies." In general, however, the stories that follow are true.

In both urban and rural areas of the South, speakers share narratives daily for many reasons, and what is apparent from the study of these stories is that they are important to both the tellers and the listeners. Stories are shared and circulated: there may be variation in the story as it is told multiple times by the original narrator or others, or there may be stability; yet the core elements in most cases remain the same, with the variations illustrating the importance of personalizing a story.

LISA ABNEY
Northwestern State University

John Baugh, *Black Street Speech: Its History, Structure, and Survival* (1985); Shirley Brice Heath, *Ways with Words* (1982); Fred Hobson, *Tell about the South: The Southern Rage to Explain* (1983); Barbara Johnstone, *Stories, Community, and Place: Narratives from Middle America* (1990); William Labov and Joshua Waletzky, in *Essays on the Verbal and Visual Arts*, ed. J. Helm (1967).

North Carolina Language and Life Project

The North Carolina Language and Life Project (NCLLP) was established at North Carolina State University in 1993 to provide a research and outreach center for languages of the American South. The goals of the NCLLP are (1) to gather information about language varieties in order to understand the nature of language variation and change, (2) to document language varieties in North Carolina and beyond as they reflect the cultural traditions of their speakers, (3) to provide information about language differences to the public and to educational communities, and (4) to use research material for the improvement of educational programs about language and culture. Initial funding came from the William C. Friday Endowment at North Carolina State University, with subsequent external funding from such federal agencies as the National Science Foundation and the National Endowment for the Humanities supporting many of its research and dissemination efforts.

Since the inception of the NCLLP, its staff has conducted more than 1,500 sociolinguistic interviews with residents of North Carolina and other regions connected to language varieties spoken in the Old North State. These interviews cover topics from history and remembrances to current livelihood and lifestyle changes. Archives of NCLLP interviews, as well as copies of those for most southern states recorded by *Dictionary of American Regional English* field-workers from 1965 to 1970, are available at the project office.

NCLLP staff members have engaged in community-based sociolinguistic research projects on many regional, social, and ethnic varieties of Southern English. These include studies of Outer Banks English; African American English in remote communities (in the Appalachian Mountains, the Coastal Plain, and the Outer Banks); the varieties of English spoken in tri-ethnic communities having people of Native American, European American,

(l–r) David Esham of Ocracoke Island in the Outer Banks with sociolinguistic researchers Natalie Schilling-Estes and Walt Wolfram (Walt Wolfram)

and African American ancestry in several areas in North Carolina; and the emerging varieties of English spoken by Latinos in rural and metropolitan areas.

In addition to its sociolinguistic research, the NCLLP engages in public outreach programs related to language diversity. These activities have led to the production of television documentaries that range from a general profile of language variation across North Carolina (*Voices of North Carolina* in 2005) to documentaries on particular dialects, such as the English of the Outer Banks (*The Ocracoke Brogue* in 1996; *The Hoi Toider Brogue* in 2005), the Highlands in western North Carolina (*Mountain Talk* in 2004), and the Lumbee (*Indian by Birth: The Lumbee Dialect* in 2001). The NCLLP has produced compact disc collections of local narratives and trade books on Lumbee English and Outer Banks English. It has constructed exhibits on dialects at local museums and cultural centers in partnership with local communities and created an experimental dialect awareness curriculum for middle school students throughout the state. Staff members routinely give presentations and conduct workshops on language diversity in the public schools and to local civic organizations, particularly preservation and historical societies.

WALT WOLFRAM
North Carolina State University

Mountain Talk, North Carolina Language and Life Project documentary (2004); *Voices of North Carolina*, North Carolina Language and Life Project documentary (2005); Walt Wolfram, Clare Dannenberg, Stanley Knick, and Linda Oxendine, *Fine in the World: Lumbee Language in Time and Place* (2002).

Oratorical Themes

The mythical southern orator is a white male said to possess qualities that distinguish him from speakers heard in other regions. This regional persona speaks emotionally, in ornate symbolic language with expansive gestures and a thunderous voice, about sacred themes. Confederate ex-general John B. Gordon speaking against Reconstruction policies embodied this mythical presence. Exhibiting a "rare physical vigor," this scar-faced veteran dramatically trumpeted "Dixie," "our soil," "sacrifice," "our fathers," and the "spirit of Lee." Prideful public performance became the hallmark of the southern orator, no matter that John C. Calhoun talked "impersonally" with "few gestures" and that Joseph Brown rejected "sickly sentimentality" for unadorned speech about financial prosperity.

Conceived in Old South culture and created in suffering and defeat, this ostentatious persona tried to shield the region from federal encroachment, economic exploitation, social change, and outside criticism, while maintaining traditional thought and policies at home. Even as veterans of the Confederacy died and their children and grandchildren forgot the war, this fictive image of the raging public warrior persisted, providing speakers with stock rhetorical forms of delivery, argument, and language and with topics for their oratory.

A second type of southern oratory consists of the real-life performances of whites, blacks, males, and females of different postures and persuasions from the 1800s on. White males held communicative dominance in the region, developing the authoritative strategies of white superiority, southern manhood, and southern ladyhood. Some women spoke effectively in public, but always in a manner considered suitable to their low social status. More recently, although women had won the vote and a wider voice in society, defeat of the Equal Rights Amendment in the South demonstrated that many persons still preferred traditional social and rhetorical roles for women and men in the region.

Until the 1960s black men and women experienced few safe and meaningful opportunities to speak in the general cultural institutions. As slaves, blacks confronted coercive sanctions with both a defensive posture of accommodation and an aggressive assertion of exploitation. Former slaves from the South did become influential orators in the northern antislavery movement. Drawing on their southern experiences, they offered dramatic testimonials about slavery. Frederick Douglass, a former slave from Maryland, became one of the 19th century's greatest orators. With the physical gifts of a great orator — tall in stature, melodious in voice — Douglass won converts to abolition throughout the North and in Britain. During Reconstruction some blacks spoke a new rhetoric that rejected racist stereotypes and called for equal opportunities. The black church became the most significant forum for black public speaking. Audience interaction with the preacher and the use of biblical language, musical rhythms, and sometimes even chanted sermons—all in a passionate religious setting—characterized speaking in the black church. After the judicial and legislative decisions of the 1950s and 1960s, blacks had increased opportunities for open communication. They marched in streets and talked in churches, on campuses, and over television about constitutional rights, basic freedoms, human dignity, economic opportunities, and cruel discrimination.

Prior to the Civil War, white leaders saw the threat to their slave society and responded with a "rhetoric of desperation." They differed on the nature and future of the Union, and a new sectional awareness emerged. Confronting social and economic change, orators perfected defensive rhetorical forms dealing with the recurring themes of constitutionality, states' rights, regional pride, Old South culture, white superiority, agrarianism, and God. Equally important was the omission from public discourse of the topic of civil rights for blacks.

During Reconstruction most white speakers supported the restoration of white rule in state government. Initially, some leaders refused to participate in Reconstruction politics and thereby legitimize the political role of former slaves. A few whites called for submission to northern conquerors as a means of reclaiming economic security and political control and, as a consequence, were ostracized from public office for a number of years. To resist Reconstruction laws and to restore white authority, the majority of white orators constructed regionally appealing arguments from mythic themes of the Old South, white superiority, threats to southern womanhood, regional pride, states' rights, constitutional claims, violence, economic prosperity, and regional security. Supplementing these stock southern appeals were emotional references to God, sacred principles, and past loyalties, as well as to Civil War experiences, including heroic acts by soldiers, sacrifices of women left behind, regional suffering, and economic ruin.

From 1800 to 1954 whites relied on racial authority, hoping to hold blacks in their rhetorically impotent status as obedient listeners. At the same time, to communicate with northerners, white orators practiced a "rhetoric of accommodation," a stance opposite to their Reconstruction discourse of resistance. This conciliatory posture combined a regional loyalty oath with an emphasis on sectional prosperity. Listeners heard the same orators talk of Old South themes of "southern honor" and New South appeals of "practical progress" for the "new age." Between 1880 and 1946 a number of southern demagogues, noted for their fiery delivery, belligerence, magnetism, assumed infallibility, and monopolizing strategies, governed the region. During the 1940s, when courts ruled that blacks could participate in white primaries, these demagogues and other, less dogmatic whites began a new round of intimidating bribes and threats.

The most dramatic change in southern oratory occurred from 1954 to the 1980s, as the Supreme Court ruled against racially segregated public schools and the Congress passed civil rights legislation. Blacks challenged the dominant rhetorical status of whites. A pluralistic public speaking emerged, with a variety of views being stated on questions of race, economy, political parties, crime, national defense, ecology, industry, and education. Blacks were able publicly to communicate feelings, convictions, and aspirations previously kept private. Blacks and some whites directly confronted the morality, expediency, economy, and legality of racial discrimination. Many blacks abandoned their former accommodating posture and developed more candid and assertive language, strategies, topics, and arguments appropriate for newly won freedom.

Martin Luther King Jr. used oratory as a key weapon in the civil rights movement. He drew from the communication styles of the black folk church and combined biblical themes with national egalitarian ideals. His "I Have a Dream" speech at the 1963 March on Washington echoed Lincoln's language in the Gettysburg Address, portraying the South as the locale of a hoped-for racial reconciliation.

To oppose social changes resulting from legal and judicial decisions, many whites escalated their defensive rhetoric of white superiority, black inferiority, constitutional interpretations, states' rights, God, free enterprise, and racial segregation. Increasingly, however, whites were forced to share the public forum with blacks. As more blacks registered to vote and campaigned for

Dr. Martin Luther King Jr. speaking at a civil rights march on Washington, D.C., August 1963 (U.S. Information Agency, Press and Publication Service [NWDNS-306-SSM-4C (51)13])

office, whites for the first time since Reconstruction were required to communicate directly and respectfully with the new minority audience. Although awkward initially, white orators experimented with rhetoric appropriate to their new, less-powerful status. In the 1970s a few governors actually called for an end to racial discrimination. Some writers have called this new white male speech an "oratory of optimism," but a more accurate characterization would be a public admission of the expediency of social change and shared authority.

CAL M. LOGUE
University of Georgia

Waldo W. Braden, ed., *Oratory in the New South* (1979), *Oratory in the Old South, 1828–1860* (1970), *Southern Speech Journal* (vol. 29, 1964); Kevin E. Kearney, *South-*

ern Speech Journal (vol. 31, 1966); Cal M.
Logue, *Quarterly Journal of Speech* (vol. 67,
1981); Cal M. Logue and Howard Dorgan,
eds., *The Oratory of Southern Demagogues*
(1981); John D. Saxon, *Southern Speech
Communication Journal* (vol. 40, 1975).

Perceptions of Southern English

The South is the touchstone for the
perception of differences in American
English. When surveyed, respondents
from all over the United States identify
it as the region with the most distinctive
speech. Studies confirm the existence
of a stereotype of a distinctive southern
speech, but is southern speech itself
readily identifiable? Research shows
that Americans can indeed identify
southern speech as unique and that
they can identify it on pronunciation alone.

The linguistic salience of the South
is not purely geographical, however.
Map 7 shows that when southeastern
Michigan respondents rated the 50
states, New York City, and Washington,
D.C., on a 10-point scale for language
correctness, the states in the South were
rated lowest, although New York City
and New Jersey were rated low as well.

These findings suggest that an overwhelming linguistic concern among
Americans is the distribution of good
English and bad English. The most
important locus of bad English is the
South. Good English is the white-bread
stuff of the mythical national news-
caster variety, which is supposed to
have its origins and provenance somewhere in the Midwest. As Map 7 shows,
Michiganders clearly believe they speak
this variety.

One cannot, however, paint a completely negative picture of southern
English. To do so would ignore one-
half of the findings uncovered by years
of scholarly research on language attitudes. Typically when respondents are
asked how they feel about language,
they exploit two dimensions. The first
is the one discussed above: language is
correct or incorrect, and speech either
reflects the practices of the dominant
culture and stands for conservative,
mainstream educational norms or it
does not. Many nonsoutherners believe
they are speakers of that norm and that
southerners are not.

Not all speakers, however, place exclusive value on such a standard. Many,
perhaps especially speakers of varieties
that are denigrated and who experience
prejudice themselves in nonlinguistic
ways as well, value nonstandard, small-
group, and local varieties of language
for the solidarity and identity they
provide. Respondents have also been
asked, therefore, to rate regions for
language pleasantness as well as correctness. Map 8 shows the results of such
an investigation of university-enrolled
southern respondents, primarily from
Alabama. These southerners appear to
feel as strongly about language pleasantness (and believe that they have it)
as Michiganders do about language
correctness, but the ranking of southern speech as pleasant does not result
exclusively from in-group solidarity;
even many nonsoutherners have a tendency to rate southern speech highly
for pleasantness. For example, Michigan residents rate southerners as more
casual, friendlier, more down-to-earth,

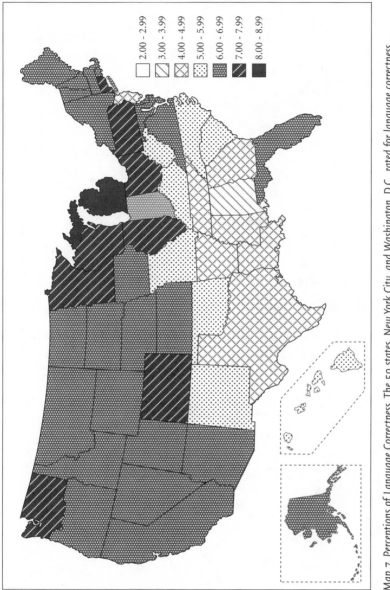

2.00 - 2.99
3.00 - 3.99
4.00 - 4.99
5.00 - 5.99
6.00 - 6.99
7.00 - 7.99
8.00 - 8.99

Map 7. Perceptions of Language Correctness. The 50 states, New York City, and Washington, D.C., rated for language correctness (1 = least correct, 10 = most correct) by southeastern Michigan respondents (results are shaded by means score ranges)

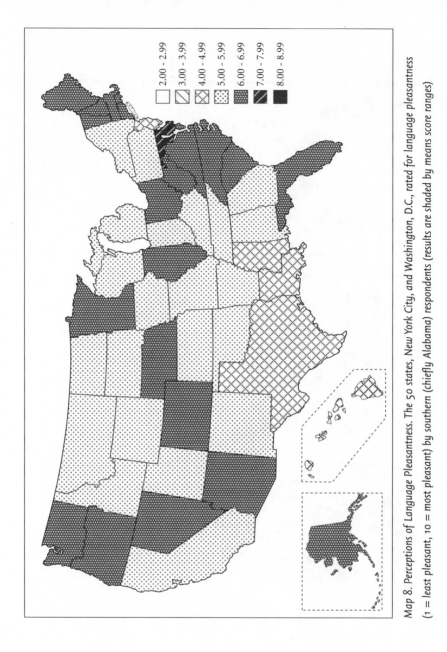

Map 8. Perceptions of Language Pleasantness. The 50 states, New York City, and Washington, D.C., rated for language pleasantness
(1 = least pleasant, 10 = most pleasant) by southern (chiefly Alabama) respondents (results are shaded by means score ranges)

2.00 - 2.99
3.00 - 3.99
4.00 - 4.99
5.00 - 5.99
6.00 - 6.99
7.00 - 7.99
8.00 - 8.99

and more polite than they rate themselves.

Since Michiganders obviously are not dissatisfied with the local Michigan speech as a variety of correct English, what is the source of their preference for southern varieties in the pleasantness dimension? Young Michiganders assign a kind of prestige to southern speech, which they imagine has more value than their own for casual interaction. Thus, one American linguistic option appears to be to use a popularly identified Standard English in settings that require it and to prefer varieties that are perceived as nonstandard in settings that require casual use. Southern English appears to function very well for the latter.

The studies outlined above all focus on southern speech as an abstract or global fact, but studies of attitudes toward southern speech have also looked at specific features. At the grammatical level, the stigmatized construction *I done told him* was strongly associated by Texans with the South, along with other indicators of nonstandardness. Raters said it would more likely be used by a person with less than a high school education and associated it with male, rural, and working-class speakers. Raters also said it would be preferred by younger and older rather than middle-aged speakers.

Pronunciation features of Southern English have been even more thoroughly investigated. One study looked at the following:

d for *z* before negative contractions (*isn't* pronounced as *idn't*)

i for *e* before *m* and *n* (*ten* pronounced as *tin*)
the presence of a *y*-glide before *oo* (*news* pronounced as *nyuz*)
a for *i* before *ng* (*thing* pronounced to rhyme with *rang*)
the loss of the diphthong so that *time* sounds like *Tom*
the "drawling" or lengthening of vowels before *r*.

For language correctness, a southern voice was rated significantly lower than a northern one for every pronunciation feature above, but most dramatically for *z* replacing *d*, and *a* replacing *i* before *ng*. This study makes it clear that not all authentic southern features have equal value for the perceiver. In another study, several southern vowels were rated as less educated than northern equivalents.

bait pronounced as *bite*
beet pronounced as *bait*
the vowels of *boat* and *good* pronounced further forward in the mouth
bet pronounced as *bait*
bit pronounced as *beet*

Studies of the perception of southern speech have provided new methodologies for linguists, particularly methodologies that focus on the influence of single linguistic features. Many of these features can be studied within the area of phonetics, making full use of newer acoustic and synthesizing techniques and technologies.

In conclusion, southern speech is the regional variety perceived as most distinct in the United States, and linguistic prejudice seems to be the prime reason for that evaluation. On the other hand, analyses of perceptions have shown that, even for northern speakers, southern speech has a strong, general affective appeal or "pleasantness" in addition to its strong solidarity appeal for southerners themselves.

DENNIS PRESTON
Michigan State University

Nancy Niedzielski and Dennis R. Preston, *Folk Linguistics* (1999); Dennis R. Preston, in *Focus on the USA*, ed. E. Schneider (1996), in *Language Variety in the South Revisited*, ed. Cynthia Bernstein, Thomas Nunnally, and Robin Sabino (1997); Dennis R. Preston, ed., *Handbook of Perceptual Dialectology*, vols. 1 and 2 (1999, 2002).

Personal Names

Personal names document the settlement history of the South. Surnames and given names of British and Irish colonists (the most numerous), the Spanish, the French, Germans, Sephardic Jews, and others are linked to the towns, counties, and other places they founded. But personal names do much more than substantiate historical facts; they convey a southern ethos.

Commemorative given names have long been popular in the South. Surnames of the first families of the South, such as Byrd, Carroll, Clay, Jefferson, Pinckney, Spencer, Taylor, Warner, and Washington, are bestowed on yeoman and patrician, men and women alike, and are numerous in any southern telephone directory. In particular, the first and third presidents have had great influence on names. George Washington Cable was the novelist of the Louisiana

Creoles; George Washington Harris, a journalist and humorist of east Tennessee; and George Washington Carver, an accomplished black botanist and inventor. (*Washington* was also adopted as a surname by many African Americans after emancipation.) Jefferson Davis, the first president of the Confederate States of America, was named for the famous president from Virginia, as was Thomas Jefferson Wertenbacker, the historian.

Southern naming practice has consistently honored military heroes. Andrew Jackson Hamilton was a governor of Texas and Andrew Jackson Montague a governor of Virginia. Francis Marion Cockrell, a Confederate general and Missouri governor, pays tribute to the Swamp Fox. Robert E. Lee's name has been perpetuated by many southern lads; Robert E. Lee Prewitt, the protagonist of James Jones's *From Here to Eternity*, possessed the heroism if not the gallantry of his namesake. French and Latin American heroes are also honored: Florida governor Napoleon Bonaparte Broward and the distinguished Confederate hero Simon Bolivar Buckner illustrate such christening. Some southern magnificoes have been remembered ironically. The shiftless and nocturnal Gowrie Twins, Bilbo and Vardaman, in Faulkner's *Intruder in the Dust*, satirize the two Mississippi politicians for whom the boys are named.

The most common type of commemorative naming, however, does not invoke the heroic or illustrious but passes on a family name, like an heirloom, from one generation to another. Often a surname is given as a first or middle name, for example, Carson McCullers, Harper Lee, Reese Witherspoon, Davis Smith, Bobby Brown Travis, or James Strom Thurmond, the Dixiecrat-turned-Republican, who was called by his mother's maiden name.

In naming, as in southern architecture, the classics have been influential. Many southerners have borne a first or middle name of Greco-Roman origin, Augustus being among the most popular. This practice reveals the South's respect for antiquity as well as its hope that Herculean feats would be replicated in Dixie. Without rival, onomastically speaking, was Lucius Quintus Cincinnatus Lamar (born in Georgia, later a senator from Mississippi), the South's "Redeemer Politician" and later Supreme Court justice. Although diminishing in recent decades, this naming custom flourished for centuries. Cadmus Marcellus Wilcox distinguished himself on the battlefields of Virginia; Civil War heroine Phoebe Pember was from Charleston; Cassius Marcellus Clay (after whom the pugilist more popularly known as Muhammad Ali was named) was a famous Kentucky abolitionist; Augustus Baldwin Longstreet portrayed the South movingly in fiction and was an educator. Virginius Dabney was an award-winning journalist; Cleanth Brooks, a highly respected literary critic; and Thomas Dionysius Clark, an eminent historian. Virgil H. Goode represents Virginia's 5th Congressional District. In southern literature, characters with classical names perpetuate a noble tradition (Atticus Finch in Harper Lee's *To Kill a Mockingbird*) or suggest mythic models (Phoenix Jackson in Eudora Welty's "A Worn Path"). In the popular arts, Homer and his biblically christened partner Jethro offered bardic entertainment, mountain style.

Although long known as the Bible Belt, the South does not surpass the North in using biblical first names, but the practice remains strong. Such names have been borne by senators from North Carolina (Jesse Helms), Alabama (Jeremiah Denton), Tennessee (James Sasser), and Georgia (Rebecca Latimer Felton) and by Maryland congressman Elijah E. Cummings. Some southerners have been named for religious figures. Texas outlaw John Wesley Hardin, whose father was a circuit-riding Methodist preacher, carried the name of the early leader of that denomination. Martin Luther King Sr. and his more famous son, the civil rights leader, were named for the Protestant reformer, and many other young southerners have later carried King's first name.

If southern names reflect the grandeur and formality of tradition, they also embody the folksy congeniality cherished by the region, a practice that may be waning because of the homogenization of culture in the United States. More than in other parts of the nation, names in the South are diminutives, ending in -*y* or -*ie*, making them appear friendlier, less pretentious. The Carter brothers Jimmy and Billy typified in name and character an affection for popularism. Other similarly named southern dignitaries in the U.S. House of Representatives now and in years past include Ronnie Flippo (Alabama); Andy Ireland and Ginny Brown-Waite (Florida); Larry Hopkins (Kentucky); Lindy Boggs, Billy Tauzin, Jerry Huckaby, Bobby Jindal, Charlie Melancon, and Cathy Long (Louisiana); and Jamie Whitten and Bennie Thompson (Mississippi). Several southern congressmen court votes with chummy, monosyllabic first names: Zach Wamp (Tennessee), Mac Thornberry (Texas), and Ric Keller (Florida). Southern governors also sport short, memorable first names: Jeb Bush (Florida), Sonny Perdue (Georgia), Ernie Fletcher (Kentucky), and Rick Perry (Texas). Some in America would recognize the name of William Franklin Graham, although Billy Graham is much more of a household name. Nor are these folksy names considered inappropriate for someone of status. Diminutives such as Bubba (which approximates a young southerner's pronunciation of *brother*), Buddy, Lonnie, Sissy, Sonny, and Stoney are recorded legal given names.

Many southerners have a double given name, with one or both parts often a diminutive or shortened form. Such names suggest the southern ideals of youthful vigor and inviting informality. Among males, characteristic doublets are Billy Bob, Danny Lee, Eddie Ray, and Larry Gene. For belles, popular names are Bonnie Jean, Connie Ann, Ellie Mae (Jed Clampett's daughter in *The Beverly Hillbillies*), Kelly Lynn, Kerry Leigh, Suzy Kay, or Tammy Jo. A subpattern for females combines a male and a female name— Billy Sue, George Jean, Johnnie Mae,

Jimmy Carter (Thomas J. O'Halloran, photographer, Library of Congress [LC-U9-33286-19], Washington, D.C.)

Ronnie Gayle, Tara Lyn, Tommy Ruth, or Willie Jean.

An extreme example of unpretentious names is the use of initials in place of first names in the South. Sometimes these initials stand for first names (J. R. of *Dallas* fame), but the initials are also given as legal first names—B. J., B. W., J. T., and T. W. Initial names discomfit the U.S. government, especially the military, which adds *only* after such initial first names for easier processing of recruits.

Perhaps more than any other section of the country, the South has been distinguished by picturesque names, including nicknames, especially for men. There are the ubiquitous southern Bubbas, Busters, Goobers, Macks, Pudgies, Slicks, and Zacks. In one Tennessee Williams play alone (*Cat on a Hot Tin Roof*) we encounter Gooper, Big Mama, Big Daddy, and Sookey. From politics come William "Fishbait" Miller, the longtime doorkeeper of the U.S. House of Representatives; Goat Harris, an official in Durham, N.C.; Foxy Robinson, the water commissioner of Laurel, Miss.; Shag Pyron, a former Mississippi football star and highway commissioner; and Scooter Borgman, who ran for city council in Hattiesburg. The world of sports, too, glitters with southern luminaries having unusual nicknames: Bear Bryant, Dizzy Dean, Mudcat Grant, Catfish Hunter, Bum Phillips, Vinegar Bend Mizell, and Oil Can Boyd. God bless them all.

PHILIP C. KOLIN
University of Southern Mississippi

John Algeo and Adele Algeo, *Names* (vol. 31, 1983); Timothy C. Frazer, *Midwestern Folklore* (vol. 21, 1995); Kelsie B. Harder, *Bucknell Review* (vol. 8, 1959); Philip C. Kolin, *Names* (vol. 25, 1977); Forrest McDonald and Ellen Shapiro McDonald, *William and Mary Quarterly* (ser. 3, vol. 37, 1980); Grady McWhiney and Forrest McDonald, *Names* (vol. 31, 1983); Pauline C. Pharr, *American Speech* (vol. 68, 1993); Thomas Pyles, *Names* (vol. 7, 1959).

Place-Names

Place-names label the landscape, identifying both natural and man-made features. They are common to all cultures, and although the kinds of names may vary, nearly all consist of two parts, a generic and a specific. For ex-

ample, the generic *River* identifies the kind of feature, and the specific *Mississippi* tells us what this particular river is called. Both the generic and the specific depend on the namer's linguistic experience, and their order usually follows the grammatical pattern of the language (or the language from which the name is translated). In English, the specific usually precedes the generic, just as an adjective precedes the noun it modifies, while in French and Spanish, for example, the pattern is reversed. Names with the generic before the specific, such as *Lake Pontchartrain* or *Rio Grande*, show French and Spanish grammatical patterns, respectively. In many cases, however, the generic may precede the specific either in an attempt to make the name sound more elegant or because the combination seems to sound better in that order (*Lake Murray*, *Mount Mitchell*). Further, people in one part of the country, though they may speak the same language, often use different standards for choosing generics, especially for streams. In New England, *brook* is used for most small streams, while most of the rest of the country favors *creek*. In Tennessee, Kentucky, and western North Carolina, however, more than half of the small streams are *branches*. West Virginia has a large number of streams called *runs*, and most small streams in Louisiana are called *bayous*. Another regional feature name is *cove*, used for a mountain valley. This generic, though it appears sporadically in the West, is mostly concentrated in the Appalachian Mountains of North Carolina, Tennessee, and Alabama. *Key*, for a small island, is limited almost entirely to Florida.

The place-names of the South reflect the speech, history, observations, and values of the people who have lived there. As artifacts of language that give the landscape its linguistic identity, they are a result of the significant contributions of Spanish, French, English, and various indigenous languages.

Names from indigenous languages are scattered across the entire region, and Spanish names are common in Florida and Texas, reflecting the importance of Spain in the early colonization of the Americas and the continuing influence of Hispanic culture in the Southwest. The Gulf Coast, especially Louisiana and the lower Mississippi Valley, were occupied by French speakers in the early naming days, resulting in a strong legacy of names from that language. Most states in the South are in areas that have been dominated by English speakers, and the history of settlement is clearly seen in naming patterns across the region, from the British orientation of the colonial period through the period of nation building that followed the Revolutionary War to the Civil War era and beyond.

Most place-names either grow out of descriptions of places or are chosen for commemorative reasons, as to honor individuals or other places. Descriptive names, usually of natural features, are functions of observation—what a feature may look like, what animals or plants may be associated with it, or what human activities may have taken place nearby. The other kind of name often reflects the values of the namers. The South has numerous names of both sorts.

Names of indigenous origin in the South come from many different languages and language families, especially Muskogean (Creek, Choctaw, Chickasaw, etc.), Iroquoian (Cherokee, Tuscarora, etc.), Siouan (Biloxi), and Caddoan (Caddo). These names appear mostly on rivers: beyond the largest of these (*Mississippi*, *Ohio*, and *Tennessee*), many other rivers in all of the states of the South have names traceable to indigenous languages: *Atchafalaya*, *Chattahoochee*, *Kanawha*, *Kentucky*, *Ouachita*, *Pecos*, *Potomac*, *Roanoke*, *Santee*, *Tallahatchie*, and *Tombigbee*, to name just a few.

Names of the states in the South reflect the historical development of the various regions. The earliest region to be named was Florida, which shows the Spanish pattern of naming features for the day of discovery. On Easter Sunday 1513, Ponce de León spotted a land covered with abundant flowering groves and called it *Pasqua de Flores* 'Easter flowering.' The other South Atlantic states trace their names to the British royal family. Virginia (named in 1584) is a Latin form honoring Queen Elizabeth I, the "Virgin Queen." The colony of Carolina (originally spelled *Carolana*) received its name in 1629 in honor of King Charles I, although it was not settled until 1670 under Charles II. The colony was officially divided into North and South in 1735. Georgia, founded as a colony in 1732, honors King George II. The use of feminine Latinate forms, ending in -*a*, seemed appropriate for place-names and was extended throughout the nation (*Louisiana*, from *Louisiane*, honoring the French King Louis XIV in 1681; *Columbia*, from *Columbus*: the city in South Carolina in 1786, the District of Columbia in 1791, the river in the Northwest in 1792).

Most other states in the South are named for major rivers within or along their boundaries. These include Alabama, Arkansas, Kentucky, Mississippi, and Tennessee. Since West Virginia, which separated from Virginia during the Civil War, also has a royal name, the only southern state (other than Florida) that is neither a descriptive nor a commemorative name is Texas, whose name comes from *Tejas*, a Spanish rendering of a Caddo word meaning "friends." *Tejas* appears as a name for the region as early as 1541 and *Texas* by 1683.

Values and concerns of local people are seen more clearly in county names. Many counties in states settled by British subjects before the American Revolution show British dominion, loyalty toward monarchs, or nostalgia for British counties and towns, and they remain today. In the Carolinas are counties recognizing the proprietary noblemen who were granted a charter for the original colony: *Albemarle, Berkeley, Carteret, Clarendon, Colleton*, and *Craven*. In Virginia and South Carolina are counties honoring the royal family: *King* and *Queen, Prince Edward, Prince George, Prince William, Georgetown*, and *Williamsburg*. In Virginia and the Carolinas names of towns, counties, or noblemen of Britain are echoed: *Amherst, Bath, Beaufort* (for Lord Beaufort, an English nobleman), *Bedford, Buckingham, Camden, Chester, Chesterfield, Cumberland, Dorchester, Isle of Wight, Lancaster, New Kent, Northampton, Northumberland, Richmond, Scotland, Southampton, Stafford, Surry, Sussex, Westmoreland*, and *York*.

In the late 18th and early 19th centuries the South expanded westward, and the political necessity of new counties required a large number of names. Many came from prominent Revolutionary War and early Federalist figures. George Washington, in addition to giving his name to the new capital city, is recognized in the names of 10 southern counties, matched by the number named *Marion* (for Francis Marion, "The Swamp Fox") and followed closely by *Franklin* and *Madison*, both with nine. *Jefferson* and *Lafayette* (usually as *Fayette*) have eight each. Most of these names are also common in those parts of the Midwest settled in the early 19th century.

By the time of the Civil War most counties throughout the South were already organized and named, but after the war many divided and reorganized and took names to commemorate southern heroes of the war and the years leading up to it. Nine southern states have counties named *Lee*, for example. In every southern state, more counties are named for local or state political figures than for national ones. This is not surprising, since state legislatures usually have naming rights to counties. Many other counties bear names of local historical importance, such as indigenous groups or natural features. Examples are *Tuscaloosa*

(Ala.), *Okeechobee* (Fla.), *Chattahoochee* (Ga.), *Prairie* (Ark.), *Rockcastle* (Ky.), *Point Coupee Parish* (La.), *Chickasaw* (Miss.), *Transylvania* (N.C.), *Cherokee* (S.C. and N.C.), *Lake* (Tenn.), *Palo Pinto* (Tex.), *Alleghany* (Va.), and *Mineral* (W.Va.).

The names of towns and cities have origins even more diverse than those of counties. To take as examples the names of the state capitals, we see cities named for physical features (*Little Rock, Baton Rouge* — apparently from a red post used as a boundary marker), a Native American place (*Tallahassee*), a town in England (*Richmond*), a rail company (*Atlanta*, terminus of Western and Atlantic Railroad), local settlers (*Frankfort, Austin, Charleston*), Revolutionary War generals (*Montgomery, Nashville*), and near-legendary figures of American history (*Jackson, Raleigh, Columbia,* and of course, *Washington*, D.C.).

The South has a rich variety of names for both natural and cultural features, reflecting its nearly five centuries of European exploration and settlement and the centuries of habitation of indigenous peoples.

THOMAS J. GASQUE
University of South Dakota

William Bright, *Native American Place-Names* (2004); Virginia Foscue, *Place Names in Alabama* (1989); Kenneth Krakow, *Georgia Place Names* (3d ed., 1999); Allen Morris, *Florida Place Names* (1995); Margaret S. Powell and Stephen D. Powell, *Names* (vol. 38, 1990); Robert Rennick, *Kentucky Place Names* (1984); Richard B. Sealock, Margaret M. Sealock, and Margaret S. Powell, *Bibliography of Place-Name Literature: United States and Canada* (3d ed., 1982); George R. Stewart, *Names on the Land* (1945), *American Place-Names* (1970); U.S. Board on Geographic Names, Geographic Names Information System, Reston, Va.: Geological Survey, <http://geonames.usgs.gov/>.

Politeness

A common observation about southerners of all backgrounds is that they are "polite." The South is known for its cultivation of traditional manners. The ethos of any group or region can be seen as having a particular balance of linguistic strategies designed to meet two basic, potentially conflicting needs of individuals when interacting: on one hand, to be recognized as sharing common ground with the group ("positive politeness") and, on the other, to be free from imposition and to preserve individual autonomy ("negative politeness"). Positive politeness, sometimes referred to as solidarity politeness, is based on how individuals approach one another and highlights a lack of social distance; negative politeness is based on avoidance and serves to maintain or increase social distance. The linguistic dimensions of "southern courtesy" offer an opportunity to explore how the southern ethos combines expectations for both types of politeness in civil interaction. To highlight southern linguistic dimensions of politeness, it is useful to consider the potential for miscommunication with nonsouthern Americans who speak "the same language" but who operate within a different ethos having different expectations for how that language is appropriate to use in interaction.

Perhaps the most distinctive politeness strategy in the South, compared with the rest of the United States, is the greater use of the address terms *Ma'am* and *Sir* with the intent to show respect. This strategy is a classic form of negative politeness in which social hierarchy is linguistically signaled. A clear indication of this norm is that within the last decade legislation was proposed in Alabama and actually passed in Louisiana that mandated the use of these terms by elementary school students to their teachers. They are used not only in addressing someone as part of a question or request (as "May I help you, Sir?" or "Ma'am, would you mind passing me the salt?") but also elsewhere, especially added to the response to a yes/no question (as "Yes, sir" or "No, ma'am"). A southerner can take failure to soften the bald *yes* or *no* with the address term as a serious breach of politeness or etiquette.

In the usage of *Ma'am* and *Sir* there is significant potential for miscommunication. It is not that nonsoutherners are not familiar with these terms and do not use them, but that they use them in much more limited contexts. Nonsoutherners associate them with addressing a person of an older generation or with marking a social hierarchy; for example, in a service encounter the server will ask, "May I help you, Sir?" and in the well-defined hierarchy of the military these address terms are strictly enforced. Within the context of an ideologically democratic American society, however, these terms have for nonsouthern speakers acquired the uncomfortable connotation of explicit social ranking, of "knowing one's place," a type of ranking nonsoutherners prefer to avoid. The problem arises when the nonsoutherner does not realize that the southerner is trying simply to be "polite" without necessarily intending to signal hierarchy, and the southerner does not realize that the nonsoutherner can be "polite" within a nonsouthern framework without using the terms, that is, with a stronger tilt toward positive politeness strategies.

Whereas *Ma'am* and *Sir* are gendered address terms, many southerners also have a set of honorific titles specifically for women. There is a long-standing tradition in the South to use *Miss* with a given name and *Miz* with a surname, regardless of marital status. This variation is found in both direct address and third-person reference. Thus, Jimmy Carter's mother was known as both "Miss Lillian" and "Miz Carter." The use of these forms is complex, socially graded, and highly contextualized, as is the case with other markers, and they are employed mainly for a woman a generation older than the speaker. While they may be most often used for an older woman, there is evidence that young student teachers are addressed by their pupils as "Miss Laura," "Miss Susan," and so forth. This set of two honorific titles for women, interestingly without a comparable set for men (although *Mister* can be used with either a given or a surname, especially to an older man), is another example of negative politeness, here used to show respect. The potential for misunderstanding across subcultures is similar to that discussed in the case of

Ma'am and *Sir* usage, involving shared terms applied in different contexts with different interpretations. Non-southerners view *Miss* as a relatively old-fashioned honorific that signals unmarried status. They interpret *Miz* as the identical-sounding *Ms.*, which, since the women's movement and the publication of *Ms.* magazine, has come to indicate something like "a woman who doesn't want to indicate her marital status," a likely feminist. Ironically, the traditional southern *Miz* accomplishes the same purpose but without the same ideological baggage.

On the other hand, a form of southern positive politeness is reflected in the use, typically by women, of conventionalized terms of endearment, such as *honey, sugar, sweetie,* and so forth. These are much more common in the South than elsewhere between people who are not familiarly acquainted; they may even be used with people who are strangers in the context of service encounters, as by a cashier to a customer. The dimension of positive politeness that is invoked here is the reduction of social distance, in which the speaker claims the right to use a term of endearment with a stranger, in an interactional bid to claim conventional closeness. In this case, such usage does not necessarily lead to misunderstanding, unless a man being addressed in this way misreads the intent of the female speaker. Instead, the effect would normally be to bring the subcultural difference in discourse patterns into the addressee's awareness, potentially triggering a positive or negative judgmental response.

A slightly different dimension of politeness is the degree to which one communicates in a "direct" fashion. Southerners are notoriously indirect, a classic negative politeness strategy. Such indirectness can appear in the overall structure of interaction, as in the length of time spent before getting to the main business of a conversation. A negative politeness strategy is probably most clearly demonstrated in the form of "indirect speech acts." In these interactional moves the force of a request or order is softened, often through its grammatical formulation as a question. "Would it be too much trouble for you to carry me up the road a mile or so?" is an indirect form of the imperative "Give me a ride to the store." Such strategies conventionally allow the addressee more freedom to refuse the imposition. Southern English even has a very common and distinctive set of grammatical constructions called "double modals" (such as *might could*) that combines and represents possibility and probability in a more indirect way than in nonsouthern formal English, which allows only one modal auxiliary before a verb. The past tense of the verb creates metaphorical distance (in the same way that a questioner uses a past-tense verb to hedge a direct request by saying, "I was wondering . . ." rather than "I want to know . . ."). Southern English allows the distance created by the past tense to be doubled in *might could.* Thus while the nonsoutherner has the sole option of saying, "I might be able to go," the southerner can also say, "I might could go." The speaker uses the grammatical potential of southern English to protect his or her own autonomy from a commitment to future action. Here and elsewhere a greater degree of indirectness than expected is a prime source of misunderstanding between people who speak the same language. On the part of the nonsoutherner, the communicative intent of a request or command may be missed, the strength of a commitment to action may be misjudged, and an interaction may be assessed as somehow vague or inscrutable. The southerner may experience the more direct style of the nonsoutherner as pushy and rude.

Finally, an important positive politeness dimension of southern courtesy is the elaborate ritual of social conversations. Such interactions have different phases, from the initial greeting, through the main body of the conversation, and to the parting. Important positive politeness strategies characterize the conversation: noticing and attending to the interlocutor ("Is that a new dress?"), exaggerating interest and sympathy ("I love your hair"), asserting knowledge of the interlocutor ("How's your mama doin'?"), providing empathy and cooperation ("I know just how you feel"), and so on. Particularly among women, the greeting and leave-taking phases of an interaction can be much more complex and extended than in other parts of the United States. Such elaboration is often a manifestation of a greater cultural value attached to the verbal dimension of sociability. The potential for discomfort and misunderstanding across subcultures is substantial, as the impatient nonsoutherner who tries to cut these phases short risks being labeled

"rude." Such interaction is perceived as excessive by someone whose ethos does not require such elaboration to signal and maintain solidarity politeness.

Southern politeness, to the extent that it conforms to traditional manners of the sort found in etiquette books, is essentially a form of negative politeness that highlights social distance. This ethos is reflected in the frequent use of *Ma'am* and *Sir* as address terms, in distinctive honorifics for women, and in patterns of indirectness in interaction. On the other hand, positive politeness strategies, in which social distance is reduced as the individual is affirmed as part of the group, is found in the use of certain terms of endearment in service encounters and in the elaborated greetings and leave-takings of sociable conversation. Cultural practices are always changing, however, and some of the deference politeness practices, such as honorific titles for women, appear to be falling away. It is also important to keep in mind that every conversation is a delicate negotiation in which people shift strategies, within a broader ethos, as they attempt to achieve their interactional goals.

CATHERINE EVANS DAVIES
University of Alabama

Penelope Brown and Stephen Levinson, *Politeness: Some Universals in Language Usage* (1987); Marvin K. L. Ching, in *Methods in Dialectology*, ed. Alan R. Thomas (1988); Catherine E. Davies, in *Language Variety in the South Revisited*, ed. Cynthia Bernstein, Thomas Nunnally, and Robin Sabino (1997); Barbara Johnstone, in *English in the Southern United States*, ed. Stephen J. Nagle and Sara L. Sanders

(2003), in *The Text and Beyond: Essays in Literary Linguistics*, ed. Cynthia Goldin Bernstein (1994); Margaret Mishoe and Michael Montgomery, *American Speech* (vol. 69, 1994); Deborah Tannen, *Conversational Style: Analyzing Talk among Friends* (2005).

Preaching Style, Black

During the Second Great Awakening of the early 1800s and for years after, many itinerant preachers found that their listeners for religious services often numbered in the thousands. To accommodate such large congregations, the camp meeting was institutionalized. These large-scale worship services were especially successful in the border states of Kentucky and Tennessee, where many clergymen from the North traveled. This new form of divine worship, sometimes attracting as many as 20,000 or more at events such as the one held at Cane Ridge, Ky., included black as well as white worshipers. Although this form of worship never caught on in the Northeast, it was highly successful in the South and Southwest. Many black ministers were inspired to preach at such gatherings, though at first only to other blacks, and a characteristic oral style of delivery emerged from this experience.

These sermons were characterized by the preacher's chanting the Word of God rather than delivering it conventionally. The sermon began traditionally enough with a statement of the day's text and its application to contemporary morals. Then, as the preacher got further into the day's message, he began to chant his lines; the metrics and time intervals of the lines became more and more regular and consistent; and as he became further imbued with the Holy Spirit, the preacher's delivery slid into song. The sermons were—and still are—characterized by an increase in emotional and spiritual intensity, expressed by the gradual transition from conventional pulpit oratorical style, through chanting, to highly emotional singing. Many black folk preachers are excellent singers and have had several years' experience with church choirs, if not on the professional stage. Quite a number have been choirmasters, and nearly all these men have from an early age attended church services in which music played a major role. A musical sense has thus been acquired, and its rhythms, intonations, timbres, and verbal phrasing are inextricable parts of the tradition. Foreign visitors to black church services in the early 19th century remarked not only on the minister's chanting but on the congregation's equally emotional responses. Such witnesses were appalled by the unbridled emotionalism of such services.

The African heritage of black preachers influenced the style of their performances and of the congregations' responses. The African folksong tradition of call-and-response was carried over; not only was the preacher directly in this tradition, but in holy services the congregants felt free to call out to the preacher, or to the other congregants, as the Spirit moved them. The service became, and still is, however, something more than the regulated, orchestrated, and patterned response of one individual or group to another;

in black services each member of the congregation actually creates his or her own sacred communion simultaneously with the holy service that is proceeding. Members of the congregation call out spontaneously, and such exclamations may not have been anticipated by the minister.

During a service in which the preacher has been successful in arousing the Spirit of the Lord or in bringing his congregation to a high emotional level, individual cries are frequent, some of the congregation will enter an altered state during which they may lose consciousness or dance seemingly involuntarily, and the preacher will be visibly ecstatic as well. Many people laugh aloud; a few cry unashamedly. When the service is over, they will say that they have had a happy time.

Research on this phenomenon suggests that while much of the sermon cannot possibly be heard distinctly, something is being communicated, and the congregation will feel that it has received God's Word. This may happen because many in the congregation know the Bible almost as thoroughly as does the preacher, and they creatively anticipate his message; also, in these services the congregation participates actively and creatively in the service and may for long periods be "hearing" their own celebrations.

Both preacher and flock share many common traditions, not only inherited Christianity but also an African American interpretation of that faith flavored by the experience of living in the South. Few preachers have had extensive seminary training, and many of their beliefs,

like those of their congregations, are derived from popular traditions. For instance, many preachers prefer to use popular, folk versions of stories and parables in Scripture. Hence, although their Christianity is in the main "official," it is heavily influenced by folkloric elements. In some urban areas these preachers are often known as "old-time country preachers," though many of them have migrated away from the rural South to the urban North. The Reverend C. L. Franklin, for instance, became most famous after he left the South and moved to Detroit.

The ministers do not use manuscripts but believe that when they are in front of congregations, the Holy Ghost is using them to communicate his message to the people. This spontaneous preaching style is accurately and movingly reproduced by William Faulkner in the last portion of *The Sound and the Fury*. In those pages the Reverend Shegog from St. Louis delivers a moving sermon in a style indistinguishable from the authentic oral performance. Significantly, this sermon is placed near the novel's conclusion; Faulkner recognized the great emotive and spiritual power that is the potential of this medium and chose to end his book on an affirming note.

Some white preachers also still preach in this mode; the style is not the exclusive property of one ethnic group. But most practitioners are black and usually Methodist or Baptist. The practice is characteristically southern, though many preachers have now moved to the cities of the North or to the West Coast. These preachers continue to evoke the South in their services. Many professional black singers have vocal qualities that carry heavy echoes of this preaching style. Examples are Aretha Franklin (daughter of the Reverend C. L. Franklin), Sarah Vaughn, and Lou Rawls. Much of the "Motown sound" owes a debt to southern country preaching.

The influence of black folk preachers on the nation extends well beyond the contributions of musical entertainment and the popular arts. The Reverend Martin Luther King Jr. was a "spiritual" preacher whose "I Have a Dream" speech was in large measure a sermon on racial equality; he is well known for this oral performance, which profoundly moved his listeners, regardless of their race or ethnic backgrounds. This art has been prominently practiced by Chicago's Jesse Jackson, a southerner by birth and raising. His address to the Democratic National Convention (1984) was a spontaneous sermon, a moving oration delivered by electronic media to the nation and the world. More recently, one sees the survival and adaptation of this black preaching style in contemporary televangelists. West Virginia–born T. D. Jakes is one of the most prominent black televangelists, preaching from his church, The Potter's House, located on some 50 acres in southwest Dallas, Tex. He bridges the gap between a rural, southern constituency and the upwardly mobile black (and white) middle class. He can speak, as one observer notes, with "a strong country contour," pronouncing, for instance, Kenya as Keen-ya. He begins his sermon conventionally with a conversa-tional tone, delivered from the pulpit, but when he steps down to the floor, he becomes a showman, influenced as much by Las Vegas as by black church tradition. Still, as in that tradition, his sermons bring the congregation to increasingly intense emotional levels as he hops around the stage, his voice rising and falling in a sophisticated version of a chant. As with earlier preachers, Jakes knows his Bible, and the Scriptures, along with his own personal experiences, give him his sermon lessons. He is likely to preach a message of self-betterment, perhaps shouting it, perhaps whispering of its promises. Men and women rise from their seats at the end and move in excitement, often with tears in their eyes—evidence of the continuing power of the black preaching style.

BRUCE A. ROSENBERG
Brown University

Richard Allen, in *Black American Literature: 1760 to Present*, ed. Ruth Miller (1971); Paul C. Brownlow, *Quarterly Journal of Speech* (vol. 58, 1972); Gerald L. Davis, *"I Got The Word in Me and I Can Sing It, You Know": A Study of the Performed Afro-American Sermon* (1986); Charles V. Hamilton, *The Black Preacher in America* (1972); Henry H. Mitchell, *Black Preaching* (1970); Sridhar Pappu, *Atlantic Monthly* (March 2006); Albert J. Raboteau, *A Fire in the Bones: Reflections on African-American Religious History* (1995), *Slave Religion: The "Invisible Institution" in the Antebellum South* (1978); Joseph R. Washington Jr., *Black Religion; The Negro and Christianity in the United States* (1964).

Preaching Style, White

Whether by miter, robe, collar, licensing and ordination, honorific title, or even slicked-back hair, society sets its ministers apart from run-of-the-mill mortals. Naturally this obsession with difference includes that most basic element of identity: speech, especially in preaching, the principal public enterprise of ministers. Preaching is marked as special speech by particular stylistic traits or, more accurately, by a register, that is, a language variety used for a specific purpose and having a set of linguistic characteristics that define it.

While there is demonstrably an African American preaching style, the question of whether a specifically southern white preaching style exists is more complex and less explored. Unlike the scholarly interest and research on (southern-originating) African American preaching, research on southern white preaching styles is a virtual wasteland. Religion in general in the South has spawned much study, but the linguistic/rhetorical nature of preaching styles in white church traditions, southern or otherwise, has received relatively little scholarly attention, perhaps because the churches and preachers are such an eclectic lot.

Against a reality of diverse styles, two stereotypes of southern white preaching merit mention: folk preaching and loud preaching. The characteristics of folk preaching may be more common in the South than in more urban sections of the nation because of the South's greater demographic rurality (the 2000 census places the East South Central Division [Kentucky, Tennessee, Alabama, and Mississippi] at 43 percent rural). Also, the folk preacher model is embraced by many white southerners. Baptists in Alabama and elsewhere developed a long tradition of bivocational farmer-preachers with little formal education but possessing folk wisdom and wit esteemed by pioneer and rural society, but the model does not play out universally. Although many top televangelists during their heyday in the late 1980s were white southerners, the preaching or presenting styles of the major ones differed mightily, from Jimmy Swaggart's "country preacher" style, with its folk elements, to Pat Robertson's urbane television talk-show format.

Some southern white preachers have certainly been stentorian in their exhorting, such as the late Southern Baptist leader W. A. Criswell, reputedly audible five miles away. Preaching at an extreme volume, though more frequent in rural and southern white preaching, is not a universal trait, even less so after the Rural Electrification Act of 1936 eventually brought the advent of sound systems to rural churches.

The eclecticism of southern white preaching results in part from settlement history. The lack of homogeneity in settlement patterns and religiocultural development across the South as a whole gave rise to a socially motivated multiplicity of styles. Founding groups of English, Ulster Scots and Lowland Scots, Germans, French, and other Europeans arrived with set linguistic homiletic expectations. These various Protestant groups lacked the formational matrix found in African

American settlement history. That is, the slaves' social experience of being separated from their individual tribal historical roots and forced to form new mixed tribe communities necessitated a synthesis of generic expectations of theme and delivery out of African oratorical antecedents and southern folk Christianity. In Geneva Smitherman's words, "As the only independent African-American institution, the Black church [did] not have to answer to white folk!" Protestant settlers, on the other hand, brought their styles with them as they set up communities within communities, with social groups often highly tied to denominations such as German Lutherans; English Baptists, Methodists, and Episcopalians; and Scots and Irish Presbyterians. Constituting social networks, every denomination, denominational subgroup, or even loose association of like-minded congregants developed preferred styles, that is, a linguistic register recognized as effective preaching, serving not only to mark "the message" but also to create and sustain solidarity among the group's members and to differentiate it from other groups.

Over time, as ethnocentric blocks blended somewhat into a community edifice (with certain groups, such as Catholic congregations, fairly well ostracized by Protestant suspicion and by their claims—and those of other groups—to exclusivity), so did the criteria for acceptable preaching/sermon presentation blend, but with enough distinct features that the Baptist sermon could still be distinguished from Methodist or Presbyterian ones, not only

by emphasis and theology, but also by linguistic features as well as discourse and register. Within large denominations strong within the South, such as United Methodists and Southern Baptists, stylistic traits of preaching seem as adoptable as Arminian or Calvinistic theology: soft, upper-class, *r*-less, Coastal Southern pleading from pastors of large urban United Methodist churches, or loud, wrathful *r*-ful Inland Southern berating from conservative-camp Southern Baptist preachers.

However, certain parts of the South did approach the sort of closed, close-knit, beleaguered community that gave rise to typical African American preaching. One area that has been studied is Appalachia. Although Appalachia hosts a variety of denominations that differ fiercely in doctrinal principles (Baptists, Presbyterians, Methodists, and Pentecostals), it is generally accepted that rural churches and working-class ones in more urban areas often share what can be termed the Southern Appalachian Preaching Style. In Howard Dorgan's study of preaching styles in rural Appalachia, he notes that sermons are often impromptu (with no written notes) and require that the preacher "have the spirit" in order to communicate the Word of God to the congregation. Rural Appalachian preachers rely heavily on rhythm, with sermons switching quickly from fast bursts of biblical rhetoric to singing and back to a trancelike preaching state. These cycles are repeated several times during the sermon. Like African American preaching styles, a dialogue similar to call-and-response patterns is demanded of the congregation, and an "amen corner" of exhorters near the pulpit reinforces the minister's message.

A major point of southern white preaching not to be overlooked is that it is still largely a male enterprise. More conservative views in the South about women as preachers were strong even in colonial days and grew stronger over time. Even as the South became politically more separate over the issue of slavery, male slaves were afforded preaching opportunities denied to both black and white women. With the recent advent of several very popular southern women preachers, research is needed to understand the use of gendered linguistic resources in preaching, especially the extent to which female styles can or cannot be identified.

Considered as a register, preaching is unique in requiring both an overlay of "otherness" characteristics to separate it from regular, nonsacred speech and also rhetorically motivated intimacy strategies to ensure persuasive success. This otherness is achieved in strikingly different ways according to denominational expectations and conditioning. For example, southern preaching styles (not uniquely) range from the intoning of very formal written sermons prepared in the study and delivered with minimal extemporaneous comment in some denominations to almost completely extemporaneous rant-style messages delivered in a loud, physically altered voice, punctuated by panting, thought-marking ejaculations (*haah*), holy catchwords such as *glory* and *hallelujah*, and glossalalic outbursts.

The formal preacher may descend to the level of the congregation's vernacular to promote oneness and earnestness, while the inspired preacher may attempt to elevate a segment of discourse by exploiting his or her most formal language features. Southern white preaching is therefore especially well equipped for stylistic variation because of the bidialectalism of the region. The formal southern white preacher can strike a plain-folks stance with a simple "Ain't no way" or "He done good" and greater use of the monophthongized /ai/ (i.e., modification of long *i* as in *It's the sahns* [signs] *of the tahms* [times]). The "Holy Ghost" preacher, conversely, may set a tone of intimate soul searching by "just talking to you from my heart" while correcting *it don't* to *it doesn't* and *we ain't* to *we haven't* and by pronouncing *the signs of the times* with the standard diphthong.

Much research into southern white preaching is needed to identify clearly the linguistic hallmarks of its varieties and their social meanings. Nevertheless, a rough taxonomy of the major styles of southern white preaching, often but not always associated with particular denominations or other groupings, can be described as follows:

1. Inspired-Impromptu (in a range from simple notes and outline to no specific preparation): often loud, emotional, and combative, as the "Spirit leads." Commonly, the more improvised the sermon, the more it invites and incorporates a "dialogue" between the

preacher and the congregation, similar to the call-and-response patterns observed in African American preaching. Generally speaking, this type of sermon is more common among preachers lacking theological training, while the following three styles are taught in homiletics classes in formal theological study.

2. Narrative-loaded: a sermon built around a short biblical text, with emphasis on a few key words, explicated usually by three points, with each point illustrated by one or more narratives of some length. This type of sermon is carefully written and many times memorized for no-note delivery.

3. Doctrinal-treatise: a sermon built on topical scriptural use, with unemotional delivery until a climax is reached. At the climax of the sermon, the minister may, as it were, drop his persona of the theologian and "speak from the heart" in a more extemporaneous style marked by more informal vocabulary, including perceived solecisms such as *ain't* for proof of sincerity.

4. Expository-Exegesis: preaching that methodically proceeds verse by verse through a scripture passage or serially through a complete book of the Bible, with a chunk presented at each meeting (with time out for major theme Sundays such as Mother's Day). The sermon might employ a mixture of methods as called for in order to unhull the meat of the passage in question and to keep the verse-by-verse exegesis from becoming unrelenting. Usually its fervor, as linguistically marked by greater volume, higher pitch, vocal stress, and tempo, rises according to the applicable value of the content.

These four styles are not presented as uniquely southern but are certainly prevalent across the South. This taxonomy represents a starting point for linguistic research into a neglected area of southern culture.

THOMAS E. NUNNALLY
Auburn University

JENNIFER REID
Auburn University

Catherine A. Brekus, *Strangers and Pilgrims: Female Preaching in America, 1740–1845* (1998); Howard Dorgan, *Giving Glory to God in Appalachia* (1987); Wayne Flynt, *Alabama Baptists: Southern Baptists in the Heart of Dixie* (1998); Janice Peck, *The Gods of Televangelism: The Crisis of Meaning and the Appeal of Religious Television* (1993); Bruce A. Rosenberg, *Can These Bones Live? The Art of the American Folk Preacher*, rev. ed. (1988); Geneva Smitherman, in *African-American English: Structure, History, and Use*, ed. Salikoko S. Muifwene, John Russell Rickford, Guy Bailey, and John Baugh (1998).

Pronunciation, Changes in

"Southern accents" are legendary in the landscape of American English. From the southern Appalachian Mountains to the former plantation areas to the coastal regions of the South, the region's accents are as diverse as the population itself and as characteristic of the South as summer heat and grits. Although many people perceive southern accents as "old-fashioned" or even as uniform, they are actually dynamic, changing over time and space as the landscape and social demography also change. Many of the hallmark features of southern pronunciation have developed in the past century and a half.

The pronunciation of long *i* as *tahd* 'tide' and *taht* 'tight' is an important marker of southern identity. The southern long *i* is a sound midway between the *ah* sound in *all* and the *a* sound in the word *at*, usually represented as *ah* in dialect respellings. This prominent southern vowel pronunciation is frequently commented on by outsiders. In some parts of the Lower South, the long *i* is pronounced as *ah* before voiced consonants, as in *side*, but not before voiceless ones, as in *sight*. In contrast, in other parts of the South, such as the Great Smoky Mountains and Texas, people pronounce long *i* as *ah* before both voiced sounds (*sahd* 'side') and voiceless ones (*nahs whaht rahs* 'nice white rice'). This quintessential southern pronunciation developed primarily after the Civil War and is still changing. For example, the pattern in which the southern long *i* appears before both voiced and voiceless consonants is now spreading outside the Appalachian Mountains and Texas to other parts of the South. Although the southern long *i* is still found in the urban centers of the South, it is competing there with the nonsouthern pronunciation *ah-ee* (*tah-eed* 'tide') and may or may not appear in the speech of young, urban southerners.

Another important southern pronunciation involves pronouncing short *e* and short *i* the same before nasal consonants, so that *pen* and *pin* both sound like *pin*, and *gem* and *gym* sound like *gym*. Like the pronunciation of long *i*, this change was not widespread until after the Civil War. It remains strong in the South, regardless of the social class or generation of the speaker.

In the South, the vowels /o/, /ʊ/, and /u/ are often pronounced somewhat toward the front of the mouth instead of at the back: for example, *buh-oot* 'boat' and *bih-oot* 'boot.' These vowel pronunciations emerged in the last quarter of the 19th century but did not spread across the South until after World War II. They are continuing to increase among younger speakers in the region. Another southern sound pattern is pronouncing long *a* and short *e* before /l/ the same (*sale* and *sell* both sound like *sell*); by the same token *peel* is often pronounced like *pill*.

Some changes in southern pronunciation are just beginning. For example, some southerners, especially younger, urban ones, now pronounce words such as *cot/caught* and *Don/Dawn* the same (as the first member of these pairs), much like people in the rest of the country. In traditional southern speech, however, these two vowels are pronounced differently. Traditional southern speech distinguishes between the short *o* in *cot* and the vowel sound of *caught*, which is made with rounded lips.

In terms of consonants, one change in southern pronunciation involves the loss of the initial *h* sound in words starting with *wh-*, such as *which* and *witch*. For example, *where* and *wear* were once pronounced differently, but they underwent a change in the early 20th century and are now usually pronounced the same, so that *which* sounds like *witch*, and *where* like *wear*.

Another consonant undergoing change in pronunciation in the South is *r* after a vowel in words like *car* and *fear*. In traditional southern speech, especially in the Lower South, this consonant is pronounced as *uh* or is not present at all: *cah* 'car' and *fe-uh* 'fear.' In other areas of the South, such as the Appalachian Mountains, the *r* is pronounced in these words, and this pattern is now spreading across the South. However, the absence of *r* after vowels persists in African American varieties, both in the South and elsewhere.

One feature that has endured across time and cultural change is the southern pronunciation of *greasy* with a *z* (so pronounced as *greazy*), identified by one of the earliest published dialect studies in America (in 1896 by George Hempl) as distinguishing northern from southern pronunciation. The pronunciation with *z* is still widespread today.

Southern pronunciations have changed over time alongside cultural and demographic characteristics. Two important periods in the evolution of southern pronunciations occurred after 1875 and after World War II. After 1875 many southerners moved from the countryside to towns to work in cotton mills, in lumber production, in mines, in steel mills, and for the railroads, setting the stage for dialect contact between different groups of people and subsequent language change. After World War II many southerners moved to midwestern cities to work in factories, creating another opportunity for new dialect contact. Many migrants and even their midwestern-born descendants maintain quintessential southern pronunciations such as *ah* in *side*, but southern sounds appear to be fading with each new generation. In the South, rural populations continue to decline, and current and future changes in the culture and demography of the region will no doubt have effects on southern pronunciations. For example, southern sounds are not as typical of southern cities such as Atlanta, Raleigh, Richmond, Nashville, and Charlotte as they were before the mass migration of outsiders to these cities. However, southern pronunciations are not dying or decaying but, rather, are adapting to new situations and new blends of voices.

BRIDGET L. ANDERSON
Old Dominion University

Bridget L. Anderson, *Migration, Accommodation, and Language Change: At the Intersection of Regional and Ethnic Identity* (2007); George Dorrill, in *English in the Southern United States*, ed. Stephen J. Nagle and Sara L. Sanders (2003); Judy Reed, "Evolution of the Loss of /h/ before /w/ Word Initially in Texas" (M.A. thesis, University of Texas, 1991); Jan Tillery and Guy Bailey, in *English in the Southern United*

States, ed. Stephen J. Nagle and Sara L. Sanders (2003).

Proverbs

As expressions of collective experience, southern proverbs embody generalized wisdom. The proverb repertoire seems to serve some southerners as a set of universal laws against which individual experience is measured. With their characteristic use of metaphor and their claims of similarity and difference, southern proverbs remain close to both poetry and philosophy. Proverbs have served generations of southerners as guides to appropriate behavior and as informal channels of education. They are still in widespread use today.

Southern proverbs have their roots in the Old World, especially in Europe and Africa. Europeans and Africans alike adapted their traditions of proverb usage to a new natural and social environment in the South. The African preference for indirect and highly ambiguous speech, both as an aesthetic variation on drab everyday discourse and as a means of avoiding the sometimes painful effects and insults of direct commentary, had a counterpart in the South in the European proverb tradition. That tradition included British proverbs stretching from the 16th century's "Beggars cannot be choosers" and the 15th century's "eat us out of house and home" to the 14th century's "Look before you leap" and the 12th century's "You can lead a horse to water, but you can't make him drink." European tradition also included such literary proverbs as St. Augustine's "When in Rome, do as the Romans do" and the classical Greek proverb "A rolling stone gathers no moss." Biblical proverbs, such as "Cast your bread upon the waters," "Pride goeth before a fall," and "The love of money is the root of all evil" are particularly widespread in the South. In the colonial period southern folk tradition also absorbed proverbs from Benjamin Franklin's *Poor Richard's Almanac*, such as "A word to the wise is sufficient" and "Early to bed and early to rise makes a man healthy, wealthy, and wise."

Like all forms of folklore, proverb wording is subject to variation, but structural patterns of proverbs are relatively fixed. The most common structural forms in southern proverbs are simple positive or negative propositions, such as "Beauty is in the eye of the beholder" or "Nobody's perfect." But double propositions ("Everybody talks about the weather, but nobody does anything about it" or "Young folks, listen to what old folks say, when danger is near keep out of the way") are common in southern tradition, and triple propositions ("So I totes my powder and sulphur and I carries my stick in my hand and I puts my trust in God") are not unknown. Multiple propositions provide an apt structure for making invidious distinctions, as "Man proposes, but God disposes."

In their proverbs, southerners make distinctions by comparison and contrast. They emphasize the equivalence of things ("Seeing is believing") or they deny it ("All that glitters is not gold"). Or they emphasize that one thing is bigger or of greater value than another, as in "His eyes are bigger than his belly,"

"A bird in the hand is worth two in the bush," and "Half a loaf is better than none." Proverbs purport to explain how things come about ("Politics makes strange bedfellows" and "New brooms sweep clean") or to deny causation or justification ("Barking dogs don't bite" and "Two wrongs don't make a right").

An important attribute of southern proverbs is their sense of authority, deriving partly from their detachment from common speech and partly from their allusive poetic nature. They are set off from ordinary discourse by such poetic devices as alliteration ("The proof of the pudding is in the eating" and "A miss is as good as a mile"); rhyme ("A friend in need is a friend indeed" and "Haste makes waste"); repetition ("All's well that ends well" and "No news is good news"); meter ("Nothing ventured, nothing gained" and "A word to the wise is sufficient"); and parallelism ("Like father, like son" and "The more he has, the more he wants").

Because of their poetic qualities (their allusiveness and ambiguity), proverbs may be cited with authority in a broad range of situations. Their flexibility has sometimes made proverbs seem contradictory to modern readers. Are two heads better than one, or do too many cooks spoil the broth? Some proverbs used by southerners tout the virtues of cautious conservatism ("Look before you leap," "Rome wasn't built in a day," and "Haste makes waste"), whereas others, equally authentic, urge hearers to "Strike while the iron is hot" (similarly, "Time and tide wait for no man" and "He who hesitates

is lost"). But proverbs are not really contradictory. Just as a language gives its speakers words with which to praise or to criticize as necessary, the southern proverb repertory enables southerners to offer whatever advice seems appropriate to a particular situation, to advise either action or inaction, and to do so through heightened poetic language.

In offering advice, a southern proverb might pursue either of two strategies. It might recommend acceptance of the situation or it might recommend action to relieve the situation. "Put up or shut up" and "Nothing ventured, nothing gained" are examples of the action strategy. Some proverbs counsel defensive action, such as "A stitch in time saves nine" and "An apple a day keeps the doctor away." Some acceptance strategy proverbs suggest that the situation is normal ("Accidents will happen" and "Boys will be boys"); thus, no action is called for. Some urge their hearers not to overreact ("Look before you leap" and "Barking dogs don't bite"). Others counsel patience, for troubles come and troubles go ("March comes in like a lion but goes out like a lamb"). Some even suggest that the hearer is responsible for the situation and must accept the consequences ("You've made your bed, now you have to lie in it"). Yet other proverbs maintain that no matter how hard the misfortune may seem, it can be borne ("Every back is fitted to the burden").

Though relatively simple in form, proverbs are perhaps the most complex of all folklore genres in their extreme sensitivity to context. The meaning and distinctiveness of the southern proverb does not lie in its form or content, but in the context of its use. And those contexts range as widely and deeply as southern life itself.

Coastal Carolina University

F. A. DeCaro and W. K. McNeil, *American Proverb Literature* (1970); Alan Dundes, *Analytic Essays in Folklore* (1975); Charles Joyner, *Down by the Riverside: A South Carolina Slave Community* (1984); Wolfgang Mieder et al., *A Dictionary of American Proverbs* (1992); P. Seitel, *Genre* (1969); Archer Taylor, *The Proverb* (1931); Archer Taylor and Bartlett J. Whiting, comps., *A Dictionary of American Proverbs and Proverbial Phrases, 1820–1880* (1958); Newman I. White, ed., *Frank C. Brown Collection of North Carolina Folklore*, vol. 1 (1952).

R in Southern English

The pronunciation of *r* has been a stereotypical feature of southern speech since at least the early 20th century but has been widespread in the region since at least the 18th century. Southerners are often characterized as replacing *r* with a schwa vowel or deleting it altogether, so that *here* is pronounced *heah*, *better* as *bettuh*, *part* as *paht*, and *four* as *foah* or *fo*. Linguists call such pronunciations *r*-less, or non-rhotic, as opposed to *r*-ful, or rhotic, utterances, in which the *r* is pronounced. While *r*-lessness remains a stock feature of depictions of southern speech in movies and television shows and in the dialogue of fiction, the reality is far more complex and is also changing.

R is not indiscriminately absent in *r*-less speech. It is not absent at the beginning of a syllable, as in *run*. It is usually absent in only two places: before another consonant sound, as in *part* and *bird*, and at the end of a word, as in *here*, *four*, and *better*. Some southerners, mainly older whites from the Deep South and African Americans, also delete *r* when it falls between two vowels, as in *carry*. When *r* occurs at the end of a word, *r*-less speakers do not pronounce an *r* before a pause or when the next word begins with a consonant sound (*cah trouble*), but they often pronounce the *r* when the next word begins with a vowel (*car engine*). Many *r*-less southerners show some variability, with inconsistent *r*-ful pronunciations of words in which the *r* could be absent.

Not all parts of the South are *r*-less. Generally speaking, regions where the plantation culture once dominated, including the cotton belt, the Virginia Piedmont and some other tobacco-producing areas, and the rice- and sugar-producing areas of South Carolina, Georgia, and Louisiana, are *r*-less. Other regions, such as the Appalachians, the Ozarks, the Pamlico Sound region of North Carolina, the Delmarva peninsula, northern Texas, and to a lesser extent the sandy "Piney Woods" belt of the Gulf states, are *r*-ful. Some *r*-ful speakers even add "intrusive" *r* where it did not occur historically: usually in unstressed syllables, such as *idear*, *hallelujar*, and *holler* (for *hollow*), but also in a few other words, as in *warsh* for *wash* or *ort* for *ought*. Such pronunciations are most common in traditionally *r*-ful areas, but they also occur in formerly *r*-less regions among speakers who are "restoring"

R IN SOUTHERN ENGLISH 189

r and have fallen into what linguists call *hypercorrection*. African Americans are largely r-less in most regions of the country both inside and outside the South. However, younger African Americans usually pronounce the r in words such as *bird*, *certain*, and *turn* in which there is no true vowel sound before the r but the syllable is stressed.

Linguists have proposed three theories for the origin of southern r-lessness. One is that English settlers brought it with them in the 17th and 18th centuries. Some settlers probably did show inconsistent r-lessness in unstressed syllables, as in *better*. In addition, an earlier process in which r disappeared before a consonant made with the tip of the tongue (*t, d, s, z, n,* or *th*) was certainly prevalent among settlers. It accounts for pronunciations such as *bust* for *burst*, *hoss* for *horse*, and *catridge* for *cartridge* and perhaps could have led to later full-fledged r-lessness. Another theory is that r-lessness began only in the latter part of the 18th century as an imitation of fashionable British usage, since planters with adequate resources sent their children to England for education. Other features of British English, such as the broad *a* in *past*, *aunt*, and similar words, were quite likely established in Virginia and elsewhere through prestige imitation, and r-lessness could have followed suit. A third theory is that r-lessness was due to African influence. European American children on plantations often had primarily slave children as playmates, and African Americans have always been the most r-less group. Furthermore, a large fraction of west-

ern African languages cannot have a consonant at the end of a syllable, so that r-lessness could have developed as slaves tried to learn English using the patterns of their native languages, passing them on to their children and thence to white plantation children.

In the past, r-lessness was prestigious and was spreading. However, studies in North Carolina, Alabama, and Texas have shown that it is the full pronunciation of r that is now prestigious, and young white southerners, especially females, are now quite r-ful. Possible reasons for this turnabout include migration of r-ful Appalachian natives to mill towns in r-less areas, migration of r-ful northerners to the Sunbelt, racial tension accompanied by reaction against r-less African American speech, and increased awareness of what is prestigious nationwide. It appears that, in the future, r-lessness will be restricted to African American speech in the South, a significant change from the past.

ERIK R. THOMAS
North Carolina State University

Crawford Feagin, in *Development and Diversity: Linguistic Variation across Time and Space. A Festschrift for Charles-James N. Bailey*, ed. Jerold Edmondson, Crawford Feagin, and Peter Mühlhäusler (1990), in *Language Variety in the South Revisited*, ed. Cynthia Bernstein, Thomas Nunnally, and Robin Sabino (1997); Maverick Marvin Harris, *American Speech* (vol. 44, 1969); Archibald A. Hill, *Publications of the Modern Language Society of America* (*PMLA*) (vol. 55, 1940); Hans Kurath and Raven I. McDavid Jr., *Pronunciation of English in the Atlantic States* (1961); Lewis

Levine and Harry J. Crockett Jr., *Socio-
logical Inquiry* (vol. 36, 1966); Raven I.
McDavid Jr., *American Speech* (vol. 23,
1948); Thomas Schönweitz, *American
Speech* (vol. 76, 2001).

Randolph, Vance

(1892–1980) FOLKLORIST.

Vance Randolph's academic training
was in psychology (M.A., Clark University, 1915), and Randolph described
himself most often as a "hack writer."
To be sure, for many years he supported himself by writing, often under
a pseudonym, pulp fiction and non-
fiction on a vast range of subjects. The
shelf of books resulting from his long
lifetime's work in the Arkansas and
Missouri Ozarks, however, is responsible for his continuing reputation as
one of the nation's premier regional
folklorists. Driven by an encyclopedic,
curious mind, he collected all facets of
Ozark lore. His works on the region's
speech offer unparalleled insight and
are the foundation of all subsequent
scholarship in this field.

Randolph was born in Pittsburg,
Kans., just west of the Ozarks, but he
lived his adult life in small towns in
Missouri (Pineville and Galena) and
Arkansas (Eureka Springs and Fayetteville), where he assiduously sought
out and perpetuated in print and on
recordings the sayings, doings, sing-
ings, and believings of his Ozark neighbors. His first books, *The Ozarks: An
American Survival of Primitive Society*
(1931) and *Ozark Mountain Folks* (1932),
are long out of print but remain notable
excellent examples of what later were
called folklife studies. His methods and

definitions were often in advance of
their time—he included, for example,
discographical references to "hillbilly"
records in his four-volume folksong
collection *Ozark Folksongs* (1946–50) at
a time when many scholars found such
recordings unworthy of notice.

Randolph first achieved renown as a
student of dialect when H. L. Mencken
lavishly praised his numerous article-
length studies published beginning in
1926 in two American Dialect Society
periodicals, *American Speech* and *Dialect Notes*. His major work in this area,
*Down in the Holler: A Gallery of Ozark
Folk Speech* (1953), gathered material
from more than 30 years of study and
observation and covered Ozark grammar, pronunciation, archaisms, taboo
terms and euphemisms, and wisecracks, along with the use of the dialect
in fiction. The book also provided
an extensive, scholarly glossary. Like
others working on Ozark dialect until
recent years, he frequently identified
archaisms that could also be found in
Renaissance-era English literature, but
he kept any ideas about the Elizabethan
character of Ozark speech in perspective with its other qualities, unlike his
peers. Along with his massive folksong
collection, the 1940s saw the publication of Randolph's major study of folk
belief, *Ozark Superstitions* (1947). In the
1950s Randolph published five volumes
of folktales, including *We Always Lie
to Strangers: Tall Tales from the Ozarks*.
A collection of jokes, *Hot Springs and
Hell* (1965), and Randolph's huge bib-
liographic work, *Ozark Folklore: A Bibliography* (1972), were followed by his
classic collection of bawdy humor, *Piss-*

ing in the Snow (1976). Taken together, Randolph's many publications provide a detailed and sympathetic portrait of Ozark traditional life and speech. Academic folklorists honored Randolph in 1978 by electing him a Fellow of the American Folklore Society.

ROBERT COCHRAN
University of Arkansas

Robert Cochran, *Vance Randolph: An Ozark Life* (1995); Vance Randolph, *The Ozarks: A Bibliography* (1972, 1987); Vance Randolph and George P. Wilson, *Down in the Holler: A Gallery of Ozark Folkspeech* (1953).

Southern Drawl

One of the most noticeable aspects of southern speech, particularly among whites, is what is called "the southern drawl." (Drawling is much less frequent and less dramatic among African American speakers.) However, pinning down exactly what the drawl is, much less the details of who uses it, when, and why, is challenging. Despite the popular recognition of the term *drawl* and the explosion of studies of southern speech by linguists in recent decades, very little has been written about it.

One problem is that the term has been applied loosely to southern speech or a southern accent in general. For linguists it relates to the pronunciation of vowels in stressed syllables, and its salient characteristics include the lengthening of vowels, the changing of simple vowels into diphthongs and triphthongs, and the producing of noticeable changes of pitch on the drawled word. Diphthongs are combinations of two vowel sounds in the same syllable. The second one is called a glide, since the tongue glides from the initial vowel position to another position in the mouth. Triphthongs have more than one glide. The glide sound(s) inserted after a vowel that is drawled can vary for the same vowel, even in the same word, sometimes producing a diphthong with tongue movement toward the front of the mouth and at other times one with centering movement. For example, *ask* can be pronounced [æsk], [æisk], [æəsk], or [æiyisk] (roughly *ăsk, ă-isk, ă-uhsk,* or *ă-i-yisk*). The same vowel in the same word can occur as a simple vowel or become a diphthong or even a triphthong with the insertion of glides.

The drawl is sometimes characterized by extreme changes of pitch. In white southern speech, any vowel under stress in a one-syllable word can be lengthened, whether it is what is traditionally called a long vowel (*wide, cake, moon*), a short vowel (*cab, bed, kid*), or a diphthong (*boy, cow*). This lengthening can simply extend the duration of the vowel, or it can occur in conjunction with a change of pitch. Acoustic studies show that the drawled form of a one-syllable word is at least twice as long as the "plain" form (e.g., 300 vs. 140 milliseconds, 360 vs. 100 milliseconds).

Drawled words most often appear at the end of a clause or sentence. Words that are under sentence stress but that have even one word following before a pause or at the end of a sentence are less likely to be drawled, as *They come and pay my* bills *for me* (with plain, undrawled pronunciation) versus *Then [we] went down the* hill (with drawled pronunciation). The drawl varies from speaker to speaker for reasons having to do with geography, demographics (age, sex, and social class), situation, topic, and self-identification. Moreover, the same speaker, in the same discourse, using the same word in the same environment, and under the same amount of stress, may drawl a word in one instance but not in another.

The drawl is associated more with women, with informality and intimacy, and with rural and small-town interests. It is used in exaggerated speech, such as baby talk and in "kindergarten teacher" style. Drawling is considered very feminine, even sexy. Because drawling is used by women in "hostess" mode, it is observed more often by outsiders than drawling by men is. Men use the drawl with their wives, children, close friends, horses, and dogs and in discussions of hunting, fishing, football, and similar topics to express solidarity and informality. Pediatricians often drawl with young patients in order to set them at ease. Avoidance of the drawl is found in more formal situations, in discussions of serious topics, and among professional men, especially in urban settings. Similarly, professional women are usually careful not to drawl in a business/professional context. Finally, the drawl is often used to establish one's identity as a southerner. Some people who live within the South identify themselves more closely with being southern than do others, and for many complex reasons, some people who leave the South jettison all vestiges of southern speech—especially the drawl—while others not

only maintain it but perfect it, polish it, and exaggerate it to make sure that their identity as southerners is clear to all. The variability of the drawl, then, while presenting difficulties of linguistic analysis, is a very useful part of a southerner's repertoire and an integral part of the speech of many people in or from the region.

CRAWFORD FEAGIN
Arlington, Virginia

Crawford Feagin, in *Variation in Language: NWAVE XV at Stanford*, ed. Keith M. Denning, Sharon Inkelas, Faye C. McNair-Knox, and John R. Rickford (1987), in *Towards a Social Science of Language: Variation and Change in Language and Society*, ed. Gregory R. Guy, Crawford Feagin, Deborah Schiffrin, and John Baugh (1996).

Southern English in Television and Film

From the southern belles of *Designing Women* to the country bumpkins of *Forrest Gump*, depictions of southern culture and characters are frequently found in television programs and films and can reflect attitudes about the South and southerners. These media portrayals necessarily include representations of Southern English, some accurate and some less so, that can affect how southerners see themselves and how others see them. Writers and other creators of television and film often use references to (supposedly) regionally distinctive foods (grits and sweet tea) or observances (Mardi Gras and Civil War reenactments) to indicate "southernness," but most often they use regional speech to indicate this sense to the audience, if not also something about character personality, intelligence, and other attributes. Though tremendously diverse in nature, portrayals share traits in their motivation and construction. Characters depicted through southern speech or as southern tend to fall into several types, many corresponding to stereotypical ideas about the South and southerners.

Precepts drawn from the analysis of dialects in literary works help us understand how television and films use Southern English. These consider the author's skills, intentions, and knowledge of dialects. The use of dialect to construct character is an artistic tool and is not necessarily intended to be completely accurate. When dialect is addressed to an audience of nonsoutherners, the ability of the audience to understand regional language varieties must be considered since a completely accurate depiction may interfere with comprehension of the actor's utterances. The goal may not be to convey all the nuances of a language variety realistically but to provide information about a character's background or personality. Decisions regarding dialect depictions may be made by several persons, including scriptwriters, directors, and dialect coaches. Even southerners who make television shows and films may consider it necessary to share only part of the linguistic picture to achieve the desired characterization. Further, if those involved in the television or film production have only limited acquaintance with the language varieties in question, creating an accurate dialect depiction may be implausible.

Thus, several factors affect which features of Southern English are included in television or film dialogue, depending on the value of each feature as an indicator of southernness or in character development. To choose a linguistic feature not recognized as southern by at least some audience members would defeat the purpose of using Southern English. Features may come from any level of dialect, including phonology, lexicon, pragmatics, or grammar. In many cases scriptwriters use these features in ways deviating from the actual usage of any southerners. In others, the features may not be appropriate to the part of the South being depicted. For example, in *Cold Mountain* Nicole Kidman's character from Charleston, S.C., shows no sign of the distinctive Lowcountry pronunciation but instead uses a more general southern accent. In cases such as these, the scriptwriter just might view the features as southern and therefore indicative of anyone from south of the Mason-Dixon Line.

One of the most typical features used in depicting southerners is the loss of *r* after vowels. While still occurring in the speech of some southerners, this usage is becoming less prevalent and is found in only certain social groups and certain parts of the South. Despite this, many film and television creators think that any southerner, or at least female southern characters and those from upper social classes, should be depicted as not pronouncing *r* after vowels. Even the *r*-less pronunciation is not necessarily rendered as southerners would pronounce it. In many cases southerners fill the space occupied by *r* with a schwa (the *uh* sound), so that *George* is not pronounced *joadge* but *joe-udge* or *joe-wudge* instead. An example of this is found in the speech of Ruth Jamison in *Fried Green Tomatoes*, whose filmmaker attempts a type of characterization using a Southern English pronunciation, but one that is inaccurate. While nonsoutherners may not notice this, southerners may realize that the accent is contrived because of linguistic details such as these.

More noticeable uses of Southern English in television and films occur at the word level. Vocabulary choices may be stereotypically southern (*I reckon*, the frequent use of *sir* and *ma'am*, etc.). Stereotypically southern attitudes about history can be reflected in the use of phrases such as "the recent unpleasantness" or "the war of northern aggression" for the Civil War. In some cases, however, the depictions involve usages that are nonexistent or at best rare in southern speech. The most stereotypical icon of southernness is the pronoun *y'all* or *you all*, which television programs and films often use for only one person, thus deviating from the plural usage of southerners (as in Mandy's *You all got some ice?* in the film *Midnight in the Garden of Good and Evil*). Sometimes the notion of *you all* is extended to other pronouns, creating what sounds to southerners to be completely unnatural constructions, such as Larry Steinberg's *we all* and *he all* in the film *Dill Scallion*. This is a prime example of how accuracy is sacrificed for

characterization, often because of a lack of knowledge about Southern English or simply attempts at humor.

A more subtle case of the misuse of southern features to convey character traits involves double modal verbs, most commonly *might could*. Linguistic research demonstrates that southerners who use this construction do so in very specific situations, particularly when speaking indirectly or wanting to make polite requests (as in Hoke's speech in *Driving Miss Daisy*). However, the nuanced southern usage of *might could* is not often included in films and television, which more frequently utilize the form's reputation as a typical southern verb phrase and ignore its situations of use by real-life southerners. While such features of Southern English may have the desired iconic effect of conjuring up "southernness" in the audience's mind, they can also distort ideas of how southerners speak and, to some southerners, can appear contrived, even demeaning. Southern English sometimes simply indicates a character's regional origins, but it can also depict a character as unintelligent, simpleminded, ignorant, or narrow-minded.

Iconic linguistic features are found in depictions of such stock southern character types as the Southern Belle, the Country Bumpkin, the Good Ole Boy, and others. The best known of these characters may be the Southern Belle (for example, Scarlett O'Hara in *Gone with the Wind*). Often known for her coquettish manipulation of those around her; her capricious attitude toward beaux, friends, and fashion; and a tendency to be less than intelligent, the Southern Belle debutante stereotype is usually indicated through a high-pitched, *r*-less, "Old South," upper-class accent. It may or may not be accompanied by other Southern English features. Another well-known stereotype, the Country Bumpkin, can come in many forms, as demonstrated by the poor farm boy Will Stockdale in the film *No Time for Sergeants* and the Clampett family in television's *The Beverly Hillbillies*. The film character Forrest Gump can also be seen as an example of this stereotypical southerner. Frequently ignorant of the ways of life outside his or her home area, the oft-ridiculed Country Bumpkin, or rube, can be traced to vaudeville shows such as *Arkansas Traveler* and *Hickory Bill* and to early "hillbilly" films, such as those featuring Lum and Abner. In some cases, the Country Bumpkin also has a "salt-of-the-earth" honesty and common sense, as in Jed Clampett, Andy Taylor of *The Andy Griffith Show*, or Ma Kettle of the Ma and Pa Kettle films. Another southern type that shares some traits with these salt-of-the-earth characters is found in the *Smokey and the Bandit* films and in the television series *The Dukes of Hazzard*. Bo "The Bandit" Darville and the Duke brothers can be seen as Good Ole Boys who are rebellious and mischievous but generally good natured and kindhearted. Whereas there is much variation in the speech of the Country Bumpkin and Good Ole Boy characters, their portrayals often include nonstandard features, which can be perceived by the audience as indicating poorly educated, lower-class, ignorant persons. Examples include the frequent use of *ain't* and the absence of subject-verb agreement (as *we was* and *he don't*).

Many television programs and films depict Southern English throughout, as do *The Waltons* and *Steel Magnolias*. In other cases, even the absence of southern features in a character's speech can be a tool of characterization. In the film *To Kill a Mockingbird*, language use helps distinguish the enlightened, well-schooled Atticus Finch from the bigoted, uneducated Bob Ewell. Ewell's language is riddled with nonstandard features and an accent that has come to indicate a closed-minded "redneck" character type (as in the rapists in *A Time to Kill* and Billy Hanson in *Midnight in the Garden of Good and Evil*). Gregory Peck (as Atticus Finch) has few, if any, Southern English features in his speech, which may help to indicate his liberal-mindedness and enlightenment.

Although the ways in which southern speech is depicted in films and television are myriad, these representations all aim to indicate that something about a character is "southern." The skill and intent behind a given depiction can range from a valid endeavor to portray realistic southern language use (*Sling Blade*) to a farcical, derogatory use of stereotypical southern features to convey character ignorance (*Poor White Trash*). Between these two ends of the spectrum are many uses of southern language features and character types accomplished with varying degrees of nuance and effectiveness. The motivation and techniques behind their construction in television and films tell us much about attitudes toward southern cultures and language varieties.

RACHEL SHUTTLESWORTH
University of Alabama

Cynthia Bernstein, *American Speech* (vol. 75, 2000); Warren French, ed., *The South and Film* (1981); Sumner Ives, in *A Various Language: Perspectives on American Dialects*, ed. Juanita V. Williamson and Virginia M. Burke (1971); Rosina Lippi-Green, *English with an Accent: Language, Ideology, and Discrimination in the United States* (1997); Nancy Niedzielski and Dennis Preston, *Folk Linguistics* (2000); Rachel Shuttlesworth, "Language Ideological Factors in Twentieth Century Artistic Depictions of Southern American English" (Ph.D. dissertation, University of Alabama, 2004).

Storytelling

A robust and vital storytelling tradition is part and parcel of the South's persona, probably because of the persistent image of tale spinning as a form of entertainment made for front porch socializing and family circles in isolated areas characterizing the South. Southern narrators, given social approval for their verbal artistry, typically boast extensive repertoires of folktales, legends, jests, and anecdotes. Attracted by the lure of this trove, early folklore collectors flocked to isolated pockets of the Appalachians, Ozarks, and bayous to find centuries-old tales of international circulation. But the romantic draw of pristine back-sections aside, storytelling, much of which involves creative narrative-making of recent events in urban as well as suburban areas, holds social significance throughout the South.

Folklorists found in the South versions of Old World folktales, including tales having familiar motifs of remarkable adventures or quests, magical objects or incantations, and giants or other fearsome creatures. A subgenre of the tales associated with the American South, called "Jack tales," revolves around the figure of a young crafty boy named Jack, sometimes with two older, but not as wise brothers, who outwits larger, dangerous antagonists. For the most part, the European *Märchen* types popularized by the Brothers Grimm lose their supernatural and fantastic elements in America. The tales reportedly become shorter, and often the actions or characters are made humorous. In African American tradition, the related trickster type is "John," who fools his white bosses; the theme of the tale cycle also has a relation to the African animal trickster tales of Brer Rabbit and Anansi the Spider (called Miss Nancy or Aunt Nancy in coastal Georgia and South Carolina communities).

Although the early folklorists spotlighted the New World *Märchen*, this genre actually constitutes a minor part of most narrators' repertoires. Folk humor frequently revolves around stereotypical, comical characters or "folktypes." Typically, southerners have sheafs of stories using either the mountaineer (or "hillbilly"), the poor white, the black, the preacher, or the city slicker as the butts of humor. Using the veil of laughter, the jests deal with the concerns and tensions of southern society. There is the caution against hypocrisy in fundamentalist southern religion and the fallibility of the clergy underlying the popular series of preacher jokes, for example. An irony in this storytelling cycle is that preachers are celebrated for their verbal artistry, and indeed pulpit sermons often retelling biblical stories as modern-day legends are an important source for narrative structure.

Perhaps the most celebrated genre in the narrator's repertoire is the tall tale, also called a "windy," a "whopper," or simply a "lie." The tales can be brief exclamations, such as the following boast collected in Mississippi: "You think your tomatoes are big? Well, I had a tomato so big the picture of it weighed five pounds!" Typically though, tall tales are extended narratives, such as the embellished personal experience story. Folklorist Kay L. Cothran found many such stories in the Okefenokee Swamp Rim of Georgia, where narrators delighted in relating remarkable hunting and fishing exploits. The success of the tall tale depends greatly on its delivery and the convincing expression of the teller. According to folklorist Jan Harold Brunvand, the tall tale "does not depend on belief in the details of the story, but rather on a willingness to lie and be lied to while keeping a straight face. The humor of these tales consists of telling an outrageous falsehood in the sober accents of a truthful story." Depending therefore on common situations and themes, the storyteller creatively weaves characters and remarkable exploits together and then stretches the tale to the tallest limits his or her audience will tolerate.

The South's particular folk heroes have a strong part to play in story and ballad. Yet the lines between folk and popular tradition often become blurred in accounts of Davy Crockett, Stonewall Jackson, Jesse James, and others. More common in today's oral tradition are local characters given notoriety by storytellers. In the Mississippi Delta, for instance, a local outlaw, "Bad Man Monroe," is the subject of many narratives told about his remarkable deeds, extraordinary size and strength, and difficult capture. Also in the Delta, moonshiner, outlaw, or lawman (depending on whom you listen to) Perry Martin remains an important folk hero to the river people. In southern Kentucky, the guerrilla actions of Beanie Short during the Civil War for the Confederate cause or, some say, for his own gain still circulate. Like the escapades of other legendary figures, they give rise to not one but a series of stories. Beanie Short's legend includes accounts of buried treasure, ruthless activity, and tragic death. In the communities of the South, these legends compose the rich folk history of the locality and help give residents a sense of past and place.

Storytelling often occurs in "sessions." In social centers people gather to hear and tell stories. The session provides entertainment and passes time, but by drawing people together, it also reinforces shared values and binds a group together. In the Okefenokee Swamp, for example, the storytelling custom of "talking trash," says Kay Cothran, "comes from a time when men did not work by the time clock but by cycles of nature. Talking trash today is an act of identification with that older way of life, and whether one does it as a matter of course or as something of a rebellion, talking trash is a sneer at middle-class subservience to continuous gray work and a denial of that class's identification of the materially unproductive with the counterproductive." The "liar's bench" at the courthouse, the hunting camp, or the general store may serve as an appropriate place for the activity.

The ages of participants are also contextual factors. Although the popular image exists of the grandfather warmly relating a tale to a child on his knee, storytelling occurs from early childhood on. In Mississippi, William Ferris found ghost stories limited largely to the repertoires of children and old people, whereas protest tales were found primarily among black adolescents and adults who encountered racial tension daily in their work.

Storytelling is a way of communicating ideas and concerns that may not be effectively articulated or desired in conversation. Often putting feelings and ideas on the fictive plane of a story helps clarify or act out personal and social concerns. Further, storytelling changes according to the needs and demands of the situation in which it occurs. The function of storytelling—be it entertainment, education, or social maintenance—depends on the intent of the narrator and the composition of the audience, as well as the place in which they interact and the nature of the material presented. As there are many contexts for people to gather, so there are many contexts for story-

telling. Vance Randolph thought that the isolation of places like the Ozarks and the ample time on the hands of its residents explained the vitality of the region's storytelling, but the existence of storytelling in new urban and suburban areas and in other modern contexts challenges that notion.

Since the early days of commercial recording, southern storytellers have been featured as entertainers. The telling of "The Arkansas Traveler" was released by Edison at least three times prior to 1920. Rural-styled entertainers like Arthur Collins and Cal Stewart (popularly known as Uncle Josh) captured on disc numerous folk narratives, often in the guise of "rube sketches." The record, though, placed limitations on the storyteller's performance. The story had to conform to a certain time limit, and the teller had to strain to get a clear reproduction of his voice. More often the trained voice, rather than the authentic, relaxed raconteur, found its way onto the early recordings.

Radio shows, however, like the *Grand Ole Opry*, gave many genuine southern folk humorists a chance to ply their craft effectively before a wide listening audience. Benjamin Francis (Whitey) Ford, popularly known as the Duke of Paducah, and Archie Campbell were 20th-century *Opry* humorists who combined theatrics and traditional texts in their performances. Campbell was especially adept at a tongue-twisting form of storytelling—the spoonerism. He built stories on the interchange of word sounds, such as "Rittle Led Hiding Rood."

Television spread southern storytelling further. *Hee Haw*, for instance, regularly featured genial John Henry Faulk storytelling against the backdrop of a country store and Archie Campbell holding court in a barbershop. Out on a porch another of the show's amiable raconteurs, the Reverend Grady Nutt, specialized in anecdotes and preacher jests. Their successors are Jeff Foxworthy, Larry the Cable Guy, and other denizens of *Blue Collar TV*.

Hosting his own show was Mississippi's ebullient Jerry Clower. He developed his narrating skill regaling customers with stories while working for a fertilizer company in Yazoo City. Clower achieved national popularity, but many storytellers are recognized and occasionally celebrated only in their home localities. Near Banner Elk, N.C., Marshall Ward and Ray Hicks performed Jack tales that have attracted folklore collectors. Solsberry in southern Indiana annually holds a liar's contest featuring the Ray brothers, specialists in tall tales, from whom folklorist Brunhilde Biebuyck collected 200 tales. Some local storytellers, like Ed Bell of Luling, Tex., have gone beyond their hometown to present personal experience stories and tall tales at an occasional regional or national folklife festival.

Despite the spotlights placed on the aforementioned storytellers, American folklorists have generally given more attention to the narrator's texts than to the narrator. Recently, though, some folklorists have explored the biography, repertoire, and creativity of several outstanding southern narrators, James Douglas Suggs, for example. Born in Kosciusko, Miss., in 1887, the black Suggs worked the famed Rabbit Foot Minstrel Show throughout the South in 1907. He sang and played guitar, danced, and told jokes. Later years found him working as a professional baseball player, railroad brakeman, and cook. With his wife and many children he eventually settled in Calvin, Mich., an area populated largely by southern blacks. He absorbed many narratives in his various occupations and travels, recounting them to the workers at the next job and to friends at the tavern. In 1952, while searching for storytellers in the field, folklorist Richard Dorson was directed by a local barkeep to Suggs, whom she knew as a "good talker." In Suggs's repertoire animal stories predominated, followed by equivalent numbers of ghost and hoodoo stories, tall tales, preacher jests, and Ol' Marster tales. Dorson's visit was opportune, for Suggs died two years later. Suggs's life and narratives compose a major portion of Dorson's classic study *American Negro Folktales* (1967). Another notable 20th-century narrator was Ray Lum, loquacious mule trader of Vicksburg, Miss. Lum's rapid-fire delivery unveiled a quick wit and an impressive verbal ability, which served to relax people in trades. Indeed, the trader as clever trickster and affable talker ran throughout Lum's many tales.

The image of southern storytelling has been instrumental to the growing popularity of the National Storytelling Festival in Jonesborough, Tenn., held annually since 1973. The featured storytellers inevitably are southern verbal artists, many of whom give homage to traditional tellers in hometown settings who never came on a stage. Among the new generation of professional storytellers with southern repertories featured at the festival are Donald Davis, Kathryn T. Windham, and Charlotte Blake Alston. Colquitt, Ga., claims its own storytelling legacy with a festival and a unique "storytelling museum." It not only instructs in the folk roots of southern storytelling but also encourages tradition-bearers to share their stories in a storytelling room.

Folk storytellers usually do not hang out shingles or announce their wares. Storytelling is rather an informal part of their jobs or social life. In a traditional anecdote attributed to many raconteurs, the renowned Texas *Munchausen*, Gib Morgan, when asked for a good "lie" by fellow oilworkers, told them that he was too busy to lie right then, for his brother lay sick and Gib had to leave. Later the workers discovered that indeed they were told a good lie. Such informal, impromptu exchanges recur often today at work and at play. Less easily spotted than the European wonder-tale-telling counterpart, the American storyteller nonetheless thrives on informal opportunities for a joke or anecdote. The South's sociable, leisurely image and its strong oral tradition help foster the association of the region with storytelling.

SIMON J. BRONNER
Pennsylvania State University

Richard Bauman and Roger D. Abrahams, eds., *And Other Neighborly Names: Social Process and Cultural Image in Texas Folklore* (1981); Simon J. Bronner, *Mid-South Folklore* (vol. 5, 1977), *Folklore Forum*

(vol. 13, 1981); John H. Burrison, *Storytellers: Folktales and Legends from the South* (1989); Kay L. Cothran, in *Readings in American Folklore*, ed. Jan Harold Brunvand (1979); Daryl Cumber Dance, *Shuckin' and Jivin': Folklore from Contemporary Black Americans* (1978); Richard M. Dorson, *American Negro Folktales* (1967); William Ferris, *Journal of American Folklore* (vol. 85, 1972), *Ray Lum: Mule Trader* (1977); Zora Neale Hurston, *Mules and Men* (1935); Carl Lindahl, ed., *Swapping Stories: Folktales from Louisiana* (1997); William Bernard McCarthy, ed., *Jack in Two Worlds: Contemporary North American Tales and Their Tellers* (1994); William Lynwood Montell, *Don't Go Up Kettle Creek: Verbal Legacy of the Upper Cumberland* (1983); *North Carolina Folklore Journal* (vol. 26, 1978).

Teaching English to Speakers of Other Languages

Nothing indicates the growing diversity of the South more than the rapid increase of the region's immigrant population and their many languages. At the beginning of the 21st century the number of teachers of English for Speakers of Other Languages (ESOL) was increasing dramatically. Previously, some school districts employed one English language teacher who traveled around to different schools on different days of the week, but many others, particularly in rural areas, had no ESOL teachers at all, leaving some immigrant children sitting silently in classrooms and understanding little of what was said. Only the larger urban school systems in cities where significant numbers of immigrants lived had daily classes for children learning English.

Things are different today. Of the 10 metropolitan areas with the greatest relative increase in foreign-born population during the 1990s, seven are in the South, with Nashville, Atlanta, and Louisville at the top of the list. Georgia and North Carolina, especially, have seen their Hispanic populations increase, by almost 400 percent in North Carolina. As more non–English speakers moved into the Southeast, the need for ESOL teachers became increasingly apparent. Schools in rural as well as urban areas initiated programs to introduce immigrant children to U.S. classrooms and to American English. Most schools use a system called "pullout" ESOL classes, where students leave regular classrooms for several hours of English classes per week. Other school systems have "sheltered" programs, where English learners remain with other learners for up to a year before being moved into a regular classroom. Sometimes these programs are in a separate school building called a newcomer center. Most of the instruction in the sheltered class is in English, but teachers simplify their speech and use as many visual aids as possible in order to provide comprehensible input for learners.

One innovative program is called the Georgia Project. Started by a former senator whose daughter taught in an elementary school, with support from local businesses, this program in Dalton, Ga., has become a model for school districts around the country. After establishing a relationship with the University of Monterrey in Mexico, the district welcomed Mexican teachers into the classrooms as paraprofessionals. During the summers, teachers from Georgia go to Monterrey for an intensive language and culture course. The project has even incorporated some dual-language classrooms that include both English-speaking and Spanish-speaking children, who are taught half the day in each language. Though they have met with some controversy, such programs are becoming more popular in the region, with schools in Chapel Hill, N.C., offering dual-language classes in English and Chinese, for example.

In the region's universities the most sought-after subfields for teaching faculty in linguistics are applied linguistics and second-language acquisition, as classroom teachers take the necessary courses for qualifying to teach ESOL. Such programs are increasing, and large universities in Atlanta, Memphis, and other cities offer doctorates in the field. Meanwhile, all over the South, English classes for adults are often being staffed by volunteers with little or no training in linguistics or language teaching methods. Classes are offered at churches, public libraries, and technical schools, and some public schools offer classes to parents of their students. Of course, much learning takes place outside the classroom, especially for immigrants who are not part of a local ethnic community and for those who work at jobs where English is commonly used. As new ethnic groups in the South learn English, new varieties of Southern English are developing.

ELLEN JOHNSON
Berry College

Center for Applied Linguistics, <www.cal .org>; James Crawford, *Educating English Learners* (2004); Edmund T. Hamann, *The Educational Welcome of Latinos in the New South* (2003); Stanton Wortham et al., *Education in the New Latino Diaspora* (2001).

Toasts and Dozens

In Greenville, Miss., Atlanta, Memphis, and other towns and cities in the South, you might hear preadolescent, lower-socioeconomic-class black boys playfully hurling rhymed insults at each other. The language is rough and the themes are risqué, but the composition is creative. They are playing the "dozens," as they often call it. "I fucked your momma on the levee," a Greenville youth told his playmate while others looked on. "She said, 'Get up, baby, your dick's getting too heavy.'" The onlookers roared with delight. After shouts of encouragement, the butt of the insult replied, "I fucked your momma in New Orleans; her pussy started poppin' like a sewing machine." The challenge was put to the first boy to top the retort. He came back strongly with "I fucked your momma on a fence, selling her pussy for 15 cents; a bee come along and stung her on the ass, started selling her pussy for a dollar and a half."

The dozens are social entertainment, a game to be played, but they have also sparked considerable sociopsychological comment. Folklorist Roger Abrahams observed, for example, that the dozens represent a striving for masculine identity by black boys, as they try symbolically to cast off the woman's world—indeed the black world they see

as run by the mother of the family— in favor of the gang existence of the black man's world. In dozens playing, the black boy is honing verbal and social skills he will need as an adult male. A form of dozens playing, usually called "ranking," has also been collected among white boys, but most collections have stressed the black dozens, also called "woofing," "sounding," and "joning."

Although Roger Abrahams did his classic study of black verbal contests and creativity in Philadelphia, Pa., his informants had deep roots in the South. Other southern connections to the dozens are found in a spate of southern blues songs popular from the 1920s on. "The Dirty Dozen" was first recorded by Georgia's Rufus Perryman, known as Speckled Red, in 1929. Other versions quickly followed by southern artists, including Tampa Red, Little Hat Jones, Ben Curry, Lonnie Johnson, and Kokomo Arnold. The content of the dozens was apparently in circulation prior to these recordings; folksong collectors Howard W. Odum and Newman I. White found references in the field to the dozens before World War I. Alan Dundes and Donald C. Simmons have suggested an older existence of the dozens in Africa.

Also collected from working-class blacks has been a form of narrative poetry called by its reciters "toasts." Toasts use many of the rhyming and rhythmic schemes and the rough imagery of the dozens but are performed by young men as extended poetic recitations rather than ritualized insult. Indeed, Abrahams called toasts the "greatest flowering of Negro verbal talent." Today, toasts are less common, but the related musical genres of rap and hip-hop are an important part of popular culture, not only in the U.S. South, but around the world.

The performance of toasts is intended to be dramatic. The settings are barrooms and jungles; the characters are bad men, pimps, and street people; and the props are often drugs, strong drink, and guns. Here is an excerpt, for example, from a common toast, "The Signifying Monkey."

> Down in the jungle near a dried-up
> creek,
> The signifying monkey hadn't slept
> for a week
> Remembering the ass-kicking he
> had got in the past
> He had to find somebody to kick the
> lion's ass.
> Said the signifying monkey to the
> lion that very same day,
> "There's a bad motherfucker
> heading your way.
> The way he talks about you it can't
> be right,
> And I know when you two meet
> there going to be a fight.
> He said he fucked your cousin, your
> brother, and your niece,
> And he had the nerve enough to ask
> your grandmom for a piece."
> The lion said, "Mr. Monkey, if what
> you say isn't true about me,
> Bitch, I'll run your ass up the
> highest tree."
> The monkey said, "Now look, if you
> don't believe what I say,

> Go ask the elephant. He's resting
> down the way."

Other popular toasts in oral tradition include "Stackolee" (also spelled *Stagolee* and *Stagger Lee*), "The Titanic," "Joe the Grinder," and "The Freaks (or Junkers) Ball."

Several collections of toasts come from the South. In the North most texts come from the cities. Although some southern examples are reported in cities like New Orleans and Austin, southern texts often come from the rural and small-town South. In Mississippi, David Evans, William Ferris, and Simon J. Bronner collected them in small towns. Bruce Jackson's book on toasts, *Get Your Ass in the Water and Swim Like Me* (1974), had texts primarily collected from prisons in Texas and Missouri. The connection to southern life is usually passed over by interpreters of toasts in favor of links to the life of the underworld and the urban ghetto. Relations exist, however, between the themes and heroes of the toasts and those of southern black folksongs, including "Stackolee" and "The Titanic." The blues also are influenced by the erotic and violent verses of the toasts, and toasts are believed to be the most important source for the beginnings of rap music. Other connections are found between southern black animal folktales featuring the monkey and the toast "Signifying Monkey." Indeed, Richard Dorson reported prose versions of "Signifying Monkey" in his classic collection *American Negro Folktales* (1967) taken from southern-born blacks.

Dozens and toasts stand out because they are framed as play or performance, and they contain strong themes and sounds. Dozens and toasts creatively manipulate imagery and metaphor to bring drama to words. The boy telling dozens may eventually tackle the more sophisticated toasts. Mastering the techniques in these traditional performances gives the teller an important sense of prestige and power that is reserved for the man of words in black society. Their dozens and toasts entertain friends and pass the time; they communicate values and feelings. The tellers of dozens and toasts are narrators of imagined scenes and cultural critics for the audiences for which they perform. The tellers also draw attention because they themselves are characters in the social drama of communication through folklore.

SIMON J. BRONNER
Pennsylvania State University

Roger D. Abrahams, *Deep Down in the Jungle: Negro Narrative Folklore from the Streets of Philadelphia* (1970), *Positively Black* (1970); Simon J. Bronner, *Western Folklore* (vol. 37, 1978); Richard M. Dorson, *American Negro Folktales* (1967); William Ferris, *Jazzforschung* (1974/75); Bruce Jackson, *Get Your Ass in the Water and Swim Like Me: Narrative Poetry from Black Oral Tradition* (1974); Thomas Kochman, ed., *Rappin' and Stylin' Out* (1972); William Labov, Paul Cohen, Clarence Robins, and John Lewis, in *Mother Wit from the Laughing Barrel*, ed. Alan Dundes (1973); Lawrence Levine, *Black Culture and Black Consciousness: Afro-American Folk Thought from Slavery to Freedom* (1977); John Russell Rickford and Russell John Rickford, *Spoken Soul: The Story of Black English* (2000); Dennis Wepman, Ronald B. Newman, and Murray B. Binderman, *Journal of American Folklore* (vol. 87, 1974).

Turner, Lorenzo Dow

(1890–1972) LINGUIST.

Lorenzo Dow Turner was born in Elizabeth City, N.C., to a free black family that dates its origins to 1799. His research is important to southern speech because he was the first linguist to conduct systematic interviews of Gullah speakers, the first to maintain that Gullah was a legitimate speech variety, and the first to publish a book that illustrated how and why Gullah differed from other English varieties within and outside the southern United States.

Turner's father, Rooks, and his brothers, Rooks Jr. and Arthur, all held college degrees at a time when most African Americans could expect to gain only a sixth-grade education, though the education of his mother, Elizabeth, was rudimentary. The importance that Turner's family placed on education put him on the track to achieve the extraordinary. He completed a B.A. at Howard (1914) and an M.A. at Harvard (1917), becoming, like W. E. B. Du Bois and Carter G. Woodson before him, among the first black men to attend the latter institution. Returning to Howard, he served as instructor (1917–20) and then professor of English and head of the department (1920–28), during which time he completed a Ph.D. from the University of Chicago (1926). Leaving Howard for a year to found and edit the *Washington Sun* with his brother Arthur, he reentered academia after the newspaper failed and became professor

Lorenzo Dow Turner at his desk, 1949
(Lois Turner Williams, Chicago)

and head of the Department of English
at Fisk University (1929–46).

While teaching summer school
at South Carolina State College in
Orangeburg in 1929, Turner became
acquainted with Gullah, the English-
based creole spoken on the Georgia
and South Carolina Sea Islands and
nearby mainland. He soon decided to
make recovery of the history and linguistic background of this language
variety one of his life's quests, encouraged by the historian Carter Woodson,
who had identified the Sea Islands
as an important reservoir of African
American culture. After attending two
summer Linguistic Institutes to learn
the methodology of the nascent Linguistic Atlas Project, Turner arrived in
the Sea Islands in 1932 to begin the first

scientific investigation of Gullah, which
Americans widely viewed as merely an
"incorrect" version of 17th- and 18th-
century English dialects. To counter this
view and to document the African influence on Gullah and on other creoles,
Turner studied West African languages
at the University of London (1936–37)
and then conducted fieldwork among
African descendants in northern Brazil
(1940–41), where he found that Yoruba
speakers recognized some of the same
African words, tones, and rhythms he
had identified in Gullah.

Turner's two decades of research on
Gullah, his tireless lecturing, his frequent writing, and finally his groundbreaking book *Africanisms in the Gullah
Dialect* (1949) began to reverse soci-
etal attitudes toward Gullah, a creole
like the one believed by some to be the
ancestor of modern African American
speech. He documented 4,000 terms
in Gullah that derived from approximately 30 African languages. Most of
these were personal names, but others
were common vocabulary, such as
bitty/biddy 'a bird' (Kimbundu, used in
the South to refer to baby chicks); *ninny*
'the female breast' (Mandingo), 'breast
milk' (in the South); *goober* 'peanut'
(Kimbundu and Umbundu); *jumbo*
'elephant' (Umbundu, Kimbundu, and
KiKongo); *gumbo* 'okra, stew with okra'
(Tshiluba and Umbundu); and *yam*
'yam' (Vai).

Turner's research earned him the
title "Father of Gullah Studies." He was
first in bringing linguistic training to
the analysis of Gullah, in conducting
extensive interviews among its native
speakers, in committing aspects of its

grammar to paper, and especially in establishing conclusively that elements of Niger-Congo languages had survived in North America. He was the first African American to document the African influence in the oral arts of Brazil, to collect and translate folktales and proverbs from the Yoruba in Nigeria, and to transcribe Sierra Leone Krio and prepare books in that language for the Peace Corps. He and Melville Herskovits were the premier theorists of African retentions in American culture during their lifetimes.

After World War II, Turner moved from Fisk to Roosevelt College in Chicago to become professor of English (1946–70) and lecturer in the Inter-Departmental Program in African Studies (1952–70). A Fulbright Fellowship allowed him to fulfill a lifelong goal, to conduct fieldwork in Nigeria and Sierra Leone among native speakers of African languages. From this research he prepared several dictionaries. In his career's final years, he directed the language component of Roosevelt's Peace Corps project, training teachers for Sierra Leone (1962–66). In all he published five books and numerous articles and book reviews and prepared an impressive array of additional manuscripts, many translated from Brazilian Yoruba and the Niger-Congo languages of Africa into English. His research on Gullah, Krio, and Brazilian Yoruba brought the study of creole languages into the center of linguistic interest in the United States. Gullah is now celebrated in several annual festivals and has been the focus of at least 30 Ph.D. dissertations, numer-

ous books and articles, and audio and video recordings.

MARGARET WADE-LEWIS
State University of New York at New Paltz

Julie Dash, *Daughters of the Dust* (video) (1991); Joseph Opala and Cynthia Schmidt, *The Language You Cry In* (video) (1998); South Carolina ETV, *Family across the Sea* (video) (1990); Lorenzo Dow Turner, *Africanisms in the Gullah Dialect* (1949; 2002); Lorenzo Dow Turner Jr., ed., *The Folk Tales of Africa* (2006), *Photographic Images of Brazil and Nigeria by Africanist/Linguist Lorenzo Dow Turner* (2006); Margaret Wade-Lewis, *The Black Scholar* (Fall 1991), *Dialectical Anthropology* (vol. 17, 1992; vol. 26, 2001), *Lorenzo Dow Turner: Father of Gullah Studies* (2006).

Vocabulary, Changes in

The English vocabulary is constantly changing. Unlike pronunciation and grammar, vocabulary is acquired over a speaker's entire lifetime. New words are created, people learn different words from listening to others, and words become old-fashioned and disappear. New words can result from leaving off parts of earlier terms, as when familiar compounds such as *mantel-piece*, *school-teacher* and *clothes-closet* are shortened to *mantel*, *teacher*, and *closet*. Sometimes new terms seem more descriptive, such as *chest of drawers*, as opposed to *bureau*, and *driveway*, rather than *avenue* or *lane* (all of which once referred to a private drive); sometimes the older words were more vivid, as *spew* for *vomit*, and *falling weather* for rain or snow. Probably the most obvious characteristic of vocabulary change is the way it is inextricably tied to cultural change.

The lexicon of a language tells the story of the people who speak the language. During the 20th century the South changed from a predominantly rural, agricultural region to one having a majority-urban population, giving rise to institutions from supermarkets and shopping malls to modern high schools. Revolutions in transportation and communications increasingly affected daily lives, bringing unprecedented change to the region and its English.

Urbanization, industrialization, and technological advances led to changes in occupations and in implements and items at the workplace and at home. Words like *back house* and *privy* 'outdoor toilet,' *doubletree* and *singletree* 'crossbar used to hitch mules or horses to a wagon or plow,' *tow sack* and *crocus bag* 'burlap bag,' *co-wench* and *soo-cow* 'calls to cows,' and words for calling other farm animals are unknown to most southerners today, though a century ago they were everyday expressions that distinguished the South's vocabulary from that of other regions. People know fewer terms for wildlife (*terrapin* and *cooter* for a land tortoise have declined in favor of *turtle*) and for foods formerly raised in gardens and orchards, like *press peach* and *freestone peach*. Semantic merger, the subsuming of formerly different meanings under one form, occurs when detailed knowledge is lost and distinctions are blurred, as in these two cases. Semantic extension occurs when a word takes on a broader meaning. Thus *frying pan*

now encompasses the electric version, and *siding* is now more often made of aluminum or vinyl than wood.

Eating habits and economic patterns of production and consumption changed greatly as the South moved from an agricultural to an urban society. A century ago most southerners ate bread made at home, usually cornbread. Bread made from wheat flour was bought at a store. Back then the latter was called *light bread* or *loaf bread*, but today it is known merely as *bread*, with the addition of a modifier (*homemade bread*) if it is not factory made. Similarly, in the past sweet potatoes were called just *potatoes*, while the other kind were *Irish potatoes*.

The commercialization of products, along with increasing familiarity with labels and the advertising of items sold nationwide, has replaced regionally marked vocabulary with standardized terms. Prior to modern grocery stores (led by Piggly Wiggly in the South), customers made a list of items they wanted, which were then brought to them by clerks; the new kind of store ushered in a change from bulk sales to individual packaging with labels. Words that had been known mostly within family or neighborhood circles (e.g., terms for vegetables canned at home or parts from animals butchered on the farm) entered the larger public domain in supermarkets and became open to change. Today the Upper South term *green beans* has almost replaced Deep South variants like *snap bean* and *pole bean*, and *cottage cheese* is no longer called *curds* or *clabber cheese*. Southerners buy *green onions* instead of *shallots*;

Stores like Piggly Wiggly contributed to the standardization of southern vocabulary. (Darren Fleeger)

peanuts instead of *ground peas, goobers,* or *pinders*; and a mix for making *pancakes* rather than *battercakes, flitters,* or *slapjacks.*

However, many terms still survive that are identifiably southern. *Butter bean* is used alongside *lima bean,* though for some people it has narrowed to refer to a specific type of lima. *Cold drink* and *coke* still often mean a carbonated soft drink in general, and even though the older *family pie* has been replaced by *cobbler,* the latter is also a southern term. Many other southernisms can be heard every day: *like(d) to* 'almost,' *carry* 'to take or escort (a person) somewhere,' *wore out* or *give out* 'exhausted,' *puny* 'sickly,' *slouch* 'lazy person,' and *pallet* 'makeshift bed on the floor.' This list shows that regionalisms are often forms that are in general use but that have a special sense in one region.

Sometimes words are borrowed from other regions. *Toilet* and *outhouse* are from New England. From Pennsylvania come *kindling* (for *lightwood*) and *chipmunk* (for *ground squirrel*). *School gets out* (rather than *lets out* or *turns out*) was once a local expression confined to New York City. *Bacon* (previously called *breakfast bacon* in the South) and *burlap bag* are from the North, as are *wishbone, skunk, moo,* and *Merry Christmas!* (replacing southern *pulley bone, polecat, hum* or *low,* and *Christmas Gift!*). Some terms that are becoming less common were brought by settlers; for example, the mountain terms *fireboard* 'mantel,' *hull* 'to shell (peas or beans),' and *poke* 'paper bag' all came from Ulster. *Attics* are rarer in modern houses, and this book word has supplanted the traditional terms used by the lower classes (*loft*) and the upper classes (*garret*).

Lexical change is often led by speakers having more education or higher social status. Introduced in this way are names for members of a wedding party like *best man* and *maid of honor*. At one time, a wedding attendant, whether a male or a female, was called a *waiter* in the South. Until relatively recent times, only the wealthy hosted formal weddings. The practice known as *shivaree* in the Mississippi Valley and as *serenading* in the Southeast has dwindled to shaving cream and tin cans on the car in which the just married ride. Education played a role in replacing *rheumatism* by *bursitis*, *neuritis*, and *arthritis*, though the last of these is still sometimes anthropomorphized as *Arthur-itis*.

Other newer, nationally known words do not replace regional words but are used alongside them. Some research indicates that the size of the Southern English vocabulary has increased by as much as 40 percent from adding new words to preexisting ones. Television, movies, radio, and the Internet have a larger effect on the choice of words southerners use than on the accents to pronounce them, but even new words spread through the media may have a regional association. For example, hip-hop slang can vary by region, and the popular word *crunk* (as a noun, "a rowdy style of rap music"; as an adjective, "wild, drunk, loud, excited, etc.") originated in the South. Regional differences persist especially in vocabulary used mostly around home or within the family, like the words children use to address their grandparents (*pawpaw*, *peepaw*, *mamaw*, *nanny*, etc.).

Adequate funding for public school systems in many parts of the South was not established until the mid-20th century. With more southerners attending school, words entered the southern vocabulary because of increasing literacy. The educational level of the population in the South improved tremendously during the 20th century, and as it did, the number of synonyms for concepts increased, with older words continuing to exist alongside newer ones, the choice of words in any given situation depending on what style of speech is appropriate. Words used in one situation with a particular listener might be inappropriate in a different situation with another listener. Language is a dynamic entity, especially in its words and meanings. As our world changes, so does our vocabulary.

ELLEN JOHNSON
Berry College

Craig Carver, *American Regional Dialects* (1987); Wayne Glowka et al., *American Speech* (vol. 80, 2005); Ellen Johnson, *Lexical Change and Variation in the Southeastern United States, 1930–1990* (1996); Hans Kurath, *A Word Geography of the Eastern United States* (1949); Gordon Wood, *Vocabulary Change* (1971).

Y'all

There is no more signature southernism than *y'all*. It and its close relative *you all*, with the stress on *you*, are symbolic, immediately signaling an affinity for the American South, and northerners of all levels of education who move to

Misspelled Stuckey's sign, Vaiden, Miss. (Charles Reagan Wilson Collection, Center for the Study of Southern Culture, University of Mississippi)

the region often acquire one or both of them, even if they never adopt any other southern usages. Their down-home character conveys hospitality and makes those to whom they are addressed feel welcome. *Y'all*, and to a lesser extent *you all*, set a tone of familiarity and informality, including when directed at strangers.

The early history of *y'all* is unclear. It is unknown in the British Isles, though the Ulster form *ye aw* (i.e., *you* plus *all*), attested as early as the 1730s, is one possible source. That early form and the frequently observed modern spelling *ya'll* suggest that *y'all* may not be (or may not be perceived to be) simply a contraction of *you* plus *all*. By 1600 singular *thou* and *thee* had largely disappeared from British speech, and

plural *you* had shifted to become a singular as well as a plural pronoun. This loss of distinction opened the door to the eventual development of *y'all* and similar second-person-plural pronouns and compounds in varieties of English (*yous*, *you'uns*, and most recently, *you guys*).

Y'all and *you all* have sparked as much argument and controversy, in both scholarly and popular circles, as any other forms in Southern English, with respect to whether they are ever singular, an issue arising from the fact that they are sometimes addressed to a single individual. At the simplest level, *y'all* and *you all* differ from plural *you* in emphasizing inclusiveness; they mean *all of you*. This is the case when addressing not only a group but also a single person with whom other individuals (family members, friends, colleagues, etc.) are associated in the speaker's mind. Thus, a southerner normally understands "What did y'all do last night?" to be a question about one or more people in addition to a single person addressed. But a third party who does not use *y'all* may mistakenly interpret this use of it as a singular pronoun. In similar fashion, *y'all* is sometimes addressed to one person who represents an institution, business, or other indeterminable number of individuals collectively. The customer who asks a salesperson, "Do y'all have any fresh orange juice?" may not see or know who or how many others work for the establishment, but the speaker may nonetheless associate those others (if any) with the salesperson. Thus, cognitively the pronoun is plural. *Y'all* may also be a "distributive plural" addressed to a group of people directly, each of whom is a potential referent, as in asking the question, "Did y'all take

out the garbage?" As a practical matter, only one person takes (or needs to take) action. *Y'all* is also used in direct address (as in partings, "Bye, y'all"), greetings ("Good morning, y'all"), invitations ("Y'all come"), and so on. In these expressions the form is equivalent to *everyone* (that is, an indefinite pronoun), and more than one person is clearly present.

Taken together, these many and diverse usages indicate that *y'all* and *you all* likely have a secure future in southern speech. Accounting for their vitality is not only their strong identification with the South but the fact that they are highly functional and have diverse usages beyond being a plural personal pronoun equivalent to *you.*

MICHAEL MONTGOMERY
University of South Carolina

Michael Montgomery, SECOL *Review* (vol. 20, 1996), *Southern Journal of Linguistics* (vol. 26, 2002); Gina Richardson, *American Speech* (vol. 59, 1984).

INDEX OF CONTRIBUTORS

INDEX

Page numbers in boldface refer to articles.

Atlanta, Ga., 17, 75, 76, 77, 89, 186, 202, 203
Atwood, E. Bagby, 22
Augusta County, Va., 67
Austin, Tex., 204
Austria, 66, 115
Avoyelles Parish, La., 63

Bahamas, 2, 15, 36, 57
Bahamian Creole English, 45
Bahamian English, **45–47**
Bailey, Guy, 31–32, 33, 34
Baltimore, Md., 89, 117
Bambara, 53
Banner Elk, N.C., 200
Bantu, 70
Barbadian Creole, 70
Barbados, 15, 53, 69, 70
Bassa, 92
Baton Rouge, La., 49, 77
Beaumont, Tex., 76
Belize, 15, 100
Bell, Ed, 200
Benin, 53
Béranger, Jean, 83
Bermuda, 46, 57
Beverly Hillbillies, The, 21, 196
Biebuyck, Brunhilde, 200
Bilingualism. *See* Education: bilingual
Biloxi, 3, 107–8, 172
Biloxi, Miss., 60
Birmingham, Ala., 17, 77
Blue, Chief Sam, 51
Blue, Louise, 51
Blue Collar TV, 200
Blues (music), 29, 203, 204
Body language, 123
Bracketville, Tex., 36, 37
Braggs, Okla., 98
Brantford, Ontario, 108
Brazil, 2, 10, 58–59, 75, 206, 207
Britain, 10, 11, 14, 15, 30, 168
British English, 26, 31, 32, 46, 47, 57, 58, 93, 104, 190, 211
Bronner, Simon J., 204
Brooks, Cleanth, 12, 26

Brown, Joseph, 161
Brunvand, Jan Harold, 198
Bush, George W., 18

Cable, George Washington, 152
Caddo, 6, **47–48**, 82, 172
Caddoan, 3, 6, 78, 80, 83, 172
Cajun English, 12, **49–50**
Cajun French, 9, 63–64, 100
Cajun Kosher, 100
Cajun Renaissance, 63
Cajuns, 49–50, 62, 63, 64, 65, 129
Calhoun, John C., 161
California, 78, 109, 112
Calusa, 83
Calvin, Mich., 200
Camarota, Steven, 75
Campbell, Archie, 199, 200
Canada, 54, 82
Canadians, French, 63
Canary Islands, 8, 100
Cane Ridge, Ky., 178
Cantonese, 76
Cape Palmas, Liberia, 91
Caribbean, 7, 8, 11, 15, 29, 30, 46, 47
Carolina, 46, 172. *See also* North Carolina; South Carolina
Carolina Algonquian, 38–39
Carter, Jimmy, 1, 21
Cary, N.C., 77
Cassidy, Frederic G., 131
Catawba, 5, **50–52**, 79, 82, 107
Cavaliers, 118
Celtic, 9
Chacato, 82
Chafe, Wallace, 48
Chakchiuma, 82
Chalaque, 85
Chapel Hill, N.C., 75, 77, 202
Charlefort, S.C., 60
Charleston, S.C., 2, 15, 16, 52–54, 60, 89, 129, 137, 194; English, **52–54**
Charlotte, N.C., 17, 67, 77, 111, 186
Chattanooga, Tenn., 77
Chaucer, 26, 42, 55

Indigenous languages, 3–7, **82–85**. *See also individual languages and language families*

Indirectness, in speech, 123, 130, 131, 138, 176–77, 187, 195

Intruder in the Dust (Faulkner), 133, 168

Iran, 10, 75

Iraq, 10, 75

Ireland, 9, 14, 15, 30, 43, 53, 100, 104, 137, 168

Iroquoian, 3, 5, 50, 78, 79, 82, **85–88**, 108, 172

Isleños, 8, 100

Italy, 75, 100, 115

Jackson, Andrew, 95, 174

Jackson, Bruce, 204

Jackson, Jesse, 21, 180

Jackson County, N.C., 86

Jakes, T. D., 180

Jamaica, 15, 29, 30, 36, 46, 69

Jamaican Creole, 70

Jamestown, Va., 38, 117

Japan, 58

Jasper, Ark., 105

Jasper County, Miss., 141

Jefferson, Thomas, 173

Jefferson Parish, La., 100

Jewish English, 20, 88–90

Jewish language, **88–90**

Johnson, Lonnie, 203

Jones, Little Hat, 203

Jonesborough, Tenn., 200

Kansa, 107

Karankawa, 6

Kentucky, 11, 23, 42, 75, 147, 171, 178, 198; school for the deaf in, 40; name of, 173

Kenya, 10, 75

Key West, Fla., 57

Kidman, Nicole, 194

KiKongo, 206

Kimbundu, 206

King, Martin Luther, Jr., 163, 180

Kiowa, 6

Kituwha, 86

Klao, 92

Koasati, 5, 83, 94, 95, 99

Korea, 75

Kosciusko, Miss., 200

Kretzschmar, William A., Jr., 149

Krio, 207

Kru, 70

Kurath, Hans, 22, 23, 26, 147, 148, 149, 154, 155

Kwa languages, 70

Labov, William, 31–32, 157, 158

Ladino, 7, 88–89

Lake Charles, La., 49

Laos, 10, 75

Larry the Cable Guy, 200

Last of the Ofos, The (Hobson), 108

Latinos, 109–15, 160

Lawson, John, 50

Lederer, John, 108

Lee, Harper, 169

Lewis, Henry Clay, 151

Liberia, 2, 32, 70, 91

Liberian Settler English (LSE), **91–92**

Lieber, Francis, 150

Linguistic Atlas of New England (Kurath), 147

Linguistic Atlas of the Gulf States (LAGS), 23, 135, 139, 140, **142–46**

Linguistic Atlas of the Middle and South Atlantic States (LAMSAS), 22, 135, **147–49**, 155

Linguistic Atlas of the North-Central States, 26, 155

Linguistic Atlas of the United States and Canada, 149

Linguistic Atlas Project. *See* American Linguistic Atlas Project

Linguists and linguistics, **149–50**; university having academic program in, 150

Lipan, 6, 36

Literary dialect, **150–54**, 189, 194

Livingston, Tex., 95

London, 19, 118, 119
Longstreet, Augustus Baldwin, 151
Louisiana, 11, 23, 132, 142, 144, 151, 171, 175, 189; indigenous languages in, 6, 47, 80, 82, 83, 95, 98, 108; French in, 7, 8–9, 12, 49, 50, 60–65, 73, 81, 129, 172; Spanish in, 8, 78; Cajun English in, 12, 49–50; black signers in, 42; Acadians in, 49; German in, 66; Vietnamese in, 75; New Orleans English in, 100–103; storytelling in, 158–59; name of, 173
Louisiana Creole, 61–65, 130
Louisiana French Creole, 8, 37, 65, 100, 152
Louisville, Ky., 202
Lowcountry, 11, 129, 130, 194
Lower South, 11, 17, 18, 19, 23, 42, 59, 92, 116, 185
Lowman, Guy, 147
Lucayan Indians, 46
Luling, Tex., 200
Lumbee English, **93–94**, 160
Lutherans, 9, 66, 67

Malinke, 53
Mandarin Chinese, 77
Mande, 70
Mandingo, 53, 206
Mandinka, 7
Marion, Francis, 60, 173
Marksville, La., 107, 108
Marshallese, 75
Maryland, 54, 55, 91, 104, 132
Maryland in Africa, 91
Maskogo, 36
Mayaguana, 45
McDavid, Raven I., Jr., 23, 147, 148, 149, 150, **154–56**
McDavid, Virginia G., 156
McMillan, James B., 149
McPherson, James Alan, 154
Mecklenburg County, N.C., 67, 111
Media, 21, 34, 45, 63, 114, 193, 210
Melnar, Lynette, 48
Memphis, Tenn., 77, 89, 202, 203

Mencken, H. L., 155, 191
Mende, 7, 53
Mennonites, 9, 67
Metaphors, 43, 135
Mexico, 10, 36, 58, 75, 109, 114, 202
Miami, Fla., 113
Miami, Okla., 107
Michigan, 164
Midnight in the Garden of Good and Evil (film), 195, 196
Mikasuki (Miccosukee), 5, 83, 94, 95
Mirvis, Tova, 90
Mississippi, 3, 11, 23, 73, 92, 100, 132, 142, 144, 151, 198, 199; indigenous languages in, 5, 6, 82, 95, 97, 98, 107, 108; school for the deaf in, 40; name of, 173
Mississippi Delta, 198
Mississippi in Africa, 91, 92
Missouri, 105, 132, 151, 191, 204
Mithun, Marianne, 108
Mobila, 82
Mobile, Ala., 60, 80
Mobilian Jargon, 6, 37, 60, 80–82, 94
Mohawk, 85
Mongolia, 10, 75
Monrovia, Liberia, 91
Monterrey, Mexico, 202
Montgomery, Ala., 89
Montgomery, Michael, 26
Moneton, 107, 108
Mooney, James, 87
Moravians, 9, 66
Morgan, Gib, 201
Morocco, 100
Mosopelea, 108
Mules and Men (Hurston), 129
Murfree, Mary, 152
Muscogee Creek, 120
Muskogean languages, 3, 5, 6, 50, 78, 80–81, 82, 83, **94–97**, 98, 172
Muskogee, 5, 79, 94

Nacimiento, Mexico, 36
Names. *See* Personal names; Place-names
Nantahala, N.C., 85

Narrative, **156–59**. *See also* Storytelling
Nashville, Tenn., 17, 21, 77, 186, 202
Nassau, 45
Natchez, 6, 82, **98–99**
Natchez, Miss., 90, 129
Natchitoches, La., 60
National Storytelling Festival, 200
New Braunfels, Tex., 9, 68
New Brunswick, 9, 49, 61
New Orleans, La., 2, 12, 49, 60, 65, 89, 129, 137, 204; English, **100–103**
Newport News, Va., 117
New Providence, 46
New York, 5, 40, 45, 85, 109, 147
New York (City), 32, 90, 209
Ngola, 7
Niger-Congo, 7, 34, 92, 207
Nigeria, 10, 53, 70, 75, 207
No Time for Sergeants, 196
Nolan, Charles F. M., 151
Norfolk, Va., 117, 118
North Carolina, 7, 11, 22, 33, 42, 44, 91, 92, 104, 132, 139, 149, 159–60, 171, 189, 190; indigenous languages in, 5, 6, 38, 50, 51, 82, 85, 86, 107; Spanish in, 8, 109, 110, 111, 202; Moravians in, 9; Gaelic in, 10; English in, 10; school for the deaf in, 40, 41; German in, 66, 67; Gullah in, 69; Asians in, 75–77; Lumbee Indians in, 93; name of, 172
North Carolina Language and Life Project (NCLLP), **159–60**
Nottoway, 85
Nova Scotia, 2, 9, 15, 32, 49, 61
Nutt, Grady, 200

Oakland, Calif., 14, 34
O'Cain, Raymond K., 156
Occaneechi, 79, 107, 108
O'Connor, Flannery, 133
Odum, Howard W., 203
Ofo, 107, 108
Ohio, 67, 68, 132, 147
Okefenokee Swamp, 198
Oklahoma, 132; as Indian Territory, 5, 36, 98, 120; indigenous languages/peoples in, 5, 6, 38, 47, 71, 80, 86, 95, 96, 97, 107
Oklahoma Creek (Muskogee), 5, 94
Oklahoma Seminole, 5, 94
Old English, 26
Oliverio, Giulia R. M., 108
Omaha, 107
Ontario, 85
Orangeburg, S.C., 66, 206
Oratorical themes, **161–63**
Orleans Parish, La., 100, 103
Osage, 48, 81, 107
Oto, 81
Outer Banks (islands), 1, 11, 19, 94, 138, 139, 159
Outer Banks English, **104–5**, 159, 160
Ozark English, 42, **105–6**
Ozark Folklore (Randolph), 191
Ozark Folksongs (Randolph), 191
Ozark Mountain Folks (Randolph), 191
Ozarks, 1, 11, 105, 138, 144, 189, 191–92, 197, 199
Ozarks, The (Randolph), 191
Ozark Superstitions (Randolph), 191

Page, Thomas Nelson, 128, 153
Pakistan, 10, 75
Pamlico, 79
Pardo, Juan, 50
Pareja, Francisco, 83
Parks, Suzan-Lori, 154
Pascagoula (language), 82
Paul, Benjamin, 84
Pawnee, 47
Peck, Gregory, 196
Pederson, Lee, 23, 142, 149
Pendleton County, W.Va., 67
Pennsylvania, 11, 23, 38, 209; German in, 9, 65–68
Pennsylvania Dutch, 67
Perryman, Rufus, 203
Personal names, 15, 20, 83, 136, **168–71**; of African Americans, **124–27**, 130–31, 206
Philadelphia, Miss., 95

Philadelphia, Pa., 31, 117, 203
Philippines, 10, 75
Phonology, 40–41
Pidgin Powhatan, 79
Piedmont, 11, 50, 79, 158, 189
Pissing in the Snow (Randolph), 191
Pittsburg, Kans., 191
Place-names, 3, 6, 7, 8, 20, 83, 85, 118, 119, 125, 136, **171–74**; of states, 172–73
Plantation Society French, 62–63, 64
Plaquemines Parish, La., 65, 100
Pleasantness, of language, 164, 167, 168
Point Coupee Parish, La., 63
Poland, 115
Politeness, 19, 138, **174–77**, 195
Ponca, 107
Ponce de León, Juan, 171
Poor Richard's Almanac (Franklin), 187
Poor White Trash, 196
Port Arthur, Tex., 76
Portsmouth, Va., 117
Portugal, 89
Portuguese, 58, 59
Powhatan, 5, 6, 38–39, 79
Powhatan Renape Nation, 40
Preaching style: black, **178–80**; white, **181–84**
Prince Edward Island, 49
Pronunciation, 12, 17, 18–19, 22, 23, 29, 31, 133, 167, 194–95; archaic, 26; of Appalachia, 44–45; of Cajun English, 50; of Charleston English, 54; of Chesapeake Bay English, 55; of Conch, 58; of Cherokee, 87; of New Orleans English, 102–3; of Outer Banks English, 104; of Texas English, 116; of Tidewater English, 118–19; of *fixin' to*, 134; of folk speech, 135; changes in, **184–86**
Pronunciation of English in the Atlantic States (Kurath and McDavid), 23, 155
Proto-Muskogean, 99
Proverbs, 19, 43, 130, 136, **187–89**

Qualla Cherokee, 86, 88
Quapaw, 107, 108

R, 1, 17, 18, 55, 58, 59, 116, 118, 156, 186, **189–90**, 194–95, 196
Rabbit Foot Minstrel Show, 200
Raleigh, N.C., 40, 113, 115, 186
Randolph, Vance, 106, 136, **191–92**, 199
Rankin, Robert, 107, 108
Rankokus, N.J., 40
Rap music, 123, 204
Raven, Nancy, 98
Rawls, Lou, 180
Ray brothers, 200
Reconstruction, 138, 153, 161–62
Red Thunder Cloud, 51
Richmond, Va., 17, 89, 117, 186
Ritter, William, 41
Robertson, Lexie Dean, 152
Robertson, Pat, 181
Robeson County, N.C., 93
Rock Hill, S.C., 51
Rockingham County, Va., 67
Roots (Haley), 124
Russian, 72

St. Bernard Parish, La., 100
St. Charles Parish, La., 100
Saint Domingue/Haiti, 62
St. James Parish, La., 100
St. John the Baptist Parish, La., 100
St. Martin Parish, La., 63
St. Marys, Ga., 69
St. Simons, Ga., 69
St. Tammany Parish, La., 100
Sam, Watt, 98
San Antonio, Tex., 75, 76, 77, 114
Sanchez, Sonia, 154
Sandy Island, S.C., 69
Sapir, Edward, 120
Saponi, 79, 107, 108
Sarasota, Fla., 67
Savannah, Ga., 17, 77, 89, 90, 137
Sawokli, 82
Saxe Gotha Township, S.C., 66
Schools, 5, 12, 14, 29, 34, 40, 52, 62, 63, 75, 76, 77, 86, 88, 112, 141, 175, 201–2, 210. *See also* Education

Scotch-Irish, 11, 19, 26, 43, 44
Scotland, 9, 10, 14, 19, 30, 31, 53, 137
Scots, 9, 105, 181
Sea Islands, 1, 8, 37, 69, 71, 129, 138, 206
Sea Island Creole (SIC), 36–37, 69. *See also* Gullah
Seminole, 5, 6, 80, 94, 95, 96, 97
Seneca, 85
Senegal, 53
Senegambia, 11, 70
Sephardic Jews, 53, 88–90, 100, 168
Sequoyah, 5, 87
Sermons. *See* Preaching style
Settlers, Liberian, 91–92
Shakespearean English, 11, 26, 42, 43, 55, 105, 118
Shawnee, 38–39, 79
Shawnee, Okla., 38
Shenandoah Valley, 67
Shiminol, 36
Siebert, Frank T., 50
Sierra Leone, 2, 53, 70, 207
Siler City, N.C., 113
Silva-Corvalán, Carmen, 113
Simmons, Donald C., 203
Simms, William Gilmore, 151
Sinoe County (Mississippi in Africa), 92
Siouan languages, 3, 5, 50, 78, 79, 80, 82, **106–9**, 120, 172
Slavery/slave trade, 3, 7, 36, 61–63, 69–70, 138, 183
Sling Blade, 196
Smith, John, 6
Smith, Lee, 154
Smitherman, Geneva, 182
Smith Island, Md., 55
Smokey and the Bandit, 196
Snowbird Cherokee, 86
Solsberry, Ind., 200
Somalia, 75
Sound and the Fury, The (Faulkner), 179
South, as a speech region, 2–3, 12
South Carolina, 1, 7, 11, 22, 23, 42, 91, 92, 129, 132, 149, 189; indigenous languages in, 3, 5, 50, 51–52, 107; Spanish in, 8, 110;

German in, 9, 66, 67, 68; English in, 10; Gullah in, 29, 36, 37, 45, 46, 70, 71, 125, 130, 206; Charleston English in, 52–54; and work of McDavid, 147, 148, 154, 156; name of, 172
Southeastern Conference on Linguistics (SECOL), 150
Southern Belle, 195–96
Southern drawl. *See* Drawl, southern
Southern English: formation of, 10–11; changes in, 16, 17, 137–40, 184–87, 207–10; perceptions of, **164–68**; in television and film, **193–97**
Southern Journal of Linguistics, 150
Southern shift, 17, 19, 32
Southern White Vernacular English, 92
South Korea, 10
Spain, 89, 100, 109
Spanish, 7, 8, 12, 37, 38, 43, 68, 72, 78, 83, 88, **109–15**, 115–16, 168, 171, 202
Speck, Frank, 51
Springdale, Ark., 75
Sranan, 70
Starkville, Miss., 77
Staunton, Va., 40, 67
Steel Magnolias, 196
Stewart, Cal, 199
Storytelling, 19, 43, 131, 156–59, **197–201**
Stuart, Jesse, 152
Stuart, Ruth McEnery, 152
Sudan, 75
Sugar Land, Tex., 77
Suggs, James Douglas, 200
Surinam, 70
Survey of Verb Forms in the Eastern United States (Atwood), 22
Swadesh, Morris, 84
Swaggart, Jimmy, 181
Swain County, N.C., 86
Swanton, John R., 83, 84, 98, 108
Switzerland, 60, 66
Syria, 100

Taiwan, 10, 75, 76
Taliaferro, Hardin E., 151

of Louisiana Creole and Cajun French,
64; of Lumbee English, 93; of Ozark
English, 106; of folk speech, 135; in television and film, 195; of Gullah, 206;
changes in, **207–10**
Von Reck, Philip Georg Friedrich, 120

Wales, 9
Waletzky, Joshua, 157, 158
Walker, Alice, 129, 154
Waltons, The, 196
Ward, Marshall, 200
Washington, D.C., 32, 40, 75, 91, 117
Washington, George, 173
Washington Parish, La., 100
We Always Lie to Strangers (Randolph),
191
Webster, Noah, 12
Welty, Eudora, 133, 152, 169
West Africa, 15, 47, 53, 54, 61, 69, 71, 91,
92, 100, 108, 123, 124, 125, 206
West African Pidgin English, 69–70
West Indies, 15, 123
West Point, Va., 117
West Virginia, 23, 42, 108, 171; German in,
9, 67; name of, 173
Wewoka, Okla., 36
White, Newman I., 203
Whiting, Bartlett J., 136
Wichita, 47
Williams, Robert, 34
Williams, Tennessee, 171

Williamson, Juanita, 149
Wilson, George P., 136
Windham, Kathryn T., 201
Windward Coast, 70
Wise, Claude Merton, 149
Wise, Isaac Mayer, 90
Witherspoon, John, 12
Woccon, 50, 79, 82
Wolfram, Walt, 33
Wolof, 53
Woman Within, The (Glasgow), 127
Woodson, Carter, 206
*Worcester's Dictionary of the English Lan-
guage* (1860), 56
*Word Geography of the Eastern United
States* (Kurath), 22, 148
Wright, Richard, 153

Y'all, 1–2, 18, 19, 29, 90, 113, 116, 133, 135,
138, 195, **210–12**
Yamacraw, 83
Yamasee, 82
Yazoo City, Miss., 200
Yiddish, 89, 90
Yoruba, 206, 207
Youchigant, Sesostrie, 84
Young, Martha Strudwick, 152
Youngblood, Shay, 154
Yuchi (Euchee), 6, 50, 82, 107, **120–21**

Zéphir, Flore, 78